Religion of Peace?

Religion of Peace?

Why Christianity Is and Islam Isn't

Robert Spencer

Since 1947
REGNERY
PUBLISHING, INC.
An Eagle Publishing Company • Washington, DC

Library of Congress Cataloging-in-Publication Data

Spencer, Robert, 1962–
   Religion of peace? : why Christianity is and Islam isn't / Robert Spencer.
     p. cm.
   Includes bibliographical references and index.
   ISBN 978-1-59698-515-5
   1. Peace—Religious aspects. 2. Christianity and other religions. 3. Apologetics. 4. Jihad. 5. Islam—Relations. I. Title.
   BL65.P4S645 2007
   261.2'7—dc22
2007025026

Published in the United States by
Regnery Publishing, Inc.
One Massachusetts Avenue, NW
Washington, DC 20001
www.regnery.com

Manufactured in the United States of America

10 9 8 7 6 5 4 3 2 1

Books are available in quantity for promotional or premium use. Write to Director of Special Sales, Regnery Publishing, Inc., One Massachusetts Avenue NW, Washington, DC 20001, for information on discounts and terms or call (202) 216-0600.

For the Magnificent Seven,
with love

CONTENTS

CHAPTER ONE

NO, VIRGINIA,
ALL RELIGIONS AREN'T EQUAL

The "war on terror" is an ideological conflict—one in which Christians, Jews, Buddhists, Hindus, atheists, secular Muslims, and others have a stake. But on that ideological front the West has been notably deficient. And this is due, in no small part, not only to a lack of cultural self-confidence, but also to a sense that Christianity—upon which Western civilization is largely based—and Islam are at best morally equal. In the view of many left-liberal leaders, Christianity itself (or religion in general) is the real problem.

These days, Western bookstore shelves groan under an avalanche of anti-Christian books. In 2006 alone, major New York publishing houses unleashed such titles as *American Theocracy: The Peril and Politics of Radical Religion, Oil, and Borrowed Money in the 21st Century* by Kevin Phillips; *The Baptizing of America: The Religious Right's Plans for the Rest of Us* by James Rudin; *The Theocons: Secular America Under Siege* by Damon Linker; *Kingdom Coming: The Rise of Christian Nationalism* by Michelle Goldberg; *Thy Kingdom Come: How the Religious Right Distorts the Faith and Threatens America: An Evangelical's Lament* by Randall Balmer; *Piety & Politics: The Right-Wing Assault on Religious Freedom* by Barry Lynn; *Religion Gone Bad: The Hidden Dangers of the Christian Right* by Mel White; *American Fascists: The Christian Right and the War on America* by Chris Hedges.

Other popular books sound many of the same themes, including *The Conservative Soul* by homosexual activist and blogger Andrew Sullivan and the atheist apologetics *The God Delusion* by Richard Dawkins and *Letter to a Christian Nation* by Sam Harris. The parade of anti-Christian books of several years ago, like *Papal Sin* by Garry Wills, *Constantine's Sword* by James Carroll, and *Hitler's Pope* by John Cornwell, targeted Catholics. Now Protestants are finding themselves in the crosshairs.

Attacks on Christian history and doctrine are an integral part of a larger effort to instill a sense of cultural shame in even non-Christian European and American youth—a shame that militates against their thinking the West is even worth defending.

A white American student, "Rachel," unwittingly summed up this attitude when she told American Indian professor Dr. David Yeagley in 2001: "Look, Dr. Yeagley, I don't see anything about my culture to be proud of. It's all nothing. My race is just nothing. . . . Look at your culture. Look at American Indian tradition. Now I think that's really great. You have something to be proud of. My culture is nothing."

Yeagley mused: "The Cheyenne people have a saying: A nation is never conquered until the hearts of its women are on the ground. . . . When Rachel denounced her people, she did it with the serene self-confidence of a High Priestess reciting a liturgy. She said it without fear of criticism or censure. And she received none. The other students listened in silence, their eyes moving timidly back and forth between me and Rachel, as if unsure which of us constituted a higher authority. . . . Who had conquered Rachel's people? What had led her to disrespect them? Why did she behave like a woman of a defeated tribe?"[1]

Rachel's spirit is pandemic in Europe. Historian Bernard Lewis was quoted in January 2007 that "Europeans are losing their own loyalties and their own self-confidence. They have no respect for their own culture." According to Lewis, Europeans, in a spirit of "self-abasement," with its hallmarks of political correctness and multiculturalism, have "surrendered" to Islam's increasingly shrill demands.[2] Nor is Rachel alone in America: columnist Alicia Colon wrote in April 2007 that "sadly, my generation has spawned self-loathing Americans who actually believe that this country is evil. They have neither respect nor love for this nation. Rather they are being taught by today's academic community that America and its institutions should be held in contempt."[3]

A principal aspect of this abject condition of Western hearts is disgust with Christianity and Judeo-Christian civilization—which for most Americans amounts to contempt for our forefathers. Christianity and the Jewish tradition from which it was born are at the heart of Western civilization. It has formed who we are as Americans, and has influenced Europeans and others around the globe for even longer. Like it or not, it has even shaped many who reject the Christian faith. For although the West has largely cast off its Christianity, and a war against Christianity has been raging in the courts for several decades, many of the societal values of Western countries remain rooted in Christian premises. Christianity also shares key moral principles with Judaism—principles that do not carry over into Islam. These principles are the fount from which modern ethicists have drawn the concept of universal human rights—the foundation of Western secular culture.

But apparently despite all this, Rachel—and those who equate Christian and Islamic "fundamentalism"—posits that Christianity poses just as much or more of a threat to the free world than does Islam.

American high schools, colleges, and universities have now created millions of Americans who think and speak like Rachel. They have been subjected to decades of anti-American, anti-Western, and anti-Christian conditioning by our educational establishment. And many like Rachel are today in positions that affect public policy.

This is why the truth must be told about Christianity and the Judeo-Christian culture. Americans and Europeans—as well as Christians in the Middle East and elsewhere—need to stop apologizing for all our forefathers allegedly and actually did wrong, and for the culture they built (which is not identical to today's popular culture) and remember what they did right, recognizing what Judeo-Christian civilization has brought to the world. We must look honestly at Islam and Christianity and recognize how they differ. Although human nature is everywhere the same, and people have justified violence in the name of every faith, religions are not the same. We must not allow politically incorrect censors to stifle statements like this.

Ultimately this must be done because, as Yeagley points out, people who are ashamed of their own culture will not defend it.

This is why telling the truth about Christianity and Western civilization is not a matter of cultural cheerleading or even of religious apologetics. It is essential to the defense of the West against today's global jihad. I myself am a Christian, but I believe this book could have been written by a Buddhist, a Hindu, a Jew, an atheist, or anyone else interested in the facts of the case. The Islamic jihad and the defense against it, in the West and elsewhere, affect all of us; Jews, atheists, Muslims, and many other non-Christians live comfortably in societies shaped by Judeo-Christian values, and they need to understand that those values are not identical to Islamic ones. Judeo-Christian values have informed ideas of human rights that prevail across the globe, and which also have significant influence in the Islamic world—although there they battle with traditional Islamic values. A notable example came in December 2006, when the government of Pakistan, at the insistence of human rights and women's rights groups, instituted a new rape law based on modern canons of evidence. Islamic clerics and Muslim hard-liners immediately protested against the new law. They considered it "un-Islamic" because it did not follow the traditional Islamic standard that rape could be established only by the testimony of four male witnesses who saw the act.[4]

Western civilization has become global, not only in the mass export of American pop culture but also in human rights norms and standards, which are for the most part derived from Christianity. Yet controversies like that over the rape law in Pakistan are certain to move west—particularly in Europe, where the secular, post-Christian, and Christian premises of society are coming under increasing challenge from a growing and restive Muslim minority. If demographic trends continue, this minority will become a majority in some European states before the end of this century.

But if the conflict the West is facing is simply "terrorism," no one should be concerned if these Muslims challenge Judeo-Christian principles and work to replace them with Islamic norms. And if the War on Terror is a war against Islamic fundamentalism, there is no reason for anyone to be concerned about impending European Islamization—as long as the "Islamic fundamentalists" are neutralized by the loyal, Western-oriented

Muslims on whom Tony Blair, Jacques Chirac, and the rest have placed such hope. After all, if Christianity and Islam are essentially the same—in their values and in their capacity to inspire both violence and peace—why should Westerners resist advancing Islamization?

If it is widely recognized, however, that the War on Terror is in fact a struggle against an Islamic jihad that would conquer and subjugate Western non-Muslims, and which is well on its way to doing so in Europe, then Western countries face a choice. They can acquiesce to the demands of their Muslim populations and, little by little, adopt provisions of Islamic sharia law until the Islamic social order is fully implemented. Or they can choose to stand up for Judeo-Christian values and defend them against the ideological challenge of jihad and sharia.

Knowledge of the differences between Christianity and Islam is central to this effort. Thus we will investigate whether there is actually a Christian theocracy movement, as some in the media have charged, and if there is, how large it is compared to the jihad threat. We will also explore whether Christianity and Islam are equivalent in their capacity to inspire violence, and whether there is anything in the Judeo-Christian West worth fighting for to preserve in the face of civilizational challenge.

THE JIHAD AGAINST JEWS AND CRUSADERS

One group that has had no trouble recognizing Christianity's importance in the struggle against jihad terrorism has been the jihadists themselves. Malaysian prime minister Abdullah Ahmad Badawi told the World Council of Churches in 2004 that "in the eyes of many Muslims, events in the last three years seem to lend credence to the view that the Christian West is, once again, at war with the Muslim world."[5]

This is also the view of Osama bin Laden and those who share his religious and political ideology. "After the end of the Cold War," bin Laden declared in a 1996 interview, "America escalated its campaign against the Muslim world in its entirety, aiming to get rid of Islam itself."[6] He has repeated this view many times. "You should know," he said in a videotape delivered to al-Jazeera in October 2003, "that this war is a new Crusader campaign against the Islamic world, and it is a war of destiny for the entire *umma* [worldwide Islamic community]. God only knows what serious ramifications it might have for Islam and its people."[7]

In seeing the War on Terror not just as a war against Islam, but as a war on behalf of Christianity, the view of bin Laden and other jihad terrorists neatly coalesces with that of the anti–"Christian theocracy" writers like Chris Hedges and Kevin Phillips. Jihadists routinely refer to the American armies in Iraq and Afghanistan as "Crusaders." Al Qaeda's second in command, Ayman al-Zawahiri, who most frequently issues the group's communiqués, uses this term frequently; in an October 2006 message he issued a rather typical exhortation: "I urge you, in [the name of] the duty of jihad, which is incumbent upon every Muslim, to hurry and pursue martyrdom in order to kill the Crusaders and the Zionists."[8] The Crusader moniker apparently applies to any Western military forces. In January 2007, Abu Mussab Abdel Wadoud of the Salafist Group for Preaching and Combat (GSPC), an Algerian jihad group affiliated with al Qaeda, declared jihad on France: "Fight the nationals of France and the agents of the Crusaders occupying our land. Our fathers and our ancestors fought against the French Crusaders who were driven out in humiliation."[9]

Adam Gadahn, also known as "Azzam the American," the first American indicted for treason since World War II and a prominent al Qaeda operative, made the most direct connection between the War on Terror and Christianity in a September 2006 videotape introduced by al-Zawahiri himself. First he ridiculed the idea that the Islamic world needed democracy: "Those who think democracy is synonymous with freedom are either people who haven't experienced life in America, or Americans who haven't lived abroad." He asserted that "Muslims don't need democracy to rid themselves of their home-grown despots and tyrants. What they do need is their Islamic faith, the spirit of jihad, and the lifting of foreign troops and interference from their necks."

He went on to explain that they didn't need Christianity either. "And if Muslims don't need democracy, then they certainly have no need for what is known as Christianity." Gadahn called Christianity "that hollow shell of a religion, whose followers cling to an empty faith, and a false conviction of their inevitable salvation, regardless of what they do or believe, as long as they accept the core tenets and doctrines of Paulian Christianity, which also happen to be its most unbelievable, untenable, and illogical." He even went on to enumerate some of those negative aspects:

> Like the belief that the Bible that we have today, with all its contradictions, errors, deletions, and outright fabrications, is the infallible, revealed word of God.... Like the doctrine of the original sin, which states that man is born in sin, because of the lapse and subsequent fall of his parents, even though we know from the Qur'an that God forgave our father Adam and mother Eve when they repented.... Like the incomprehensible, illogical, non-biblical doctrine of Trinity.... Like the belief that God sent His only begotten son, who is also God in human form, to die on a cross for the sins of mankind, which, is implied, He could otherwise not have forgiven.

Gadahn sounds, aside from his references to the Qur'an, like your typical Western biblical skeptic. Does he buy into the American Left's view that the War on Terror is a war on Islam being waged on behalf of Christianity? Perhaps. But he also clearly believes that a central part of the struggle he and al Qaeda are waging is against what he regards as the false belief of Christianity on behalf of the truth of Islam. For Gadahn went on to invite Christians, Jews, and others to Islam: "Isn't it time for the unbelievers to discard these incoherent, illogical beliefs, theories, and conjecture? Isn't it time for every Christian, Jew, pagan, and atheist to cast off the cloak of spiritual darkness which enshrouds them, and emerge into the light of Islam, to live a life illuminated by faith and die the death of a believer, return to his Lord, pleased and pleasing to Him, God willing, rather than living out his days in blindness, to die as an unbeliever and be resurrected as an unbeliever, whose eternal abode is a fire from which the fire of this world screams in fright?"[10]

This is in accord with Muhammad's command that Muslims invite non-Muslims to Islam, and then fight them if they refuse both conversion and the alternative, second-class status:

Fight in the name of Allah and in the way of Allah. Fight against those who disbelieve in Allah. Make a holy war.... When you meet your enemies who are polytheists, invite them to three courses of action. If they respond to any one of these, you also accept it and withhold yourself from doing them any harm. Invite them to accept Islam; if they respond to you, accept it from them and desist from fighting against them.... If they refuse to accept Islam, demand from them the *jizya* [a tax on non-Muslims]. If they agree to pay, accept it from them and hold off your hands. If they refuse to pay the tax, seek Allah's help and fight them.[11]

Gadahn is following Muhammad's instructions, both in inviting non-Muslims to Islam and in making war on those who refuse the invitation. The unbelievers' behavior has no bearing on this war: neither their immorality nor their military matter. The unbelief of the non-Muslim world, therefore, is the ultimate "root cause" of the conflict: if we were Muslims, this war would not be happening, or it would have a radically different character.

Gadahn spoke in English, making this video unique as a direct appeal to the American people in their own language. However, no one answered Gadahn's invitation from a Christian standpoint, or even appeared to recognize its implications. The foremost of those implications is that Gadahn and others like him believe they are fighting on behalf of a superior religion and culture; while many Westerners dismiss the notion that we are engaged in a "clash of civilizations" and instead assert that we are really engaged in a clash between civilization and barbarism, Gadahn and other jihadists would most likely say the same thing.

Yet while Gadahn believes that he is fighting for a superior religion and culture, the dominant assumption among Westerners is that no religion or culture is superior to another—especially Christianity and Christian culture, Gadahn's chief foes. Tony Blair has spoken of Western culture as if it were nothing more than an empty container for other, non-Western religions and cultures, with tolerance its chief hallmark. "Christians, Jews, Muslims, Hindus, Sikhs, and other faiths have a perfect right to their own identity and religion, to practice their faith and to conform to their culture," said Blair in December 2006.

In fact, he continued, "this is what multicultural, multi-faith Britain is about. That is what is legitimately distinctive." He seemed to define "British values" only as the foundation for this multiculturalism: "But when it comes to our essential values—belief in democracy, the rule of law, tolerance, equal treatment for all, respect for this country and its shared heritage—then that is where we come together, it is what we hold in common; it is what gives us the right to call ourselves British."[12]

But all this, of course, is just what Gadahn despises. He believes that no government or culture has any legitimacy unless it is constituted according to Islamic law; he believes his struggle is against the "enemies of God." And in response Blair and other Western leaders talk endlessly about freedom, democracy, and tolerance—none of which are superior to the law of God, as Muslims view it. And Muslims recognize that these Western leaders don't care enough about their own religion and culture to defend them.

The unhappy heirs of Western civilization, in other words, are in a peculiar position. They have been eager to avoid the appearance of religious conflict, while the other side seems avid to portray it as such. Westerners are discarding Christianity only to find it identified by Islamic jihadists as the most objectionable aspect of their way of life, and as something that can't be shaken off without conversion to Islam. In this, at least, Muslims recognize what too many Westerners don't: how deeply our core beliefs—even Tony Blair's multicultural ones—are grounded in Christian ideas of morality.

Islam seeks the conversion, subjugation, or death of not only Christians but also all non-Muslims. Thus it is imperative that all the victims and potential victims of the Islamic jihad—Christians, Jews, Buddhists, Hindus, atheists, secular Muslims, and all others—recognize that, in the immortal words of Benjamin Franklin, we must all hang together, or we shall indeed all hang separately. And at the forefront of the defense, at least in the Western world, is our Judeo-Christian heritage, which has become the foundation of global values. In order to win, we cannot simply fight *against* the jihadists, or terrorists, or whatever the politically correct designation is fashionable today for those who would destroy what remains of Western civilization. We must be contending *for* something, and in the Judeo-Christian tradition there is a great deal to defend.

What the Norwegian European blogger who goes only by the name of Fjordman (an indication of the health of free speech in Europe) says about Europeans goes for Americans as well. "Europeans," Fjordman has noted, "need to understand how closely intertwined are the fates of Israel and of Europe itself. The term 'Judeo-Christian' is not a cliché. We cannot defend Western civilization without defending its Jewish component, without which modern Western culture would have been unthinkable. The religious identity of the West has two legs: The Christian and the Jewish ones. It needs both to stand upright. Sacrificing one to save the other is like fighting a battle by chopping off one of your legs, throwing it at the feet of your enemies, and shouting: 'You won't get the other one! We will never surrender!' We could always hope that our enemies will laugh themselves to death faster than we bleed to death, the Monty Python way of fighting. Maybe that works, but most likely it will leave us crippled and pathetic, if not dead."[13]

Fjordman, who has published an extensive series of insightful articles about the increasing plight of non-Muslims in Europe and related matters, is entirely correct. And his argument also goes both ways: we cannot defend Western civilization without defending both its Jewish and Christian components.

To do this, we must break through the politically correct fog that envelops us. In February 2006 I spoke at the Pim Fortuyn Memorial Conference in The Hague. After one of the sessions, one of the other speakers, Dr. Andrew Bostom, editor of the illuminating collections *The Legacy of Jihad* and *The Legacy of Islamic Antisemitism*, and I got into an animated conversation with a liberal writer from New York who is well acquainted with Islamic terror; she now resides in the Netherlands. The writer heatedly insisted that Christian fundamentalism was just as dangerous as the Islamic variety, and that equal attention should be devoted to defeating both. Shortly thereafter she told us that she had to be going, as she was on a bicycle and couldn't be out after dark, or she risked being attacked. "Who is going to attack you?" asked Dr. Bostom. "Christian fundamentalists?"

Bostom's quip illustrates several points: first, although it was clear that this woman felt threatened by the Muslim gangs that often prey on passersby, political correctness prevented her from admitting it. Also, her own actions showed that her equation of Christian and Islamic fundamentalism was absurd. Of course she had no fear that Christian fundamentalists would attack her on her way home, but about Islamic jihadists she could not be so sanguine. But that didn't stop her from loudly protesting that the two threats were essentially equivalent.

This is the prevailing malady of the West in our time. It is why this book had to be written.

CHAPTER TWO

WARS OF RELIGION

"We know who the homicidal maniacs are. They are the ones cheering and dancing right now. We should invade their countries, kill their leaders, and convert them to Christianity."[1]

So wrote Ann Coulter, two days after the September 11, 2001, jihad terror attacks in Washington and New York.

The firestorm of indignation that followed centered not so much on the first two of her recommendations, but on the third. After all, in the immediate aftermath of September 11 most Americans supported the prospect of an invasion of Afghanistan, and most would have welcomed the deaths of Osama bin Laden or Mullah Omar—but Christianity as preferable to Islam? That crossed the line. That was intolerance and bigotry.

For it quickly became conventional wisdom after September 11 that the War on Terror had no religious dimension. Analysts acknowledged that at most, it involved a struggle against "a global network of extremists who are driven by a twisted vision of Islam," as Peter Wehner, deputy assistant to the president and director of the White House's Office of Strategic Initiatives, put it in January 2007, more than five years later. This is just one indication of how resilient this notion has proven to be.[2] Few in the mainstream media or in Washington offices would even consider the possibility that Islam was part of the problem, and no one would have dreamed of suggesting that Christianity could be part of the solution.

President George W. Bush summed up mainstream assumptions
when he declared: "Our enemy doesn't follow the great traditions of
Islam. They've hijacked a great religion." Islam, he explained, "is a faith
that brings comfort to people. It inspires them to lead lives based on hon-
esty, and justice, and compassion."[3] To accompany this praise, the United
States government sponsored the building of mosques in Afghanistan
and elsewhere as a gesture of goodwill toward the Islamic world.[4]

But in 2006, many in the mainstream media began speaking in deadly
earnest about a religion that really was inciting violence and extremism,
and which was a threat to the very survival of American constitutional
government. Islam, however, was not the religion they had in mind. This
dangerous religion, of course, was Christianity. Fostering the spread of
this idea was the cascade of books that appeared that year, warning the
American public about the growth of "theocons," "Christian fascists," or,
in a conscious parallel to the term "Islamist" (which denotes the proponents of political Islam), "Christianist." These groups are supposedly not
only advancing a Christian agenda in the public sphere, but are also
working to subvert the Constitution and establish a theocracy. Sure, the
Islamists are working to impose religious rule on their own societies, but
so are the Christianists—and the Christianists pose the far more serious
threat. Some even charge that just as the Taliban practiced stonings and
beheadings, so would these Christianists if they got half a chance.

This kind of rhetoric was not uncommon among Muslims. In January
2007 the Muslim Public Affairs Committee of the United Kingdom
sounded the alarm over the Christian theocrats' alleged plot to make war
against Islam so Christianity could dominate the planet. The committee
published an article that spoke in lurid terms about a pro-Israel event
staged by prominent Evangelical pastor John Hagee: "Armed with blood-
red rhetoric and the hubris of the politically connected, Hagee filled his
5,000-seat church for a weekend-long event culminating in his Night to
Honor Israel in October. To an eager audience preparing for the end
times, analogies to Hitler and denouncement of 'appeasement' were flying. Anti-Muslim rhetoric was at a fevered pitch.... But what masquer-
aded as biblically mandated generosity toward the Jews was nothing
more than a political rally for a war not just against Iran, but against

Islam, and for the dominance of Christianity (Hagee's brand, of course)."[5]

Yet the West's generosity has not been directed solely toward Israel. Muslims have benefited from the largesse also, and not just through the building of mosques. When the West intervened in the Balkans, it was to protect Muslims. When it intervened in Somalia, it was to feed starving Muslims (for which service al Qaeda attacked it). When a tsunami devastated Muslim Indonesia and other South Asian countries in 2004, Western states pledged millions: the United States sent $950 million,[6] Great Britain almost $800 million (including aid from nongovernmental organizations),[7] Germany over $670 million,[8] Canada $400 million,[9] France about $300 million, Norway $175 million,[10] and so on. The European Union also kicked in $628 million aside from the individual contributions of its member states, making Europe's contribution two billion. The West's contributions weren't merely financial; the United States and Australian armed forces were the first responders to bring aid to people in need. This Western generosity, however, has gone largely unnoticed. What of oil-rich Muslim nations? Qatar sent $25 million. After criticism of their initial paltry responses, Saudi Arabia sent $300 million, Kuwait $100 million, and the United Arab Emirates $20 million.[11] So much for the solidarity of the *umma*.

If a Muslim looked to Western sources for a ringing defense of the countries that helped the tsunami victims, he'd be disappointed. If he attended school in a Western country, he would be taught that the West was responsible for slavery, racism, aggressive wars, and exploitation. If he watched Western television, he might be appalled at its vulgarity, but he would also note the anti-Christian values of many television programs. If he looked at the *New York Times* bestseller list, he'd see anti-Christian titles soaring to the top.

He would see what many in the West miss, because it is a common assumption among many left-liberals in the West that Christian and Muslim "extremists," "radicals," or "fundamentalists" are two sides of the same coin: indistinguishable from one another, interchangeable, and above all, both equally likely to inspire violence. In the liberal New York book publishing industry, copywriters even see this equation as a selling point. Although Mel White does not mention Islam in his book *Religion Gone Bad: The Hidden Dangers of the Christian Right*, the book's cover explains that "...White addresses the wider issue that fundamentalist Christianity—like fundamentalist Islam and the tragic ideologies of fascism—has become a threat...to all Americans who disagree with the 'absolute values' of the Christian Right."[12] The two "fundamentalisms" are supposed to have the same preoccupations. As Andrew Sullivan noted in *The Conservative Soul*, "for Osama, as with the evangelical Christian right, there was a perfect Edenic past, a fallen present, and a perfect future promised."

Often the anti–"Christian theocracy" writers deny that they are baldly equating theocratic aspirations among Christians and Muslims while affirming it in practically the same breath. Damon Linker, who is singular among the theocracy alarmists in focusing more on Catholics than on Protestant fundamentalists, wrote that "the theocons do not aim to transform the country into a Christian version of Afghanistan under the Taliban—a goal that could only be achieved by pursuing the wholesale destruction of American liberal democracy and the establishment of theocratic totalitarianism in its place. Yet they do propose to sanctify and spiritualize the nation's public life, while also eliding fundamental distinctions between church and state, the sacred and the secular. Such efforts, if successful, would not be fateful to the nation, but they would cripple it, effectively transforming the country into what would be recognized around the world as a Catholic-Christian republic."[13] Alexis de Tocqueville and most other observers of the United States have always considered the country to be a Christian republic, so it is hard to see how such a designation would cripple it. And if Linker means more than that, if he means a full-on national establishment of a denominational religion, it is unclear how that would square with the Bill of Rights and not result in "the wholesale destruction of American liberal democracy."

Equating Christian conservatives with the Taliban was a common theme on the Left for years both before and after September 11. Chris Hedges was one of its most forthright advocates, declaring that "the Christian Right and radical Islamists, although locked in a holy war, increasingly mirror each other. They share the same obsessions. They do not tolerate other forms of belief or disbelief. They are at war with artistic and cultural expression. They seek to silence the media. They call for the subjugation of women. They promote severe sexual repression, and they seek to express themselves through violence."[14] Richard Dawkins wrote of the murderous riots that broke out in the Islamic world in reaction to Danish cartoons of the prophet Muhammad, and the chastened response in the formerly free Western press, as evidence of "the disproportionate privileging of religion"—not Islam, but religion—"in our otherwise secular societies."[15] Kevin Phillips spoke darkly of "the rise of varying degrees of radical Christianity, Judaism, and Islam around the world," but he, like all the rest, was far more concerned about the Christian variety than the other two.[16]

Sam Harris wrote to Christian conservatives: "Nonbelievers like myself stand beside you, dumbstruck by the Muslim hordes who chant death to whole nations of the living. But we stand dumbstruck by *you* as well—by your denial of tangible reality, by the suffering you create in service to your religious myths, and by your attachment to an imaginary God."[17] To his credit, Harris also noted in an online debate with Andrew Sullivan that both he and Sullivan were "especially concerned about Islam at this moment—because so many Muslims appear to be 'fundamentalists' and because some of the fundamentals of Islam pose special liabilities in a world overflowing with destructive technology. I think, for instance, that we would both rank the Islamic doctrines of martyrdom and jihad pretty high on our list of humanity's worst ideas."[18]

Nevertheless, the atheist popularizers seldom resisted the temptation to enumerate the excesses of Islamic jihadists and then use them as a stick with which to beat Christians. Even conservative pundit John Derbyshire indulged in a bit of this when, in the course of explaining why he had discarded his Christian faith, he suddenly shifted ground and pulled an illustration of the point he was making from the ranks of the mujahedin: "I have now come to think that it really makes no difference, net-net. You can point to people who were improved by faith, but you can also see people made worse by it. Anyone want to argue that, say, Mohamed Atta was made a better person by his faith?"[19] Writing about atheists such as Dawkins and Harris in the *Wall Street Journal*, Sam

Schulman observed: "Naturally, the atheists focus their peevishness not on Muslim extremists (who advertise their hatred and violent intentions) but on the old-time Christian religion. ('Wisdom dwells with prudence,' the Good Book teaches.) They can always haul out the abortion-clinic bomber if they need a boogeyman; and they can always argue as if all faiths are interchangeable: persuade American Christians to give up their infantile attachment to God, and maybe Muslims will too."[20]

Movie reviewer Jim Emerson articulated the mass-market version of these ideas in a review of a documentary about cult leader Jim Jones: "The face of Jim Jones is, from a slightly different angle, the face of Stalin or Mao, of Christian or Islamic fundamentalism, of Ba'athism or American neoconservatism—any kind of ideology, rooted in certainty and the arrogance of infallibility, pursued with single-minded fervor, intolerant of free thinking or dissent, and that results, inevitably, in deadly consequences."[21] He didn't see the need to present any evidence for his assumption that Christian and Islamic fundamentalism, as well as "Ba'athism" and "American neoconservatism," were virtually identical and in all important respects equivalent.

As television personality Rosie O'Donnell put it in September 2006: "Radical Christianity is just as threatening as radical Islam in a country like America."[22] To this the British columnist David Thompson—no fundamentalist Christian—replied acidly: "But while red-faced evangelists may say, for instance, that gay people are wicked, damned to hellfire, et cetera, I don't know of any internationally renowned Christian leaders who are calling for the imprisonment and killing of gay people. Unlike the supposedly 'moderate' Grand Ayatollah Ali al-Sistani, who insists that gay men and lesbians should be 'killed in the worst manner possible.' Not condemned, 'corrected,' prayed for, or pitied, or any of the usual nonsense spouted by Jerry Falwell, Pat Robertson et al.; but murdered—as brutally as possible."[23]

CHRISTIANITY = ISLAM

Such distinctions are lost on Rosie. Of course, she and many on the political left subscribe to a relativist multiculturalism that recoils from the idea that any ideology (aside from their own) or culture could be superior to another, and particularly from any suggestion that Western Judeo-Christian civilization could possibly be superior to any non-white, non-Christian culture. The idea that Islam is a religion of peace hijacked by a few bad apples and that Christianity has just as much to apologize for as Islam does is pervasive. It has infected not only leftists and secularists, and not only politicians who think they have to spout it in today's political and social climate, but also "conservative" pundits who should know better—including Arnaud de Borchgrave, Ralph Peters, and Dinesh D'Souza.

In his famous September 2006 address in Regensberg, Germany, Pope Benedict XVI argued that, to Christians, God must act within reason, and that "spreading the faith through violence is something unreasonable. Violence is incompatible with the nature of God and the nature of the soul." But "for Muslim teaching, God is absolutely transcendent. His will is not bound up with any of our categories, even that of rationality." The pope's speech touched off murderous riots in the Islamic world, as angry Muslims protested against the idea that Islam was violent or unreasonable by rioting.

Arnaud de Borchgrave, editor at large of the conservative *Washington Times* and of United Press International, criticized the pope for speaking out, and virtually accused him of hypocrisy, given the history of the Catholic Church. Writing in the *Times*, de Borchgrave agreed that the Muslim prophet Muhammad "was no stranger to the sword." The Battle of Tours in France in the year 732, according to de Borchgrave, "saved Europe from Muslim expansionism and Islamization that had conquered Spain." However, he also noted that the victorious Franks "slaughtered the would-be conquerors down to the last man," and that "Christians also lived by the sword."

Ironically, while few in the West have even heard of the Battle of Tours, it is at the forefront of the jihadists' imagination. One wrote in April 2007 of his hope that the warriors of jihad would soon "reinvade France [and convert it into] an Islamic country." He fondly recalled the Muslim commander at Tours, Abdul Rahman al-Ghafiqi: "The Islamic army was left with a large number of martyrs, especially the great shahid [martyr] Abdul Rahman al-Ghafiqi.... this battle is mentioned in history, and is known as the battle of Tours. We ask that Allah sends us a genuine Rahman al-Ghafiqi, to finish what he started in Europe, and conquer the Vatican as promised in our beautiful Islamic verses."[24]

Equivalent to the jihad warfare that began in the seventh century and continues to this day, in de Borchgrave's view, were "the nine Crusades, or religious wars" that were waged by Christians "from the eleventh to the thirteenth century, almost all of them abject failures." De Borchgrave did not mention that they were defensive wars, seeking to reclaim lost Christian lands and defend Eastern Christians, but he did single out for special note the Crusaders' sack of Jerusalem in 1099, during which the Crusaders "made the streets of the old city run ankle-deep with Muslim and Jewish blood." De Borchgrave asserted incorrectly that "Pope John Paul II took the unprecedented step of apologizing for the violence in the Crusades in the name of Christianity," and affirmed the essential equivalence of Islam and Christianity: "Islam's promise of seventy-two virgins to suicide bombers is very similar to church leaders in the era of the Crusades that promised eternal paradise in return for martyrdom against Muslims."[25] He took no notice of the crucial distinction here between being rewarded for killing innocents (what Christians think of as homicide) and suffering death at the hands of persecution or in war (which might bring the fallen Christian peace and the "beatific vision" of God, not seventy-two virgins).

In 2006, retired Army officer Ralph Peters, author of several books on the War on Terror, unleashed a venomous attack in the *New York Post* against unnamed "Islam haters." He asserted that "the world's only hope for long-term peace is for moderate Muslims—by far the majority around the globe—to recapture their own faith. But a rotten core of American extremists is out to make it harder for them."

Who were these people? They were "right-wing extremists" who were "bent on discrediting honorable conservatism" by "insisting that Islam can never reform, that the violent conquest and subjugation of unbelievers is the faith's primary agenda—and, when you read between the lines, that all Muslims are evil and subhuman." Peters endeavored to refute these rotten extremists not by claiming that Islam wasn't inspiring violence in the modern age, but that, well, Christianity inspired violence too: "We could fill entire libraries with bloody-minded texts from the Christian past. And as a believing Christian, I must acknowledge that there's nothing in the Koran as merciless as God's behavior in the Book of Joshua."[26]

Conservative pundit Dinesh D'Souza would probably agree. In his 2007 book *The Enemy at Home: The Cultural Left and Its Responsibility for 9/11*, he notes that "Islam is notorious for the harshness of some of its punishments, such as cutting off the arms and legs of thieves, flogging adulterers, and executing drug dealers." However, "in this respect one may say, with only a hint of irony, that Muslims are in the Old Testament tradition."[27] In interviews publicizing the book, D'Souza repeatedly asserted that Christianity and Islam were just as likely to give rise to violence. He told one interviewer: "I agree with you that the classical Islamic tradition aspired to rule the whole world and bring everyone under the authority of Islamic law. This tradition was very powerful between the seventh and fifteenth centuries. But not only in Islam. The same tradition was very powerful in Christianity during that same period."[28]

Why, then, did Islam seem to have much more of a militaristic tradition than Christianity? Because of the circumstances of their early development: "There is no 'inherent conquering spirit' in Islam, any more than there is one in Christianity," declared D'Souza. "Yes, early Islam did conquer a great deal of territory and early Christianity didn't. But that's because Christianity began in defeat, with the early Christians harassed and persecuted, while Islam began with success, with the prophet Muhammad becoming the ruler of a large domain. So Islam began to spread through force and conquest, but this is no different than the Roman empire, which, let us remember, also carried Christianity to the far corners of Europe."[29]

What of violent passages in the Islamic scriptures? D'Souza finds an equivalence between Christianity and Islam there too, claiming that "the Koran, like the Old Testament, has a number of passages recommending peace and others celebrating the massacre of the enemies of God."[30]

This equivalence, particularly with reference to the Bible and the Qur'an, became a post–September 11 staple. Whenever anyone tried to tie elements of Islam to the murderous Islamist fanaticism around the globe, this was the response. Yes, we were told again and again, Islam has its violent adherents, but so does Christianity. Yes, there is Osama bin Laden, but there is also Timothy McVeigh.

To take just one of a blizzard of available examples, an Islamic apologist calling herself Sheikha Sajida stressed on al-Jazeera's website that "while Jihad is linked to Muslims and Islam-militancy, extremism and terrorism on the other hand are not limited to Muslims; we have Jewish and Christian militant groups, terror organizations, and extremists. Theodore Hertzl, a Jew, was the founder of terrorism in occupied Palestine. And we have the American Christian terrorist Timothy McVeigh, the Oklahoma bomber. But those who wish to ruin the image and the world's respect for Islam focus only on Muslim terrorists, as if the world's followers of Islam are all terrorists."[31]

The idea that Christianity and Islam have similar traditions and modern realities is not only untrue, but it is also bad logic. Even if Christianity were the most violent religion on the planet, which it is not, that fact would establish nothing whatsoever about the violence of Islamic jihadists. Nevertheless, in the minds of many, Christian religious violence, real or imagined, somehow mitigates the reality of the jihad: Everyone does it. You can't expect Muslims to behave differently from Christians. All religions have their fanatics.

WHY DOES IT MATTER?

Are Christianity and Islam really interchangeable? Could the global threat of Islamic terrorism have, in the proper combination of circumstances, arisen in a Christian context as easily as in a Muslim one? Are conservative Christians in the United States really as much of a threat to free societies as the global jihadists?

And above all, does it matter? If Christianity is or was just as violent as Islam, does it make any difference in our understanding of what we must do to defend ourselves against the Islamic terror threat?

Everyone from Dinesh D'Souza to Sheikha Sajida seems to think this is anything but tangential—and they have a point.

Because the War on Terror, a vastly imperfect term, is not a war against a conventional state, it is hard for many people to define what it really is. Prescriptions for victory depend on the diagnosis of the problem. Some think it is hardly a problem at all—merely a matter of police work. Others, like President George W. Bush, believe the War on Terror required an invasion of Afghanistan, an effort to combat al Qaeda cells around the world, an invasion of Iraq, and diplomatic pressure against Iran. Yet others, particularly on the left, continue to believe that the attacks on the World Trade Center towers and the Pentagon were engineered by the U.S. government so that it could invade Muslim countries.[32] Who, then, is the enemy?

Rich Lowry, the editor of *National Review* magazine, suggests this question doesn't matter. "I hate to say it," he wrote in September 2006, "but I don't think it's too important what we call our enemy. Yes, the 'war on terror' is flawed, but everyone knows what we're talking about. And I don't think when President Bush says (or said) 'Islamofascists' light bulbs go off for most Americans, who sit up and think, 'Oh, now I know who we are fighting.' My view is the whole naming debate is 'much ado,' and although it's very interesting, its contribution to actually winning this war will be nil."[33]

WHAT IS THE WAR ON TERROR?

"Everyone knows what we're talking about." Really? "Everyone" seems to have quite divergent views on this.

From the Left, one frequently hears that the War on Terror is war against Islam. *Boston Globe* columnist (and *New York Times* bestselling critic of the Catholic Church) James Carroll expressed it in a 2005 column: "Muslims, meanwhile, see a flood of contempt in pressures on immigrant communities in European cities, in restrictions on Islamic expression, and in openly expressed reservations about Turkey's admission to the EU precisely because of its Islamic character," he wrote. "Given escalations of the war in Iraq together with widely reported instances of Koran-denigration by U.S. interrogators, such trends in Europe make the global war on terror seem expressly a war against Islam."[34]

Western leaders, however, maintain just the opposite. President Bush has assured the world that "ours is a war not against a religion, not against the Muslim faith."[35] Australia's federal foreign affairs minister Alexander Downer told an Indonesian audience in 2006 that "one of the greatest challenges of our age is to ensure that as we fight terrorism, extremism, and intolerance, we do not at the same time trigger broader conflict between civilizations. To characterize this fight against terrorism as a fight against Islam is to invite not just a clash of civilizations, but the broadening of support for terrorists."[36]

A speech by British prime minister Tony Blair struck the same chords: "This is not our war against Islam. This is a war fought by extremists who pervert the true faith of Islam. And all of us, Western and Arab, Christian or Muslim, who put the value of tolerance, respect, and peaceful co-existence above those of sectarian hatred, should join together to defeat them."[37]

Bush and Blair may concede that while the War on Terror is not a war against Islam, it is a war against "Islamofascism" or Islamic fundamentalism. Bush stated this publicly only once, in August 2006: the "terrorists," he declared, "try to spread their jihadist message—a message I call, it's totalitarian in nature—Islamic radicalism, Islamic fascism, they try to spread it as well by taking the attack to those of us who love freedom. . . . This is the beginning of a long struggle against an ideology that is real and profound. It's Islamofascism."[38]

"Islamofascism" is generally considered as a perversion of Islam—a politicized version of a personal and peaceful faith. After the July 7, 2005, bombings in London, Blair said: "We know that these people act in the name of Islam but we also know that the vast and overwhelming majority of Muslims both here and abroad are decent and law-abiding people who abhor this kind of terrorism every bit as much as we do."[39] Bush retreated from this Islamofascism label after protests from American Muslim advocacy groups, but it was an attempt to encapsulate this in a single phrase: that the jihadists were acting in the name of Islam, but were not actually representing actual Islam or Islam as practiced today by most Muslims.

Often connected to this view is the idea that the War on Terror is ultimately a struggle against poverty and ignorance, both of which breed radicalism. This is a variant of the familiar tendency to assume that if enough money is thrown at a problem, it will go away. Despite the fact that Osama bin Laden is quite wealthy, and that study after study has shown that jihadists and even suicide bombers tend to be wealthier and better educated than their peaceful peers, most analysts assume that the problem of "radical Islam" is bred in the resentment that feeds off disadvantage, and can thus be solved by global affirmative action.[40]

A piquant example of this assumption came in December 2006, when Indian prime minister Manmohan Singh announced his support for preferential treatment for Muslims: "We will have to devise innovative plans to ensure that minorities, particularly the Muslim minority, are empowered to share equitably in the fruits of development. They must have the first claim on resources."[41]

A huge number of people in the West, including many in influential government positions, assume that poverty and disadvantage are the "root causes" of terrorism. As John Wallach, president and founder of the pacifist group Seeds of Peace, explained: "The United States needs more than a military response to terrorism. It needs a humane response as well, one that signals that we, as the greatest and richest nation on earth, care about the suffering of the hundreds of millions of less fortunate people throughout the world."[42] But it is not global humanitarianism that concerns the jihadists—it is waging war against the infidels.

We fool ourselves when we imagine that the problem is a localized "Islamic fundamentalism," a "hijacking" of an originally peaceful religion, such that the great majority of its adherents not only do not participate in religiously sanctioned violence, but also actively disapprove of it on grounds derived from the religion itself. In reality, active jihadists, while a minority among Muslims, base their actions in Islamic theology and are in the ascendancy throughout the Islamic world. Nowhere in that world is there a significant anti-jihad, anti–al Qaeda, or anti–bin Laden movement; while Muslims worldwide rioted over cartoons in a Danish newspaper and remarks by Pope Benedict XVI, they have never rioted over Osama bin Laden's supposed hijacking of their faith.

Most Muslims won't join the jihad, but not because they don't approve of it. In Islam, as in every other religious tradition, the number

of the actively devout (not to say fanatical) is always much smaller than
the number of those who identify themselves as members. A smaller
number of Muslims actively reject the jihad and Islamist ideology but
retain a cultural Islam; these moderates, however, are much more mar-
ginalized and less influential than most Westerners imagine.

But then, many Westerners think far worse of their own civilization
than they do of Islam. They believe that the War on Terror is an American imperialist power grab for Middle Eastern oil, or that it is motivated
by evangelical Christians who want a crusade against the Islamic world.
Kevin Phillips and other anti-theocracy writers tend to see the jihad
threat as one trumped up by Christian theocrats. These theocrats are
allegedly maneuvering the United States to be ruled solely by biblical law
and see the War on Terror as a means to spread Christian theocracy
around the world. This idea edges into paranoia and hysteria—as evi-
denced by those who believe that the U.S. government staged the September 11 attacks in order to create a justification for the subsequent
incursions into Afghanistan and Iraq.

In this view, George W. Bush's one-time use of "Crusade" in September 2001 to describe what came to be known as the War on Terror was
not a manifestation of his ignorance of both the history of the Crusades
and the sensitivity with which that word is met in the Islamic word, but
was instead a telling slip of the mask. "Since the collapse of the Soviet
Union," opines Phillips in *American Theocracy*, "America has taken up
the war whoops of militant Protestantism, the evangelical Christian missionary hopes and demands, the heady talk about bringing liberty and
freedom to new shores, the tingle of the old Christian-Muslim blood
feud, the biblical preoccupation with Israel, and the scenarios of the end
times and Armageddon."[43] He notes that "after the prophecy wave of the
early 1990s, the Southern Baptist Convention and other evangelicals
reorganized their missionary activity to focus on Islam in the Middle East
and North Africa, and in 2003, the *New York Times* reported that the
number of U.S. missionaries in Islamic countries had doubled since
1990."[44]

And that was what the War on Terror was all about, you see. Phillips
spoke darkly of America's "biblically stirred foreign policy" and "crusader

mentality."[45] The incursions into Iraq and Afghanistan were not a response to September 11. They were the necessary preludes to missionary efforts: the U.S. would bring the Muslims liberty and democracy, and—under the table—Christianity as well. As for jihadist activity around the world—pshaw, it was all a fabrication, as filmmaker Michael Moore affirmed when he said: "There is no terror threat in this country. This is a lie. It's the biggest lie we have been told." And it was a lie told in service of stirring up Americans to accept a new Crusade, a Crusade sponsored and led by Christian theocrats who were working to take control of this country, institute biblical law, and use America's immense might to launch their mission on a global scale.[46]

What has become clear from the success of Kevin Phillips's book and of so many others is that the imagined threat of Christian theocracy blocks many people from seeing the threat of Islamic jihad—a threat that stretches from Indonesia and the Philippines to Thailand, Kashmir, Chechnya, Iraq, Afghanistan, Israel, Nigeria, Spain, France, Britain, the United States, and elsewhere—for what it is. It is an obstacle that causes them to cast the War on Terror as simply another shameful Crusade.

The argument of moral equivalence so attractive to the Left diverts attention from the reality of an international Islamic jihad to an almost entirely imagined threat from Christianity. Although some of the anti-theocracy writers expropriate common language about Islam to assert that the theocons are "hijacking" Christianity, this is a common pattern: in its advertising for ex-Muslim Daveed Gartenstein-Ross's book *My Year Inside Radical Islam*, the publisher felt compelled to affirm that the radical form of Islam was a twisted version of the real thing, characterizing the book as "the story of how a good faith can be distorted and a decent soul can be seduced away from its principles."[47] None of the publishers of the books warning against Christian theocracy—coming from established and venerable publishing houses like Viking, Houghton Mifflin, Alfred A. Knopf, and Doubleday—feel a similar need to affirm the fundamental goodness of Christianity.

This double standard is emblematic of a general willingness of the Left to play up the notion of a Christian threat to the American republic, while downplaying the idea of an Islamic one. And even many conservatives shy away from naming the enemy, for fear that it means war against a billion Muslims. But if criticism of Islam is not allowed, if non-Muslims cannot speak forthrightly about how Islamists recruit and motivate jihadists using the Qur'an and other Islamic sources, how can we encourage genuine Muslim reformers? Nothing can be reformed if the need for reform is not even acknowledged.

We also need to be free to defend the superiority of the Judeo-Christian tradition over the Islamic one, rather than compiling facile comparisons between the Qur'an and the Old Testament. This is not, as many on the left suppose, merely special pleading and whitewashing for our own culture. The Left, and some conservative writers like Dinesh D'Souza, are much more comfortable lauding the past achievements of Islamic civilization while denigrating those of Christian Europe.

D'Souza touts the work of historian Bernard Lewis in this line, characterizing it thusly: "While firmly outlining the problems with Islamic toleration, Lewis shows that Muslims have throughout history coexisted with non-Muslims, and he goes on to make the startling point that historically speaking Islam was more tolerant than Christianity."[48]

D'Souza's point in asserting this (which he does often) is unclear. Even if Lewis is correct that the Ottomans were better to minorities than Catholic Europe, what does that prove? Certainly the evangelical Christian theocrats who inhabit the nightmares of Chris Hedges and Kevin Phillips have no interest in bringing back the Catholic Europe of the Middle Ages. But Muslim jihadists are trying to impose sharia law on the rest of the world, including second-class citizenship for non-Muslims. Is D'Souza suggesting that this isn't so bad after all?

Judeo-Christian civilization deserves a better, more spirited defense.

CHAPTER THREE

WE HAVE MET THE ENEMY AND HE IS . . .

Is it really credible that America is in danger from Christians? A growing number of writers and activists on the left think so. They are trying to convince the American people that the Establishment Clause of the First Amendment, as well as other parts of the Constitution, is in imminent danger from Christian fascists. Kevin Phillips's warning in *American Theocracy* is relatively mild: "believing constituencies" want "more of their 'government'" to "come from religious institutions, with the imprimatur of a president who openly favors at least some transfer of power."[1] Damon Linker warns in *The Theocons: Secular America Under Siege* of the possibility that "George W. Bush's presidency will come to be seen not as an electoral and historical aberration but rather as the first stage in a cultural counterrevolution whose ultimate goal is nothing less than the end of secular politics in America."[2] The anti-Bush preoccupations of these and similar writers might imply that their fears will fade once a new president takes office. But they also argue that the theocratic threat has a broader base. Phillips quotes pundit Bill Moyers asserting that "for the first time in our history, ideology and theology hold a monopoly of power in Washington," and laments that "no leading world power in modern memory has become a captive, even a partial captive, of the sort of biblical inerrancy—backwater, not mainstream—that dismisses modern knowledge and science."[3] But that, he claims, is the state of the American republic today.

In her book *Kingdom Coming: The Rise of Christian Nationalism*, Michelle Goldberg concurs, asserting that "the ultimate goal of Christian nationalist leaders isn't fairness. It's dominion. The movement is built on a theology that asserts the Christian right to rule."[4] "To the Religious Right," adds Barry Lynn of the American Civil Liberties Unions, "separation of church and state is a myth, a dangerous, anti-Christian principle imposed on the nation by judicial fiat in 1947." Mel White recounts Alabama Supreme Court chief justice Roy Moore's 2001 placement of a granite monument of the Ten Commandments in the state judiciary building (the monument was removed in 2003) and then remarks: "Judge Moore is a hero to Christian fundamentalists because placing Mosaic law over the laws of this land is exactly what they plan to do."[5]

What would happen if these "Christian fundamentalists" succeed? White worries that fundamentalist Christians might "amend the U.S. Constitution with a watered-down version of that Leviticus passage that condemns [homosexuals] to death."[6] He worries that Christian fundamentalists are "simply waiting for that day when they have accumulated enough power to enforce" the death penalty on homosexuals.[7]

Goldberg, on the other hand, sees a global struggle, "one between modernity, humanism, reason and progress on one hand, and fundamentalism, tribalism, Puritanism, and obscurantism on the other. Liberals the world over are fighting religious tyranny." She quotes Salman Rushdie on the difference between the two camps: "The fundamentalist seeks to bring down a great deal more than buildings. Such people are against, to offer just a brief list, freedom of speech, a multiparty political system, universal adult suffrage, accountable government, Jews, homosexuals, women's rights, pluralism, secularism, short skirts, dancing, beardlessness, evolution theory, sex." Goldberg informs us that "Christian nationalists have no problem with beardlessness, but except for that, Rushdie could have been describing them."[8]

In his book *American Fascists*, which made the *New York Times* bestseller list, Chris Hedges's vision of a Christian America is even darker. He sees an authoritarian, anti-democratic Christian regime in our future: "Under Christian dominion," he thunders, "America will be no longer a sinful and fallen nation, but one in which the Ten Commandments form the basis of our legal system, creationism and 'Christian values' form the basis of our educational system, and the media and the government proclaim the Good News to one and all. Labor unions, civil rights laws and public schools will be abolished. Women will be removed from the workforce to stay at home, and all those deemed insufficiently Christian will be denied citizenship.... The only legitimate voices in this state will be Christian. All others will be silenced."[9] He decries the "racist and brutal intolerance" of the founders of this Christian movement, which is "small in number but influential," and is "taking over the machinery of U.S. state and religious institutions."[10]

Not that this is genuine Christianity, we are assured. Barry Lynn echoes the conventional wisdom about Islam, asserting that these right-wingers have "hijacked Christianity."[11] Hedges says that "radical Christian dominionists have no religious legitimacy. They are manipulating Christianity, and millions of sincere believers, to build a frightening political mass movement with many similarities to other mass movements, from Fascism to Communism to the ethnic nationalist parties in the former Yugoslavia."[12] Hedges claims that "those arrayed against American democracy are waiting for a moment to strike, a national crisis that will allow them to shred the Constitution in the name of national security and strength." He even asserts that "those in the movement often speak about such a moment with gleeful anticipation."[13] For now—but only for now—the Christian Right is "forced to function within the political system it seeks to destroy."[14]

In the face of this, Lynn calls upon "Christians, Jews, Muslims, Buddhists, Wiccans, pagans, nonbelievers, humanists, the unaffiliated, and others" to "reassert the wisdom of the Founding Fathers who gave us the separation of church and state."[15] Hedges calls upon "all Americans—not only those of faith—who care about our open society" to "challenge aggressively this movement's deluded appropriation of Christianity and to do everything possible to defend tolerance. The attacks by this movement on the rights and beliefs of Muslims, Jews, immigrants, gays, lesbians, women, scholars, scientists, those they dismiss as 'nominal Christians,' and those they brand with the curse of 'secular humanist' are an attack on all of us, on our values, our freedoms, and ultimately our democracy."[16] After all, as Goldberg puts it, "it makes no sense to fight religious authoritarianism abroad while letting it take over at home."[17]

Indeed. But is there really a threat of religious authoritarianism within the United States? And if there is, is it equal in magnitude to the threat the West faces from Islam? As the Qur'an says, "Bring your proof, if you be truthful" (2:111; 27:64). Good advice. Especially given that everything these authors say seems utterly at odds not only with the Christian faith Americans know in their own lives, or in the lives of their neighbors, but with American history, in which Christianity, far from creating a theocracy, was regarded as the justification for the American system of republican government.

IS THERE ANY EVIDENCE?

In support of his claims that "those arrayed against American democracy are waiting for a moment to strike," Chris Hedges offers only a single quotation from "right-wing strategist" Howard Phillips. In a speech to the Council for National Policy, Phillips said that "it is time to leave the 'political *Titanic*' on which the conservative movement has for too long booked passage" and to "build an ark so that we can and will be ready to renew and restore our nation and our culture when God brings the tides to flood."[18]

This is a call to shred the Constitution? Phillips's words read more plausibly as a call to a conservative movement demoralized by defeat after defeat (within the Republican Party) not to give up, but to develop a new strategy and await a time when its message will be received more favorably. The Harvard-educated Phillips himself left the Republican Party in 1974 and founded the U.S. Taxpayers' Party (later the Constitution Party) in 1992 and ran for president of the United States on that ticket in 1992, 1996, and 2000. Far from wanting to shred the Constitution and impose a theocratic dictatorship, Phillips's platform was one of limited government and a return to the original intent of the Constitution and the principles of the Declaration of Independence.

Similarly, Mel White's case that Christian right-wingers are just waiting for their chance to stone homosexuals to death is based more on conjecture than actual evidence. "Even though we are certain that our fellow Americans would never go to that extreme," he says, "we need to seriously consider the question. Once fundamentalist Christians have successfully dehumanized our lives, demeaned our relationships, denied us our rights, devastated our families, destroyed our influence in church and society, and driven us back into our closets, what comes next?"[19] What indeed? Can White point to any Christian sect or denomination, Catholic, Orthodox, or Protestant, that teaches that homosexuals should be stoned to death? Of course he cannot; but he can, and does, invoke the words of several individual Christian teachers.

One of these was a Presbyterian pastor with whom White appeared on a Seattle radio show. "When I asked him," recounts White, "how he interpreted that passage in Leviticus that calls for the death of a man who sleeps with another man, he replied without hesitation, 'It means you should be killed.' After swallowing hard, I asked him, 'Who should do the killing? You church folk?' He answered without a pause: 'No, that's the civil authority's job. That's why we have to get more good men of God elected into government.'"[20]

But if this unnamed pastor got his wish and more "good men of God" were elected in America, is it really likely that Leviticus 20:13 would become the law of the land? In what Christian country in the 1950s, or the 1850s, or the 1750s, or at any time, were homosexuals sentenced to death by stoning? Almost all Christians believe, and always have believed, that the specific penal and ceremonial requirements of the Mosaic law were superseded by the new covenant. Moreover, when Jesus rebukes as hypocrites those who would stone an adulterous woman, he obviously set aside capital punishments in such matters.[21]

White notes that the pastor who spoke such frightening words on Seattle radio was a "Reconstructionist." For writers like White, Christian Reconstructionism, a Calvinist movement in the United States, is the primary foe. Christian Reconstructionism, we're told, has insinuated its adherents into the highest levels of government, and they want to stone not just homosexuals but also adulterers. Moreover, they want to subvert the U.S. Constitution and replace it with "Christian" law. (Of course, there is no Christian equivalent to sharia law; sharia, with its detailed

directives covering the minutest aspects of life as well as questions of
state governance, bears no resemblance to secular law guided by Christian principles—which is the tradition of Western law. It may be likened to
canon law, which is relevant only to the church, but even that is a stretch.)

The "proof" of a Christian Reconstructionist plot comes largely from
the writings of two American Calvinists, Rousas John Rushdoony, who
died in 2001, and his son-in-law, Gary North, the intellectual guiding
lights of the Reconstructionist movement. Rushdoony and North are the
chief villains of virtually every piece devoted to the Christian Reconstructionist menace.

They may well be cast in this villain's role, for according to some
reports they apparently do depart from Christian tradition in calling for
capital punishment for crimes such as adultery and homosexuality. In a
1998 piece in the libertarian magazine *Reason*, Rushdoony is said to
defend biblical punishments for a variety of offenders: "blasphemers,
heretics, apostate Christians, people who cursed or struck their parents,
females guilty of 'unchastity before marriage,' 'incorrigible' juvenile delin-
quents, adulterers, and (probably) telephone psychics." North is quoted in
the same article defending the ancient biblical punishment of stoning:
"Why stoning? There are many reasons. First, the implements of execution
are available to everyone at virtually no cost."[22] Perhaps, not coincidentally,
North is a libertarian economist (with a Ph.D. from the University of California–Riverside) and a professed majority-rule democrat.

The anti-theocracy writers insist that Christian Reconstructionists
intend to impose a harsh and biblically based social order upon the
United States. They point to statements like this one from the popular
Presbyterian minister and writer George Grant:

> Christians have an obligation, a mandate, a commission, a holy
> responsibility to reclaim the land for Jesus Christ—to have dominion
> in the civil structures, just as in every other aspect of life and godli-
> ness. But it is dominion that we are after. Not just a voice. It is
> dominion we are after. Not just influence. It is dominion we are after.
> Not just equal time. It is dominion we are after. World conquest.
> That's what Christ has commissioned us to accomplish. We must win

the world with the power of the Gospel. And we must never settle for anything less. . . . Thus, Christian politics has as its primary intent the conquest of the land of men, families, institutions, bureaucracies, courts, and governments for the Kingdom of Christ. It is to reinstitute the authority of God's Word as supreme over all judgments, over all legislation, over all declarations, constitutions, and confederations. True Christian political action seeks to rein the passions of men and curb the pattern of digression under God's rule.[23]

Strong words. But are statements like these a manifesto to subvert the U.S. Constitution and establish Christian Reconstructionist rule in the United States? The "theocrats" themselves deny this. Referring directly to the passage just quoted, Grant denied that it was a declaration of intent to destroy the U.S. Constitution, and added:

1. My body of work demonstrates that I am an ardent defender of the First Amendment.
2. I am an opponent of "state churches."
3. I am an opponent of confusing, blurring, or overlapping the spheres of authority and jurisdictions between church and state and family.
4. I have spent my life working in the areas of racial reconciliation, care for the poor, international relief and development, education, and advocating for the last, least and lost—so the last thing I would ever promote would be spiritual or cultural coercion.

The quoted passage is from a long discussion regarding cultural evangelism, not petty partisanship. It is from a discussion of ends, not means. The language is the culmination of a discourse in the realm of eschatological theology, not practical activism. No nation has ever willingly converted to Islam (despite what some might say about some of the Spice Islands of Indonesia). That fact speaks for itself. On the other hand, no nation has ever unwillingly been coerced into Christendom—and remained so for more than a generation. That too speaks for itself.[24]

In a similar vein, Rushdoony's Chalcedon Foundation firmly declares: "We propose an explicitly biblical system of thought and action as the exclusive basis for civilization. Only by restoring the Christian faith and biblical law as the standard of all of life can Christians hope to reestablish Christian civilizations." Theocracy? Maybe, but the statement goes on to say: "We believe that the source of godly change is regeneration by the Holy Spirit, not revolution by the violence of man. . . . No government in any form can make men Christians or truly obedient; this is the work of God's sovereign grace. Much less should civil government try to impose biblical law on an unbelieving society. Biblical law cannot be imposed; it must be embraced."[25]

Chris Ortiz of the Chalcedon Foundation amplifies this point: "Christian theocracy is not the imposition of biblical law on the unwilling. It is not the rule of a religious elite. Christian theocracy is self-government in terms of God's law. We choose the term *theocracy* very carefully, i.e., 'the rule of God.' We did not choose the term *ecclesiocracy*—the rule of the church. We do not support a religious takeover of the state. The idea is ridiculous."[26] The foundation adds in another statement:

> Because we believe that the Bible should apply to all of life, including the state; and because we believe that the Christian state should enforce biblical civil law; and finally, because we believe that the responsibility of Christians is to exercise dominion in the earth for God's glory, it is sometimes assumed that we believe that capturing state apparatus and enforcing biblical law on a pervasively unbelieving populace is one of our hidden objectives. Our critics sometimes imply or state outright that we are engaged in a subtle, covert attempt to capture conservative, right-wing politics in order to gain political power, which we will then use to 'spring' biblical law on our nation. This is flatly false. We do not believe that politics or the state are a chief sphere of dominion.[27]

In other words, if the Chalcedon Foundation does envision a Christian theocracy in the United States, it is a voluntary one that results from Christian evangelization and society-wide conversion. Under these principles, it is hardly at odds with the Constitution, which, as John Adams famously said, "was made only for a moral and religious people." In 1981 the Presbyterian theologian and philosopher Francis Schaeffer, whose writings remain highly popular and influential among Reconstructionists and many evangelical Christians, insisted that the goal is for Christianity to guide American public life, under the Constitution, as it had in the past, not to establish an unconstitutional theocracy.

> First, we must make definite that we are in no way talking about any kind of a theocracy. Let me say that with great emphasis. Witherspoon, Jefferson, the American Founders had no idea of a theocracy. That is made plain by the First Amendment, and we must continually emphasize the fact that we are not talking about some kind, or any kind, of a theocracy.
>
> We must not confuse the Kingdom of God with our country. To say it another way: "We should not wrap Christianity in our national flag."
>
> None of this, however, changes the fact that the United States was founded upon a Christian consensus, nor that we today should bring Judeo-Christian principles into play in regard to government. But that is very different from a theocracy in name or in fact.[28]

Much of the alleged "evidence" that radical right-wing Christians want to impose a theocracy on the United States is actually evidence only that Christian pastors and leaders have reasserted the right and duty of Christians to participate in public life. As journalist Bernard Goldberg puts it trenchantly, "Why is it kosher for liberal Jews to play footsie with politicians, but when the Religious Right does the exact same thing, it's the first step toward a Christian theocracy?"[29]

Of course, every interest group in the United States tries to influence the political process. They are not subverting the political process; they are participating in it. And as we have seen, the alleged Christian "theocrats" deny that they have any intention of subverting the U.S. Constitution. Indeed, right-wing Christians almost invariably see themselves as patriots who venerate the Constitution; they have no intention of overthrowing a Constitution that they believe—and that history shows—was

made by a Christian people. Paul Weyrich of the Free Congress Foundation, a longtime conservative activist who some of the anti-theocracy
writers call "the most powerful man in America," has said, "As someone
who has helped the religious right transition to the political process, I
would have nothing to do" with any attempt at replacing the American
Constitution with a theocracy.[30]

BUT OF COURSE THEY WOULD
DENY IT... OR WOULD THEY?

Conspiracy-minded anti-theocrats, however, brush aside such denials.
The whole thing is a secret plot, you see—what else would you expect
but for the plotters to deny their plotting? After all, according to Chris
Hedges, the American values of "compassion, tolerance, and belief in
justice and equality" are "being dismantled, often with stealth."[31]

There can be no definitive refutations of accusations without evidence, such as Hedges makes, but we can note that not only do the
alleged Christian theocrats deny the accusations, but no plots have been
uncovered, and the only "evidence" the anti-theocrats can point to is that
some conservative Christians are trying to advance their ideas in the public square. Put that way, perhaps the danger is not from Christians participating in America's public life, but rather the paranoid reaction of
those who think that Christians should be banned from public life.

CHAPTER FOUR

THE REAL THREAT

While the accused Christian theocrats are few in number, and they deny the allegations against them, there is no shortage of Muslim leaders who openly and unapologetically proclaim the necessity of imposing Islamic sharia law upon the world. In the same vein, Muslims pursuing Islamic holy war (jihad) are generally quite unguarded about their intentions. Abu Musab al-Zarqawi, al Qaeda's leader in Iraq before he was killed by American forces in June 2006, explained his goals in strictly religious terms: "As for our political agenda as some people call it, so we find it summarized richly in the saying of the Prophet (peace be upon him), 'I have been sent with the sword, between the hands of the hour, until Allah is worshipped alone.'"[1]

Before he left Britain (one step ahead of law enforcement) and returned to his native Lebanon, the jihadist Sheikh Omar Bakri Muhammad often boasted of his intention to "transform the West into Dar Al-Islam [the land of Islam]" and establish Islamic law on British soil. "I want to see the black flag of Islam flying over Downing Street," he said, and his now disbanded al-Muhajiroun group was dedicated to this goal.[2] The transformation of Britain into an Islamic state could come in two ways, he explained: "If an Islamic state arises and invades," in which case "we will be its army and its soldiers from within." But if no such Islamic state arises, Bakri said that Muslims would convert the West to Islam "through ideological invasion...without war and killing."[3] Bakri's fellow

British jihadist, the now imprisoned Sheikh Abu Hamza al-Masri, explained that this was a universal imperative: "Allah is the only one that must be worshipped on Earth, and the only way to guarantee this is to control all the land masses, air, and sea and give Islam the proper channel to be heard by the people."[4]

The idea that Muslims must fight in order to ensure that Islam has the "proper channel to be heard by the people" is a common teaching in the Islamic world. South African mufti Ebrahim Desai repeated it in answering a question at "Islam Q & A Online." The questioner asked: "I have a question about offensive jihad. Does it mean that we are to attack even those non-Muslims [who] don't do anything against Islam just because we have to propagate Islam?" Desai responded that "one of the primary responsibilities of the Muslim ruler is to spread Islam throughout the world, thus saving people from eternal damnation." How should a Muslim ruler fulfill this responsibility? Desai went on to explain that "if a country doesn't allow the propagation of Islam to its inhabitants in a suitable manner or creates hindrances to this, then the Muslim ruler would be justifying [sic] in waging Jihad against this country, so that the message of Islam can reach its inhabitants, thus saving them from the Fire of Jahannum [Hell]. If the Kuffaar [unbelievers] allow us to spread Islam peacefully, then we would not wage Jihad against them."[5]

Al Qaeda's second in command, Dr. Ayman al-Zawahiri, articulated a global vision in the summer of 2006: "War with Israel is not subject to a treaty, cease-fire, Sykes-Picot Treaty agreements, patriotism or disputed borders, but it is jihad for the cause of God until the entire religion is for him only. Jihad seeks the liberation of Palestine, the entire country of Palestine and to liberate every land that used to be a territory of Islam, from Spain to Iraq. The entire world is an open field for us.... With the grace of God, we have now returned to the field.... Dear Muslim brothers everywhere, today we must target the Jewish and the American interests everywhere."[6]

Until November 2003, when adverse publicity compelled them to take it down, the Islamic Affairs Department (IAD) of the Saudi Arabian embassy in Washington carried this statement of Islamic supremacism and belligerence on its website: "The Muslims are required to raise the banner of Jihad in order to make the Word of Allah supreme in this world, to remove all forms of injustice and oppression, and to defend the Muslims. If Muslims do not take up the sword, the evil tyrants of this earth will be able to continue oppressing the weak and [the] helpless."[7]

In other words, the antidote to tyranny is Islamic law, and Muslims are obliged to wage war against unbelievers to impose it. The spread of Islam must continue at all costs. There can be no half-measures or peaceful coexistence with unbelievers as equals on an indefinite basis. As Egyptian jihad theorist and activist Sayyid Qutb (1906–1966), whose works are still widely influential among Muslims worldwide, put it in his jihad manifesto *Milestones* (*Ma'alim 'ala Al-Tariq*), which has circulated throughout the world and been published in well over a thousand editions: "Islam cannot accept any mixing with Jahiliyyah [the society of unbelievers].... Islam cannot accept or agree to a situation which is half-Islam and half-Jahiliyyah.... The foremost duty of Islam in this world is to depose Jahiliyyah from the leadership of man, and to take the leadership into its own hands and enforce the particular way of life which is its permanent feature."[8]

In contrast to the completely American make-up of the Christian theocrats, Islamist jihad is an international movement. Qutb articulated for Muslims an internationalist vision transcending nationality and based on Islamic law and identity: "A Muslim has no country except that part of the earth where the Shari'ah of God is established and human relationships are based on the foundation of relationship with God; a Muslim has no nationality except his belief, which makes him a member of the Muslim community in Dar-ul-Islam."[9]

Another influential jihadist writer, Sayyid Abul A'la Maududi (1903–1979), shares Qutb's perspective. The author of several influential books, including *Jihad in Islam* and the massive *Towards Understanding the Qur'an*, Maududi was, like Qutb, not simply a theorist; in 1940 he founded the Jamaat-e-Islami (Muslim Party).[10] This organization still exists today in Pakistan, India, and Bangladesh (as well as in Jammu and Kashmir, which is one of the principal flashpoints of jihad activity), and is dedicated to making these countries Islamic states. Maududi's influence goes well beyond the subcontinent. One admirer called him "the greatest revivalist of Islam in the twentieth century" and pointed out that his "writings and thoughts inspired similar movements in a large part of the world."[11]

Maududi argued that Islam was inherently political, not just religious in the sense in which most Westerners understand the term, and that Muslims must wage war in order to impose Islamic law upon the world. To accommodationist Muslims of his day he declared: "The truth is that Islam is not the name of a 'Religion,' nor is 'Muslim' the title of a 'Nation.' In reality Islam is a revolutionary ideology and programme which seeks to alter the social order of the whole world and rebuild it in conformity with its own tenets and ideals. 'Muslim' is the title of that International Revolutionary Party organized by Islam to carry into effect its revolutionary programme. And 'Jihad' refers to that revolutionary struggle and utmost exertion which the Islamic Party brings into play to achieve this objective."

Maududi envisioned this struggle, and the hegemony of Islam that it would establish, as universal: "Islam requires the earth—not just a portion, but the whole planet—not because the sovereignty over the earth should be wrested from one Nation or several Nations and vested in one particular Nation, but because the entire mankind should benefit from . . . [Islam] which is the programme of well-being for all humanity." The well-being of all humanity would be best served by the imposition of what Maududi saw as the laws of Allah—for he regarded allegiance to merely human laws as the root of all societal evils: "No one has the right to become a self-appointed ruler of men and issue orders and prohibitions on his own volition and authority. To acknowledge the personal authority of a human being as the source of commands and prohibitions is tantamount to admitting him as the sharer in the Powers and Authority of God. And this is the root of all evils in the universe."

The Muslims, the party of Allah, are accordingly "left with no other choice except to capture State Authority, for an evil system takes root and flourishes under the patronage of an evil government and a pious cultural order can never be established until the authority of Government is wrested from the wicked and transferred into the hands of the reformers. . . . [I]f the Muslim Party commands adequate resources it will eliminate un-Islamic Governments and establish the power of Islamic Government in their stead." This is, he says, exactly what Muhammad and the first caliphs did. "It is the same policy which was executed by the Holy Prophet (peace of Allah be upon him) and his successor illustrious Caliphs (may Allah be pleased with them). Arabia, where the Muslim Party was founded, was the first country which was subjugated and brought under the rule of Islam."

Maududi explains that "as soon as the Ummah of Islam captures State power" it will therefore ban various un-Islamic practices: the lending of money at interest, "all forms of business and financial dealings which are forbidden by Islamic Law," gambling, prostitution, "and other vices," and "it will make it obligatory for non-Muslim women to observe the minimum standards of modesty in dress as required by Islamic Law and will forbid them to go about displaying their beauty like the days of ignorance." An Islamic state will also "clamp censorship on the cinema."[12]

Non-Muslims may continue to live in such a state, but they cannot hold political power within it: "Non-Muslims have been granted the freedom to stay outside the Islamic fold and to cling to their false, man-made ways if they so wish. They have, however, absolutely no right to seize the reins of power in any part of God's earth nor to direct the collective affairs of human beings according to their own misconceived doctrines.... In such a situation the believers would be under an obligation to do their utmost to dislodge them from political power and to make them live in subservience to the Islamic way of life."[13]

The political movement Maududi created, Jamaat-e-Islami, is one of the largest political parties in Pakistan today, and numerous government officials have risen through its ranks. Its current leader in Pakistan, Qazi Hussain Ahmed, states that Jamaat-e-Islami believes "NOT in the Western definition of 'democracy,' which assign[s] (in principle though) all authority to the people. We believe in the Authority of Allah and human being[s] as His vicegerents. Thus 'democracy' in Islam is guided as well as guarded." The democracy that Ahmed envisions will need no voting, for its principles are "quite clearly expounded in the Qur'an and Sunnah."[14]

Maududi's influence is international and lingering. His commentary on the Qur'an is readily available in English; the Muslim Students Association of the University of Southern California expresses a view common among Muslims today when it says, "Maududi's translation and commentary on the Qur'an, 'The Meaning of the Qur'an,' ranks as one of the best such works in existence today."[15]

Egyptian jihadist Muhammad 'Abdus Salam Faraj (1952–1982), who, like Qutb, was executed by the Egyptian government (in Faraj's case, for his role in the assassination of Egyptian president Anwar Sadat), wrote a book titled *Jihad: The Absent Obligation* that crystallized many of these ideas. "Allah revealed Islam," he asserted, "in order that humanity could be governed according to it. Unbelief is darkness and disorder. So the unbelievers, if they are not suppressed, create disorder. That is why the Muslims are responsible for the implementation of Allah's Law on the planet, that humanity may be governed by it, as opposed to corrupt man-made laws. The Muslims must make all efforts to establish the religion of Allah on the earth."[16] Faraj's book was found on the bookshelf of one of the plotters of the July 21, 2005, terror attacks in Great Britain.[17]

This is also the view of the Islamic group Hizb ut-Tahrir, which despite its protestations of peacefulness is banned in many countries for its avowed determination to establish an Islamic state. A website expounding the group's philosophy explains: "Islam makes it a duty upon all Muslims to work to change their countries from Dar al-Kufr [the land of unbelief] to Dar al-Islam, and this can be achieved by establishing the Islamic State, i.e., the Khilafah, and by electing a Khaleefah [caliph] and taking a bay'ah [oath of allegiance] on him that he will rule by the Word of Allah (Subhaanahu Wa Ta'Ala) i.e., he will implement Islamic laws in the country where the Khilafah has been established. Then the Muslims should work with the Khilafah to combine the rest of the Islamic countries with it, hence the countries will become Dar al-Islam and they will then carry Islam to the world through invitation and jihad."[18]

Okay, "invitation and jihad"—but mostly jihad; an al Qaeda manual discovered not long after September 11 in a safe house in Manchester, England, declared: "Islamic governments have never and will never be established through peaceful solutions and cooperative councils. They are established as they [always] have been by pen and gun, by word and bullet, by tongue and teeth." As Islamic governments have "never been established through peaceful solutions," it seems likely that although "word," "pen," and "tongue" are mentioned, they quickly give way to "gun," "bullet," and "teeth." The manual continues: "Islamic government would never be established except by the bomb and rifle. Islam does not coincide or make a truce with unbelief, but rather confronts it. The confrontation that Islam calls for with these godless and apostate regimes does not know Socratic debates, Platonic ideals, or Aristotelian diplomacy. But it knows the dialogue of bullets, the ideals of assassination, bombing, and destruction, and the diplomacy of the cannon and machine-gun."[19]

THE PAROCHIALISM OF LIBERALS

It seems absurd that liberals downplay the threat posed by Islamic jihadists. Jihadists are forthright about their plans and have executed devastating terrorist atrocities around the world, including the worst act of terrorism in U.S. history. But liberals dramatize a supposed threat from domestic "theocratic" Christians, who plausibly deny they have any such intention and have no record of doing anything more dangerous than trying to elect people who share their belief in the importance of reflecting Christian principles in American laws.

While writers like Chris Hedges and Kevin Phillips are busy sounding the alarm about American pastors who are urging their congregations to vote, Islamic jihadists are active on every continent. The Islamic jihadists are not just preaching hate (or absorbing the preaching of hate) and plotting terrorism—they also see themselves engaged in a worldwide holy war against unbelievers.

The Christian theocrats, we are supposed to believe, wish to establish "Christian rule" in the United States. If we suppose that to mean applying the laws found in the Old Testament, how many countries in the world today are governed today by biblical law? None. While there have been Christian states in the past, there are none today, aside from Vatican City, and even the Christian states of history held a distinction between secular and religious (or canon) law and between the authority of the king and the pope. There is no global movement today to replace secular law with biblical law. But, as we have seen, the Islamic jihadists see it as their mission to subordinate the entire globe under sharia law.

Of course, some equate Bush administration foreign policy with jihad. Kevin Phillips cites Bruce Lincoln, a University of Chicago professor of religion, to compare Bush and Osama bin Laden: "In 2002 Lincoln had dissected Bush's October 2001 speech to the nation about his planned military response to the events of September 11. He found the president's rhetoric to be not unlike Osama bin Laden's own statements in that 'both men constructed a Manichean struggle, where Sons of Light confront Sons of Darkness, and all must enlist on one side or the other, without possibility of neutrality, hesitation, or middle ground.'" Responding to the obvious objection that Bush did not use religious language while bin Laden did, Lincoln (and Phillips) resorted to claiming that the president used "'double-coding,'" through which he "signaled attentive Bible readers that he shared their private scriptural invocations—using phrases from the revelation of St. John (6:15–17, about the wrath of the lamb) and Isaiah (about evildoers hiding in caves and the lonely paths of the godless)."[20] Never mind that Bush never used the words *wrath* or *lamb* in his address, and never mind that bin Laden and other al Qaeda operatives actually do hide in caves. Why let the truth get in the way of a great theory?[21]

Phillips recounts Britain's imperial adventures in the Middle East and then opines that Britain's "post–World War I debacle" was "about to be blindly repeated by a president of the United States who shared Lloyd George's biblical frame of reference, thought the enemy was 'evil,' and failed to profit from the lessons of history." He describes Bush as an "evangelical Christian missionary," influenced by "heady talk about bringing liberty and freedom to new shores."[22] But maybe, just maybe, Bush's real mission was not biblical at all, but an attempt to defend America from a second September 11, and he was seeing the wars in Afghanistan and Iraq and the replacing of their tyrannies with democracies as part of this effort. Phillips and his ilk certainly have to stretch to portray Bush's policies in Iraq and Afghanistan as part of a Christian missionary enterprise; the new constitutions of both countries give a privileged place to Islam, and the Bush administration has taken no special measures to halt the persecution of Christians in post-Saddam Iraq. And then there's the case of Abdul Rahman.

ABDUL RAHMAN, CHRISTIANITY, AND ISLAMIC APOSTASY

An Afghani named Abdul Rahman was arrested in February 2006 for the crime of leaving Islam and becoming a Christian. Not long after this arrest, President Bush declared: "Before September 11, 2001, Afghanistan was ruled by a cruel regime that oppressed its people, brutalized women, and gave safe haven to the terrorists who attacked America. Today, the terror camps have been shut down; women are working; boys and girls are back in school; and twenty-five million people have now tasted freedom. The Afghani people are building a vibrant young democracy that is an ally in the War on Terror."[23]

Of course, when Bush spoke those words Abdul Rahman's case had not yet been reported in the West. But soon thereafter it became international news that the taste of freedom the Afghanis were enjoying under Hamid Karzai's regime was not quite what many Westerners might have expected. And certainly it had nothing to do with the Bush administration bringing Christianity, either overtly or covertly, to Afghanistan.

In reality, the constitution of the new, post-Taliban Afghani regime stipulates that "no law can be contrary to the beliefs and provisions of the sacred religion of Islam."[24] Abdul Rahman's case showed that Islam's traditional classification of apostasy as a capital crime would be included in this. The prophet Muhammad regarded apostasy from Islam as a supreme evil, and one of the main reasons the punishment is so severe is because apostates were once Muslims but "turn renegade." Muhammad decreed that no Muslim could be put to death except for murder, unlawful sexual intercourse, and apostasy.[25] He said flatly: "Whoever changed his Islamic religion, then kill him."[26] This is still the position of all the schools of Islamic jurisprudence, although there is some disagreement over whether the law applies only to men.[27] Thus it was not at all surprising that the

Afghani government, constituted so that no law could be made that contradicted Islamic law, put Abdul Rahman on trial. Yet Western analysts seem to have had trouble grasping the import of Rahman's case. A "human rights expert" quoted by the *Times* of London summed up the confusion widespread in Western countries: "The constitution says Islam is the religion of Afghanistan, yet it also mentions the Universal Declaration of Human Rights, and Article 18 specifically forbids this kind of recourse. It really highlights the problem the judiciary faces."[28]

State Department spokesman Sean McCormack tried to find a silver lining: "Under the Taliban, anybody considered an apostate was subject to torture and death. Right now, you have a legal proceeding that is under way in Afghanistan." Undersecretary of state Nicholas Burns was confident in the case's outcome: "Our government is a great supporter of freedom of religion. As the Afghani constitution affords freedom of religion to all Afghani citizens, we hope very much that those rights, the right of freedom of religion, will be upheld in an Afghani court."[29]

In the end, however, the test never came. After an international firestorm, Abdul Rahman was released, and asked for asylum in Italy, which was swiftly granted. However, the Islamic law provision in the Afghani constitution remains today. But if this episode made anything clear, it was that the Bush administration had no interest whatsoever in defending or appearing to defend the rights of a Christian prisoner in an Islamic state. American officials did nothing, after all, to prevent the approval of the constitution, despite its stipulation about Islamic law. If the American incursion into Afghanistan represented a modern-day Crusade or an exercise in evangelical Christian wish fulfillment, it was a singularly inept one.

In Iraq, likewise, the dire predicament of Christians facing jihadist persecution after the fall of Saddam Hussein demonstrated this point. If spreading Christianity was what Bush was after, he was doing a decidedly poor job of it. Ancient Christian communities that had lived in Iraq for centuries began to face persecution from both Sunni and Shi'ite jihad groups. In October 2006, a Syrian Orthodox priest, Boulos Iskander, went shopping for auto parts in the Iraqi city of Mosul. He was never seen alive again. A Muslim group kidnapped him and initially demanded $350,000 in ransom. They eventually lowered this to $40,000 and added a new demand: Iskander's parish had to denounce the remarks made the previous month by Pope Benedict XVI that had caused riots throughout the Islamic world. The ransom was paid, and the church dutifully posted thirty large signs all over Mosul, but to no avail: Iskander was not only murdered but dismembered. Five hundred Christians attended his funeral, where another priest commented: "Many more wanted to come to the funeral, but they were afraid. We are in very bad circumstances now."[30]

That is true of Christians all over the Middle East, where safe havens are dwindling rapidly. Even in Lebanon, traditionally the Middle East's sole Christian land, Christians suffer persecution, which leads to declining numbers and declining influence—and that in turn encourages more persecution. Christian communities throughout the Middle East that date back to the dawn of Christianity are decreasing so much that they are on the verge of disappearing from the area altogether. In Iraq, half the nation's prewar 700,000 Christians have fled the country since the fall of Saddam Hussein.[31] Overall the Middle Eastern Christian population has dropped from 20 percent in 1900 to less than 2 percent today.[32]

Iraqi Christians are streaming into Syria or, if they can, out of the Middle East altogether, as both Sunni and Shi'ite Islamic jihad groups do their best to make life difficult for them. Women have been threatened with kidnapping or death if they do not wear headscarves. Christian liquor store owners in Iraq have been threatened, as Islamic law restricts Christians from "openly displaying wine or pork."[33] Many Christian businesses have been destroyed, and the owners have fled.[34] A one-time Iraqi liquor store owner now living in Syria lamented that "before the war there was no separation between Christian and Muslim. Under Saddam no one asked you your religion, and we used to attend each other's religious services and weddings. After the invasion we hoped democracy would come; but instead all that came was bombs, kidnapping, and killing. Now at least 75 percent of my Christian friends have fled. There is no future for us in Iraq."[35]

It is hard to reconcile these facts with Kevin Phillips's suggestion that the Iraq adventure was undertaken because "prominent evangelical

ministers" had decided that Islam was "the primary evil force" in the
world and that Saddam Hussein was "the leading new contender for the
role of antichrist" (let alone that Saddam's Iraq was "the reembodiment
of the evil Babylon").[36] This is nothing but the most feverish conspiracy-
mongering, given what we know about the war planning that went into
Iraq, which had nothing to do with religion and everything to do with
Saddam's suspected WMD program, his ties to terrorism, and his violation of the cease-fire accords that ended the first Gulf War.

But even if one were to grant Phillips a hearing he doesn't deserve,
three points might be worth mentioning:

1. The indigenous Christians of Iraq are mostly members of the
   ancient Assyrian Church of the East or its Catholic counterpart,
   the Chaldean Catholic Church, not evangelicals.
2. Evangelicals have certainly not found an open mission field in
   Iraq.
3. If American actions in Iraq and Afghanistan represented a
   covert Christian theocratic enterprise, the emphasis must fall
   heavily upon the word "covert."

JIHADISTS VS. ABORTION CLINIC BOMBERS: WHICH IS THE BIGGER THREAT?

The September 11, 2001, terrorist attacks in New York and Washington,
D.C., the Madrid train bombings on March 11, 2004, and the London
tube bombings on July 7, 2005, are remembered in the West as shocking
acts of terrorism. But elsewhere in the world jihad attacks are a weari-
some element of daily life. Israeli civilians know that a suicide bomber
could strike anytime and virtually anywhere. In southern Thailand, two
thousand civilians—Buddhist schoolteachers, rubber tappers, and other
innocuous non-Muslims—have been killed in jihad-incited strife since
2004.[37] And the jihadists' list of victims spans the world, from Europe and
the United States to Iraq, Pakistan, Afghanistan, the Philippines, Somalia, Algeria, India, Indonesia, Chechnya, Russia, Saudi Arabia, Sudan,
Jordan, Yemen, Lebanon, and elsewhere.

But, say the secular liberals, look at Pat Robertson, George Grant, or Gary North—despite the fact that they have killed no one, and have no organization equivalent to al Qaeda. Others point to the handful of Christians who have murdered abortionists or committed acts of violence at abortion clinics: Paul Hill, Michael F. Griffin, James Kopp, Eric Rudolph, and John Salvi. To say the obvious, however, these men were not part of a larger movement in any way comparable to the global jihadists; they acted alone.

What's more, no larger Christian group supports the killing of abortionists. No Christian churches endorsed the actions of Paul Hill and the others. The Florida Catholic Conference declared that Hill's "brutal murders of Dr. John Britton and Lt. Col. James Barrett outside an abortion clinic were an unjustifiable attack on human life and we unequivocally condemn and renounce his actions."[38] Albert Mohler, president of Southern Baptist Theological Seminary in Kentucky, agreed: "Paul Hill's monumental moral error came when he assumed the roles of judge, jury, and executioner in killing Dr. Britton and his escort. The Bible instructs Christians to 'be subject to the governing authorities' [Romans 13:1]. Christians are not to take the law into their own hands. The killing of unborn human infants is murder—but so was Paul Hill's killing of John Britton and James Barrett."[39] Reconstructionist Gary North wrote to Hill: "Fortunately, your church had excommunicated you before you grabbed your shotgun. The press has not been able to tar and feather the Christian church, because the church exercised its good judgment and declared you outside the jurisdiction of Christ's ecclesiastical kingdom. It publicly announced that you are going to hell unless you repent. That cleared the church of any responsibility for you. This is an enormous blessing to the church of Jesus Christ."[40]

Christian columnist Cal Thomas summed up the view of virtually all Christians when he wrote: "Paul Hill is not a martyr, as he claims, any more than those who are members of the Taliban or Islamic jihad are martyrs."[41]

To Christians, killing an abortionist is, as Albert Mohler said, murder, and to be condemned as such. But Islam takes a different view. We need to remember that Islamic jihad terrorism is not simply an exercise in mayhem for its own sake; instead, jihad violence furthers the overall effort to "strike terror into (the hearts of) the enemies of Allah," thereby leading to the demoralization of those enemies and their ready conquest by the warriors of Allah. It is instructive to compare Islamic condemnation of terrorism with the Christian condemnations of Hill.

DO MUSLIMS REALLY CONDEMN JIHAD?

On July 28, 2005, the Fiqh Council of North America, an eighteen-member board of Islamic scholars and leaders, issued a *fatwa*, or religious ruling, against terrorism. Influential Muslim groups such as the Council on American-Islamic Relations and the Muslim Public Affairs Council immediately endorsed this fatwa, which also received international publicity. It was hailed as one of the few instances after the September 11 attacks in which Muslims unequivocally declared that those attacks were carried out in defiance of the principles of Islam, an antidote to the horrible pictures that had been televised of Palestinian Arabs dancing and clapping for joy at news of the attacks. The Fiqh Council stated that

1. All acts of terrorism targeting civilians are *haram* [forbidden] in Islam.
2. It is haram for a Muslim to cooperate with any individual or group that is involved in any act of terrorism or violence.
3. It is the civic and religious duty of Muslims to cooperate with law enforcement authorities to protect the lives of all civilians.[42]

One week before this statement was issued, 120 Canadian imams declared that "anyone who claims to be a Muslim and participates in any way in the taking of innocent life is betraying the very spirit and letter of Islam."[43] And in June 2006, the leaders of 150 mosques in Birmingham, England, jointly issued a similar statement, stating that the "killing of innocent civilians is absolutely forbidden in Islam and anyone who contemplates or commits any such act, does so against the teachings of Islam."[44]

Unfortunately, the more closely one examines such statements, the less unequivocal a condemnation of terrorism they turn out to be. The chief problem is the definition of terms. While non-Muslim Westerners may assume that they know what is meant by "terrorism," "innocent lives," and "civilians," these are in fact hotly debated terms in the Islamic world. Anjem Choudary[45] of Omar Bakri's British jihadist group told an interviewer that the victims of the July 7, 2005, bombings in London were not innocent, because they were not Muslims: "When we say innocent people, we mean Muslims. As far as non-Muslims are concerned, they have not accepted Islam. As far as we are concerned, that is a crime against God. . . . As far as Muslims are concerned, you're innocent if you are a Muslim. Then you are innocent in the eyes of God. If you are non-Muslim, then you are guilty of not believing in God."[46]

What about civilians? As one Palestinian jihadist said: "There are no civilians in Israel. All the Israelis are military, all of them. They are all military and they all have weapons and guns, and the moment they are called up they are going to be using their weapons against me."[47] Tunisian jihadist Rashid al-Ghannushi has issued a fatwa to the same effect, declaring: "There are no civilians in Israel. The population—males, females, and children—are the army reserve soldiers, and thus can be killed."[48]

The internationally influential Sheikh Yusuf al-Qaradawi, who has won praise from Islamic scholar John Esposito for engaging in a "reformist interpretation of Islam and its relationship to democracy, pluralism, and human rights," agrees. In his words, concerning jihadist "suicide" (actually homicide) bombings in Israel: "It's not suicide, it is martyrdom in the name of God, Islamic theologians and jurisprudents have debated this issue. Referring to it as a form of jihad, under the title of jeopardizing the life of the mujahideen. It is allowed to jeopardize your soul and cross the path of the enemy and be killed."[49] And what if the "enemy" is actually a noncombatant? "Israeli women are not like women in our society because Israeli women are militarized. Secondly, I consider this type of martyrdom operation as indication of justice of Allah almighty. Allah is just. Through his infinite wisdom he has given the weak what the strong do not possess and that is the ability to turn their bodies into bombs like the Palestinians do."[50]

Do all Muslims agree with these perspectives? Certainly not. But the fact that a significant number of Muslims, including such high-profile

figures as Sheikh al-Qaradawi, do hold such views illustrates the inade-
quacy of the statements issued by the Fiqh Council and the imams of
Canada and Birmingham. Were the issuers of these statements really trying to convince their fellow Muslims that contemporary jihad terrorism
is illegitimate? If so, it is not enough to condemn "terrorism" if one is trying to sway people who don't believe that what they are doing constitutes
terrorism at all. It is not enough to condemn the killing of "innocent civilians" when the jihadists don't believe their victims are either innocent or
civilian.

What's more, several prominent moderate Muslims have recently
declined to condemn Hamas and Hizballah as terrorist groups. The
Council on American-Islamic Relations (CAIR) bills itself as "America's
largest Islamic civil liberties group" and claims that "its mission is to
enhance the understanding of Islam, encourage dialogue, protect civil
liberties, empower American Muslims, and build coalitions that promote
justice and mutual understanding."[51] Yet when a reporter from the *Los
Angeles Times* asked a CAIR spokeswman, Munira Syeda, to condemn
Hamas or Hizballah as terrorist groups, she responded, "I don't understand what the relevance is."[52] Likewise, former pop star and Muslim
convert Cat Stevens (now Yusuf Islam) responded this way when a *New
York Times* interviewer asked him what he thought of Hamas: "That's an
extremely loaded question. . . . I have never supported a terrorist group or
any group that did other than charity and good to humankind." But would
he at least go on record with "contempt" for Hamas? "I wouldn't put
those words in my mouth. I wouldn't say anything on that issue. I'm here
to talk about peace. I'm a man who does want peace for this world, and
I don't think you will achieve that by putting people into corners and ask-
ing them very, very difficult questions about very contentious issues."[53]

Husham al-Husainy, imam of the Karbalaa Islamic Education Center,
a Shi'ite mosque in Dearborn, Michigan, also seemed to think the
Hizballah question a difficult one. Al-Husainy gained brief notoriety in
February 2007 when he prayed at a Democratic National Committee
meeting for an end to "oppression and occupation."[54] Subsequently, on
the television program *Hannity and Colmes* and on Sean Hannity's radio
show, al-Husainy repeatedly sidestepped Hannity's requests that he go on

record condemning Hizballah as a terrorist group. On television, al-Husainy responded to this request by saying, "Hizballah is a Lebanese organization and I got nothing to do with that."[55] On radio he grew more agitated, telling Hannity:

> God my witness, you are breaking the law and you are accusing me.... Because you are breaking the peace of this world, you wanted to create animosity between the religions, Christian and Muslim and Jewish.... You are justifying politics and the world is really burning. Let's cool it down. Let's go back to the law of Abraham and Muhammad and Jesus and Moses.... You belong to a minority of people burning the world. You just have to come back to God. Go read the Bible. Go read the Torah. And let's talk, is that the language, is that the behavior of Jesus and Moses? You are really away of your faith. So let's go back to the moral value of the Bible.... You are really making God mad at you, making Jesus mad at you, making Moses mad at you.... The trouble is, you are humiliating me and God is against that. Jesus against that.... You are against prophet Muhammad. You are against the faith of Muslims. You are against Qur'an. And God is my witness. And God's gonna get mad at you. Jesus gonna get mad at you. You are working against the unity of the world. And the unity of Muslims, and Jewish, and Christians. You are working against America. You are disturbing the peace between East and West. You are really, you are the anti-peace person.[56]

But never did he simply say that he regarded Hizballah as a terrorist organization, as does the U.S. State Department.

Are there no Muslims who genuinely condemn jihad violence and terrorism? Of course there are, but the mainstream media generally has the problem exactly backward. Even Andrew Sullivan, who has not shied away from alarmism about the Christian Right, acknowledges that "there are a few fringe groups in America—the Christian Reconstructionists, for example—who would like to replace the United States Constitution with biblical law, a Christian version of sharia. But they are marginal, extremist, and largely disowned by the fundamentalist mainstream. Evangelical

and Catholic fundamentalists have largely engaged in America in completely legitimate and democratic activity: voting, organizing, campaign-
ing, broadcasting, persuading. Even where they disagree with the
Supreme Court's interpretation of the Constitution, they do not question
that Constitution's legitimacy....A person who believes that society
should be governed only by laws consistent with his religious faith is not
a theocrat if he merely tries to persuade majorities of his case, and
restricts himself to constitutional, legal, and nonviolent activity."[57]

While the press gives ubiquitous coverage to "militants" and "insur-
gents" in places like Iraq and Afghanistan, the mainstream media pays far
less attention to the actual threat of Islamic jihad as a global movement—
despite the widespread support for jihad in the Islamic world—than it
does to the alleged Christian theocratic threat against the American Constitution. The latter is simply a matter of attacking the Christian Right, a
comfortable target. But the former means having to violate the norms of
liberal multiculturalism and attack something that is not Western.

Islamic attitudes are certainly not Western ones. In January 2007,
columnist Michael Freud summed up some disquieting survey results:

> In a poll conducted five months ago, and broadcast on Britain's
> Channel 4 TV, nearly 25 percent of British Muslims said the July 7,
> 2005, terror bombings in London, which killed fifty-two innocent
> commuters, were justified. Another 30 percent said they would pre-
> fer to live under strict Islamic sharia law rather than England's dem-
> ocratic system.
>
> Now, one in four justifying terror may not be a majority, but it cer-
> tainly isn't a "small fringe" either.
>
> In other countries, the figures are no less unsettling. A survey pub-
> lished in December found that 44 percent of Nigerian Muslims
> believe suicide bombing attacks are "often" or "sometimes" accept-
> able. Only 28 percent said they were never justified.
>
> According to the annual Pew Global Attitudes Survey, released in
> July 2006, "roughly one in seven Muslims in France, Spain, and
> Great Britain feel that suicide bombings against civilian targets can

at least sometimes be justified to defend Islam." The report also found that less than half of Jordan's Muslims believe terror attacks are never justified. In Egypt, only 45 percent of Muslims say terror is never justified.

Still think only a "tiny minority" are in favor of violence? In Israel, the percentages are even more alarming. After Cpl. Gilad Shalit was abducted by Hamas terrorists last summer, a poll conducted by the Jerusalem Media and Communications Center revealed that 77.2 percent of Palestinians supported the kidnapping, while 66.8 percent said they would back additional such attacks.

More than six out of ten Palestinians also said they were in favor of firing Kassam rockets at Israeli towns and cities.

Indeed, in various countries around the world, support for Muslim fundamentalist terror groups appears to be widespread.

On the fifth anniversary of the September 11 attacks, a survey conducted by al-Jazeera asked respondents, "Do you support Osama bin Laden?" A whopping 49.9 percent answered yes.

And the July 2006 global Pew survey found that among Muslims, a quarter of Jordanians, a third of Indonesians, 38 percent of Pakistanis, and 61 percent of Nigerians all expressed confidence in the mass murderer who founded al Qaeda.

In Lebanon six months ago, the Beirut Center for Research and Information found that over 80 percent of the Lebanese population said they supported Hizballah.[58]

On this Muslim support for jihad violence, however, the mainstream media in the United States remains largely silent. There are more than a billion Muslims in the world, and millions of them openly endorse terrorism. The moral relativism that would equate the Christian Right with Islamic jihad is no more convincing than an argument that would equate the Boy Scouts with the Hitler Youth.

CHAPTER FIVE

CHERRY-PICKING IN THE FIELDS OF THE LORD

Apologists for Islam frequently claim that violent passages from the Qur'an have been "cherry-picked" from a holy book that mainly teaches peace. And almost invariably, these apologists say that the Bible is just as violent, if not more so. Lutheran theologian Martin E. Marty, for example, has written disdainfully of "people who selectively quote the Qur'an to show how it commits Muslims to killing 'us' infidels." He then goes on to enumerate numerous violent passages in the Bible, finally quipping, "Thou shalt not bear false witness against thy neighbor's God or Book, nor witness at all until thou comest clean on what thy book portrays, a holy warrior God."[1]

As Ralph Peters put it, "As a believing Christian, I must acknowledge that there's nothing in the Koran as merciless as God's behavior in the book of Joshua."[2]

While not going as far as Peters's assertion that the Bible is actually *more* violent than the Qur'an, Dinesh D'Souza suggests that the Qur'an and the Bible are at least equivalent in their capacity to incite violence: "The Koran, like the Old Testament, has a number of passages recommending peace and others celebrating the massacre of the enemies of God."[3] He sees the problem as a matter of focus: "I realize that you can fish out this passage or that passage and make it sound like the Muslims want to convert or kill everybody. But that would be like taking passages out of the Old Testament to make Moses sound like Hitler."[4] He even claims that Moses would have pursued an aggressive policy of religious imperialism, a la Islamic jihad, if he had had the chance: "Moses wasn't exactly a believer in religious freedom. When he came down from the mountain and discovered the Israelites worshipping the golden calf he basically ordered a massacre. Don't you think that if Moses could he would have imposed the laws of Yahweh on the whole world? Of course he would."[5]

But is all this really true? Are the Bible and the Qur'an roughly equivalent in their capacity to inspire violence?

This is an important question, for it goes to the heart of whether the actual teachings of either religion have anything to do with the violence committed in its name. After all, this question cannot be wholly determined by examining the historical record of each religion; in every religious tradition the teachings of the religion are one thing and the way they are lived out is quite another. No body of people has ever lived in complete fidelity to any set of principles, religious or otherwise. Moreover, a central tenet of Christianity is that "all have sinned and fall short of the glory of God" (Romans 3:23). This is, as many have noted, one Christian dogma for which there is abundant empirical evidence: the dividing line between good and evil doesn't run between one group and another, or one race and another, or one nation and another. Nor does it run between the adherents of one religion and those of another. It is said that the British writer and superlative wit G. K. Chesterton once responded to an invitation from the *Times* of London to write a piece about what is wrong with the world by writing: "Dear Sir, I am. Yours, G. K. Chesterton." Chesterton wasn't just being flip; he was expressing the fundamental Christian belief that the dividing line between good and evil actually runs through every human heart. With this as a core assumption, neither Christians nor anyone else should ever be surprised by evil, even when it is perpetrated by Christians in the name of Christianity. That is the way human beings are.

Islam's view of this is vastly different in some ways and identical in others. While acknowledging that any human being is capable of evil, the Qur'an says that Muslims are the "best of peoples" (3:110) while the unbelievers are the "vilest of creatures" (98:6). In such a worldview it is easy to see evil in others but difficult to locate it in oneself. And that is indeed a recurring motif in the Islamic world today—an unwillingness to engage in self-reflection and self-criticism and a tendency to source all its ills on a malignant outside force: "Zionists," "the Great Satan," and the like. Still, most Muslims, like most Christians, would acknowledge that the gap between theory and practice has sometimes been quite large. Jihadists make this argument too—in their case, that Muslims are forgetting the necessity of jihad. But if we look at the teachings of each religion, as they have been understood by mainstream adherents, we can see when, through violent acts, they are actually transgressing against the teachings of the religion they claim to defend.

DOES GOD MANDATE ETHNIC CLEANSING?

So is Peters right that "there's nothing in the Koran as merciless as God's behavior in the book of Joshua"? It certainly seems so. Besieging Jericho, Joshua announces that the city is "devoted to the Lord for destruction" (Joshua 6:17). When it falls, Joshua and his men "utterly destroyed all in the city, both men and women, oxen, sheep, and asses, with the edge of the sword" (6:21). And Joshua warned: "Cursed before the Lord be the man that rises up and rebuilds this city, Jericho" (6:26).

Later God tells Joshua: "You shall do to Ai and its king as you did to Jericho and its king," except that this time they can spare the animals: "its spoil and its cattle you shall take as booty for yourselves" (8:2). Joshua complied:

> When Israel had finished slaughtering all the inhabitants of Ai in the open wilderness where they pursued them and all of them to the very last had fallen by the edge of the sword, all Israel returned to Ai, and smote it with the edge of the sword. And all who fell that day, both men and women, were twelve thousand, all the people of Ai. For Joshua did not draw back his hand, with which he stretched out the javelin, until he had utterly destroyed all the inhabitants of Ai. Only the cattle and the spoil of that city Israel took as their booty, according to the word of the Lord which he commanded Joshua. (8:24–27)

Joshua similarly kills all the inhabitants of at least ten other cities. Nowhere is there a hint of any disapproval on the part of the writer or anyone in the book. Instead, we are told that in carrying out these massacres Joshua was obeying God's will: "So Joshua defeated the whole land, the hill country and the Negeb and the lowland and the slopes, and all their kings; he left none remaining, but utterly destroyed all that breathed, as the Lord God of Israel commanded" (10:40).

Nor is the book of Joshua the only apparently morally problematic portion of the Jewish and Christian scriptures. Chris Hedges says that many Christians "often fail to acknowledge that there are hateful passages in the Bible that give sacred authority to the rage, self-aggrandizement, and intolerance of the Christian Right."[6] Joshua's behavior is rooted in the Lord's earlier behavior and other commands. The book of Numbers recounts that after the Israelites defeated the Midianites, they presented the captives and spoils of war to Moses. But the prophet "was angry with the officers of the army, the commanders of thousands and the commanders of hundreds, who had come from service in the war. Moses said to them, 'Have you let all the women live?'" He reminded them that these women had earlier caused the Israelites to "act treacherously against the Lord." Consequently, Moses told his men, "Now therefore, kill every male among the little ones, and kill every woman who has known man by lying with him. But all the young girls who have not known man by lying with him, keep alive for yourselves" (31:14–18).

This command was later extended to other enemies of the Israelites: "When the Lord your God brings you into the land which you are entering to take possession of it, and clears away many nations before you, the Hittites, the Girgashites, the Amorites, the Canaanites, the Perizzites, the Hivites, and the Jebusites, seven nations greater and mightier than yourselves, and when the Lord your God gives them over to you, and you defeat them; then you must utterly destroy them; you shall make no covenant with them, and show no mercy to them" (Deuteronomy 7:1–2). God also tells the Israelites, "When you approach a city to fight against it, you shall offer it terms of peace. If it agrees to make peace with you and opens to you, then all the people who are found in it shall become your forced labor and shall serve you. However, if it does not make peace with you, but makes war against you, then you shall besiege it. When the Lord your God gives it into your hand, you shall strike all the men in it with the edge of the sword. Only the women and the children and the animals and all that is in the city, all its spoil, you shall take as booty for yourself; and you shall use the spoil of your enemies which the Lord your God has given you. Only in the cities of these peoples that the Lord your God is giving you as an inheritance, you shall not leave alive anything that breathes" (Deuteronomy 20:10–17).

Besides passages apparently celebrating warfare and ethnic cleansing as sanctioned by God, the books of Moses also contain other passages jarring to modern sensibilities. God commands, for example, that Sabbath-breakers be put to death: "And the Lord said to Moses, 'Say to the people of Israel, You shall keep my sabbaths, for this is a sign between me and you throughout your generations, that you may know that I, the Lord, sanctify you. You shall keep the sabbath, because it is holy for you; every one who profanes it shall be put to death; whoever does any work on it, that soul shall be cut off from among his people'" (Exodus 31:12–14). So are idolaters. God tells Moses, "If there is found among you . . . a man or woman who does what is evil in the sight of the Lord your God, in transgressing his covenant, and has gone and served other gods and worshiped them, or the sun or the moon or any of the host of heaven, which I have forbidden, and it is told you and you hear of it; then you shall inquire diligently, and if it is true and certain that such an abominable thing has been done in Israel, then you shall bring forth to your gates that man or woman who has done this evil thing, and you shall stone that man or woman to death with stones" (Deuteronomy 17:2–5).

The book of Exodus contains some brief guidelines for occasions in which "a man sells his daughter as a slave" (Exodus 21:7). And there is more, here and there, that has raised eyebrows not only in modern times but throughout history.

"KILL THEM ALL," SAYS THE LORD?

But is the Bible really enjoining violence—or capital punishment—against sinners? This question cannot be answered by an evaluation of the text alone, for it does not stand apart from the way believers have understood it and acted upon it. From that perspective, the arguments of Peters and D'Souza, and the many others who have said essentially the same thing, founder upon one central fact: there are no armed Jewish or Christian groups anywhere in the world today who are committing acts of violence and justifying them by referring to these texts. Indeed, throughout history, these texts have never been taken as divine commands that either must be or may be put into practice by believers in a new age. All these passages, after all, are descriptive, not prescriptive. Nowhere do they command believers to imitate this behavior, or to believe under any circumstances that God wishes them to act as His instruments of judgment in any situation today.

Some biblical scholars suggest that the Bible depicts a process of moral evolution—a gradual advance out of barbarism to the precepts of the Gospel. Others believe that what was acceptable for, or even incumbent upon, the Israelites in their particular time and place applied only then, not to all believers for all time.[7] There are weaknesses in these and other such interpretations, but they reflect the fact that throughout history, rather than celebrating such biblical passages, Jews and Christians have regarded them as a problem to be solved. While interpretations of these passages differ widely among Jews and Christians, from the beginnings of rabbinic Judaism and Christianity one understanding has remained dominant among virtually all believers: these passages are not commands for all generations to follow, and if they have any applicability, it is only in a spiritualized, parabolic sense.

This is clear from popular scriptural commentaries and other popular treatments of this material. The Catholic edition of the Revised Standard Version of the Bible says that "the physical destruction of the enemy in obedience to the deity" was "practiced much less than a reading of Joshua might suggest"—and in any case, "it must be seen in light of the imperfect stage of moral development reached at that time."[8] Likewise the Navarre Bible, a Roman Catholic commentary series prepared by the theology faculty of the University of Navarre in Spain, calls the instructions to destroy whole cities "a policy which to us seems quite incomprehensible, savage and inhuman," but one that "needs to be seen in its historical context and to be set in the framework of the gradual development of revelation." The commentary goes on to cite Jesus's words—"love your enemies" (Matthew 5:44)—and a spiritualized interpretation of Joshua's battles by sixteenth-century mystic St. John of the Cross.[9]

Evangelical Christians Andy and Berit Kjos reflect the near-universal tendency to spiritualize such passages in a series of study questions on the book of Joshua. In connection with Joshua 6:17 they ask: "What might you 'utterly destroy' in your own life in order to fully live the holy and victorious life in union with Christ?"[10] This is similar to a footnote on Joshua 6:26 in the 1609 Douay-Rheims Roman Catholic English translation of the Bible: "Jericho, in the mystical sense, signifies iniquity: the sounding of the trumpets by the priests, the preaching of the word of God; by which the walls of Jericho are thrown down, when sinners are converted; and a dreadful curse will light on them who build them up again."[11]

Not only are such texts spiritualized, but the literal sense is also often directly rejected. The Reverend David Holwick of First Baptist Church in Ledgewood, New Jersey, quotes billionaire Andrew Carnegie: "I picked up the Bible just the other day and was reading the story of the times of Samuel. All sorts of ghastly incidents are related, and some passages are simply revolting to a mind accustomed to feel toward humanity as Christ felt. And the thing is that God is pictured as directing and helping it all. It is God who leads in the slaughter and He even inspires His children to the most unmerciful acts. Do not teach these parts to boys and girls as heroic deeds, to be admired and copied." Holwick maintains that the God of the Old Testament is the same as that of the New, but agrees with Carnegie that such tales have no exemplary value for modern believers. "Too many atrocities have been done in God's name," he said, adding, "God doesn't need human armies or politicians to win."[12]

In short, the consensus view among Jews and Christians for many centuries is that unless you happen to be a Hittite, Girgashite, Amorite, Canaanite, Perizzite, Hivite, or Jebusite, these biblical passages simply do not apply to you. The scriptures record God's commands to the

Israelites to make war against particular people only. However this may be understood, and however jarring it may be to modern sensibilities, it does not amount to any kind of marching orders for believers. That's one principal reason why Jews and Christians haven't formed terror groups around the world that quote the Bible to justify killing non-combatants.

VIOLENCE IN THE NEW TESTAMENT?

Christopher Hitchens, in his entertaining atheist apologetic *God Is Not Great: How Religion Poisons Everything*, surveys what he terms the "nightmare" of the Old Testament and then titles his next chapter "The 'New' Testament Exceeds the Evil of the 'Old' One." When it comes to backing up this assertion, however, Hitchens offers thin gruel. In his Old Testament chapter, he asks about the Ten Commandments: "Is it too modern to notice that there is nothing about the protection of children from cruelty, nothing about rape, nothing about slavery, and nothing about genocide? Or is it too exactingly 'in context' to notice that some of these very offenses are about to be positively recommended?" Yet after that buildup most of Hitchens's New Testament chapter is taken up not with allegations of iniquity, but with disquisitions on the historicity, or lack thereof, of various portions of the narrative—including one which Hitchens seems rather to like, the story of Jesus showing mercy to a woman about to be stoned for adultery (John 7:53–8:11).[13]

This is no accident. Those who comb the New Testament searching for incitement to violence come away disappointed. The best that can be done is point to two passages. The first is Luke 19:26–27: "I tell you that to everyone who has, more shall be given, but from the one who does not have, even what he does have shall be taken away. But these enemies of mine, who did not want me to reign over them, bring them here and slay them in my presence." Of course, the problem with this passage is that these are the words of a king in a parable, not Jesus's instructions to His followers. But such subtleties are often ignored.

The second is Matthew 10:34–35: "Do not think that I have come to bring peace on earth. I did not come to bring peace, but a sword. I am sent to set a man against his father, a daughter against her mother, and a daughter-in-law against her mother-in-law." If this passage is really calling for any literal violence, it would seem to be intra-familial jihad. But, of course, Christians throughout history have read it to mean nothing of the sort. Instead, it is—obviously—a statement that to convert to Christianity can mean putting oneself at odds with one's own non-Christian family. To invoke it as the equivalent of the Qur'an's jihad passages, which number more than a hundred, is absurd.

To interpret this text literally as a call to familial violence rather than as allegory is not only to misunderstand Jesus, but also the poetical nature of the Bible. Jesus did not take part in battles, as Muhammad did, and historically, even when Christians have committed violence in the name of God and the church, they have never taken these passages as marching orders.

Some New Testament critics occasionally point to passages from the Revelation to St. John. But the bloody end times scenario of death and judgment described there is not in any way a call to action for Christians to commit acts of violence. Many traditional Christians regard it as an allegory about first-century Rome or as a purely literary and symbolic work. While God is depicted as exacting judgment and punishing the wicked, nowhere does he order Christians to do so. Likewise, the popular *Left Behind* series, which dramatizes the events recounted in Revelation from an evangelical Christian perspective, doesn't depict Christians killing their non-Christian neighbors or God ordering them to do so.

BUT THE BIBLE HAS MADE PEOPLE COMMIT VIOLENT ACTS, HASN'T IT?

Certainly Christians have committed violent acts in the name of Christianity. But have they done so in obedience to or in defiance of Christian scripture and the teachings of the church? During the Crusades, it became customary for those who joined the effort to be referred to as "taking up their cross," echoing Jesus's statement: "If any man would

come after me, let him deny himself and take up his cross, and follow
me" (Matthew 16:24).

But this admonition says nothing about war or violence and has
always been understood as a call to conform one's life to the demands
of the Gospel. And so it is with all biblical passages that the Crusaders
and Crusader theologians invoked: they took clearly spiritual passages
and applied them to warfare. Bernard of Clairvaux extended St. Paul's
New Testament exhortation to "take the whole armor of God...having
girded your loins with truth, and having put on the breastplate of right-
eousness" (Ephesians 6:13–14), which clearly refers to spiritual warfare in physical terms and militarizes Paul's longing to be with Christ.
"For me to live is Christ, and to die is gain.... My desire is to depart
and be with Christ, for that is far better" (Philippians 1:21, 23).
Bernard also refers to Paul's insistence that nothing "will be able to separate us from the love of God in Christ Jesus our Lord" (Romans 8:39)
and "whether we live or whether we die, we are the Lord's" (Romans
14:8):

> He indeed is a fearless knight, and one secure from any quarter, since
> his soul is dressed in an armor of faith just as his body is dressed in
> an armor of steel. Since he is well protected by both kinds of arms,
> he fears neither the demon nor man. Nor is he afraid of death, since
> he longs to die. Why should he fear whether he lives or dies, since for
> him life is Christ and death is a reward? Faithfully and freely does he
> go forth on Christ's behalf, but he would rather be dissolved and be
> with Christ: such is the obviously better thing. So go forth in safety,
> knights, and drive out the enemies of the cross of Christ with fearless
> intention, certain that neither death nor life can separate you from
> God's love, which Jesus Christ embodies; in every moment of danger,
> fulfill through your own actions the principle: "Whether we live or
> whether we die, we are the Lord's."[14]

St. Bernard goes on to exhort his Christian knights to fight on all the
more valiantly, for their rewards will be great on earth if they are victorious and in heaven if they aren't:

How glorious the victors returned from battle! How blessed those martyrs who died in battle! Rejoice, brave fighter, if you live and conquer in the Lord; but rather exult and glory, if you die and are joined to the Lord. Life can be fruitful and victory can be glorious; but sacred death is properly to be preferred to either, for if "they are blessed who die in the Lord," are they not much more so who die on the Lord's behalf?[15]

Perhaps those who believe that any holy text can be used to justify anything will find support for their views in St. Bernard's usage of St. Paul here. However, while Bernard is able to marshal scriptural passages for the idea that God rewards martyrs, and that God is the lord of both the living and the dead, he does not and cannot adduce any scripture in support of his central assumption: warfare in the name of Christ is justified. The fact that he must instead resort to passages about spiritual warfare only makes more obvious that Christianity lacks a martial tradition in the New Testament, just as it lacks a New Testament doctrine of warfare against unbelievers.

In Islam, however, the situation is quite different.

VIOLENCE IN THE QUR'AN?

In contrast to the Bible, the Qur'an exhorts believers to fight unbelievers. The commands, taken at face value, are open-ended and universal.

Osama bin Laden, who is only the most renowned and notorious exponent of a terror network that extends from Indonesia to Nigeria and into Western Europe and the Americas, quotes the Qur'an copiously in his communiqués. In his 1996 "Declaration of War against the Americans Occupying the Land of the Two Holy Places," he quotes seven Qur'an verses: 3:145; 47:4–6; 2:154; 9:14; 47:19; 8:72; and the notorious "Verse of the Sword," 9:5.[16] In 2003, on the first day of the Muslim festival Eid al-Adha, the Feast of Sacrifice, he began a sermon: "Praise be to Allah who revealed the verse of the Sword to his servant and messenger [the prophet Muhammad] in order to establish truth and abolish falsehood."[17]

One pro–bin Laden website put it this way: "The truth is that a Muslim who reads the Qur'an with devotion is determined to reach the battlefield in order to attain the reality of Jihad. It is solely for this reason that the Kufaar [unbelievers] conspire to keep the Muslims far away from understanding the Qur'an, knowing that Muslims who understand the Qur'an will not distance themselves from Jihad."[18]

Of course, the devil can quote scripture for his own purpose, but bin Laden's use of these and other passages in his messages is consistent (as we shall see) with traditional Islamic understandings of the Qur'an. In Islam there is no interpretative tradition of the Qur'an comparable to the traditional Jewish and Christian approaches to the Bible. While Christians and Jews see an unfolding of revelation in language that is often symbolic, allegorical, historical, or poetic, Islam is much more literal, even when the text of the Qur'an itself is opaque and confusing—and the jihad passages in the Qur'an are anything but a dead letter. In Saudi Arabia, Pakistan, and elsewhere, one of the key recruiting grounds for jihad terrorist groups are Islamic schools (madrassas): the students learn that they must wage jihad warfare, and then these groups give them the opportunity. Students in these schools are made to understand that passages such as "slay the unbelievers wherever you find them" (Qur'an 9:5) and "therefore, when ye meet the unbelievers in fight, smite at their necks; at length, when ye have thoroughly subdued them, bind a bond firmly on them" (47:4) are words they need to take to heart and carry out in order to be pleasing to Allah.

In the wake of the September 11 attacks, the *Detroit Free Press* told readers that "the Quran teaches nonviolence."[19] This was repeated in essence by George W. Bush when he said that "Islam is peace," and this quickly hardened into a strict orthodoxy that could not be questioned in the mainstream.[20] Only a few dared to sound any sour notes. Christian Broadcasting Network spokesman and former presidential candidate Pat Robertson drew vehement criticism when he declared: "I'm very familiar with what goes on in the Islamic world, where our reporters are all over that area, and it's clear from the teachings of the Qur'an and also from the history of Islam that it's anything but peaceful."[21] Jerry Falwell and Franklin Graham also drew fire—as well as provoked bloody riots in India and an Iranian Muslim official's call for their deaths—for similar remarks.[22]

So what's the evidence?

TOLERANCE IN THE QUR'AN

The evidence of the Qur'anic text itself goes both ways. Within the Muslim holy book one finds verses devoted to peaceful tolerance—and also abundant verses devoted to violent intolerance.

Live-and-let-live tolerance appears in a chapter of the Qur'an that was revealed to Muhammad early in his prophetic career. (The Qur'an is not arranged in chronological or narrative order, but generally from the longest chapter to the shortest.) "Say: O disbelievers! I worship not that which ye worship; Nor worship ye that which I worship. And I shall not worship that which ye worship. Nor will ye worship that which I worship. Unto you your religion, and unto me my religion" (109:1–6).

Other verses add to this seeming indifference the contention that Allah will ultimately judge the unbelievers and cast them into hell. Thus Allah tells Muhammad not to waste his time arguing with those who reject his message, but to leave them in peace until that terrible day: "So leave them alone until they encounter that Day of theirs, wherein they shall (perforce) swoon (with terror)." (52:45–47; the sections in parentheses are added by the Muslim translator so as to express more precisely the sense of the original.)

This counsel is repeated in several places in the Qur'an: "And have patience with what they say, and leave them with noble (dignity). And leave Me (alone to deal with) those in possession of the good things of life, who (yet) deny the Truth; and bear with them for a little while" (73:10–11).

Above all, no Muslim should forcibly convert an unbeliever: "Let there be no compulsion in religion: Truth stands out clear from Error: whoever rejects evil and believes in Allah hath grasped the most trustworthy hand-hold, that never breaks. And Allah heareth and knoweth all things" (2:256). Following this celebrated verse comes another threat of hell: "Of those who reject faith the patrons are the evil ones: from light they will lead them forth into the depths of darkness. They will be companions of the fire, to dwell therein (for ever)" (2:257).

As Jews and Christians will face this dreadful judgment, Allah admonishes his prophet not to argue with them. Instead, he is to emphasize that he believes in the same God they do: "And dispute ye not with the People of the Book [primarily Jews and Christians], except with means better (than mere disputation), unless it be with those of them who inflict wrong (and injury): but say, 'We believe in the revelation which has come down to us and in that which came down to you; Our Allah and your Allah is one; and it is to Him we bow (in Islam)'" (29:46).

FIGHTING IN SELF-DEFENSE

While those verses counsel a form of tolerance, tolerance was not to be exercised in all cases. As Muhammad's prophetic career went on, and particularly after his flight to Medina and establishment there of the first Islamic political and military entity, he began to receive Qur'anic revelations allowing Muslims to fight under certain circumstances. This is emphasized in the Qur'an's eighth chapter, which is titled *Al-Anfal*—The Spoils of War:

Remember thy Lord inspired the angels (with the message): "I am with you: give firmness to the Believers: I will instill terror into the hearts of the Unbelievers: smite ye above their necks and smite all their finger-tips off them." This is because they contended against Allah and His Messenger: If any contend against Allah and His Messenger, Allah is strict in punishment. Thus (will it be said): "Taste ye then of the (punishment): for those who resist Allah, is the penalty of the Fire." O ye who believe! When ye meet the Unbelievers in hostile array, never turn your backs to them. If any do turn his back to them on such a day—unless it be in a stratagem of war, or to retreat to a troop (of his own)—he draws on himself the wrath of Allah, and his abode is Hell, an evil refuge (indeed)!" (8:12–16)

Still, the image of the Muslim warrior in these verses is one who acts in self-defense, and even in defense of all houses of worship (including churches; see Qur'an 22:39–40). The Qur'an returns elsewhere to this theme of self-defense:

> Fight in the cause of Allah those who fight you, but do not transgress limits; for Allah loveth not transgressors. [Another prominent Muslim translation renders this as "Begin not hostilities. Lo! Allah loveth not aggressors."] And slay them wherever ye catch them, and turn them out from where they have turned you out; for tumult and oppression are worse than slaughter; but fight them not at the Sacred Mosque, unless they (first) fight you there; but if they fight you, slay them. Such is the reward of those who suppress faith. But if they cease, Allah is Oft-forgiving, Most Merciful. And fight them on until there is no more tumult or oppression, and there prevail justice and faith in Allah; but if they cease, Let there be no hostility except to those who practice oppression. (2:190–193)

But here there is a change from self-defense. The command to fight against "those who fight you" until "there prevail justice and faith in Allah" (or until "religion is for Allah," in a more literal translation) indicates when Muslims should stop fighting against unbelievers: not when a peace treaty has been concluded, or when negotiations have settled disputed issues, but when Allah's religion prevails. Throughout history, Muslim jurists and theologians have understood this to refer to Islamic law being instituted over a society.

In the New Testament, of course, Jesus teaches his disciples to turn the other cheek (repudiating the Old Testament's "an eye for an eye, a tooth for a tooth"). But Islam sees self-defense in the following verse, which Abdullah Yusuf 'Ali's translation of the Qur'an renders in part: "If then any one transgresses the prohibition against you, transgress ye likewise against him" (2:194). Mohammad Marmaduke Pickthall translates this more explicitly: "And one who attacketh you, attack him in like manner as he attacked you." This is a foundation for the revenge culture that dominates so much of the Islamic world.

Fighting is defensive, but not optional: "Fighting is prescribed for you, and ye dislike it. But it is possible that ye dislike a thing which is good for you, and that ye love a thing which is bad for you. But Allah knoweth, and ye know not" (2:216).

Nor should this defensive struggle be limited in scope. Allah even tells Muhammad to take no prisoners: "It is not fitting for a prophet that he should have prisoners of war until he hath thoroughly subdued the land." This verse comes in the context of warning the Muslims not to fight simply for booty: "Ye look for the temporal goods of this world; but Allah looketh to the Hereafter: And Allah is Exalted in might, Wise" (8:67). At the battle of Uhud against the pagan Quraysh tribe of Mecca, Muhammad's own tribe that had rejected his prophetic claim, the Muslims failed to destroy their enemies utterly because of their lust for the spoils of war: "Allah did indeed fulfill His promise to you when ye with His permission were about to annihilate your enemy, until ye flinched and fell to disputing about the order, and disobeyed it after He brought you in sight (of the booty) which ye covet. Among you are some that hanker after this world and some that desire the Hereafter. Then did He divert you from your foes in order to test you but He forgave you: For Allah is full of grace to those who believe" (3:152).

However, the prohibition against taking prisoners doesn't seem to be absolute, as Allah also gives the Muslims permission to take the wives of those they have slain in battle as concubines: "O Prophet! We have made lawful to thee thy wives to whom thou hast paid their dowers; and those whom thy right hand possesses [slaves] out of the prisoners of war whom Allah has assigned to thee" (33:50).

Allah calls his people to be fearless in the face of death, mindful of the rewards he offers afterward: "And if ye are slain, or die, in the way of Allah, forgiveness and mercy from Allah are far better than all they could amass. And if ye die, or are slain, Lo! It is unto Allah that ye are brought together" (3:157–158). It is important to remember that when Bernard of Clairvaux preached the merits of dying in battle in the Crusades, he was speaking as a monk. Mohammad is speaking as the messenger of Allah. And, indeed, rather than Jesus's admonition that "blessed are the peacemakers," in Islam those who wage jihad rank highest among the believers: "Those who believe, and suffer exile and strive with might and main, in Allah's cause [*jihad fi sabil Allah*], with their goods and their persons, have the highest rank in the sight of Allah: they are the people who will achieve (salvation)" (9:19–20). *Jihad fi sabil Allah* refers to taking up arms for the Muslim cause.

OFFENSIVE WARFARE: MANDATED BY THE QUR'AN?

Alongside the verses enjoining warfare in self-defense, the Qur'an includes a cluster of verses containing general and open-ended commands to fight: "O ye who believe! Fight the unbelievers who gird you about, and let them find firmness in you: and know that Allah is with those who fear Him" (9:123).

"O Prophet! Strive hard against the unbelievers and the hypocrites, and be firm against them. Their abode is Hell, an evil refuge indeed" (9:73). The Arabic word translated here as "strive hard" is *jahidi*, a verb form of the noun *jihad*.

The command applies first to fighting those who worship other gods in addition to Allah: "Then, when the sacred months have passed, slay the idolaters wherever ye find them, and take them (captive), and besiege them, and prepare for them each ambush. But if they repent and establish worship and pay the poor-due, then leave their way free. Lo! Allah is Forgiving, Merciful" (9:5).

Muslims must fight Jews and Christians as well, although the Qur'an recognizes that as "People of the Book" they have received genuine revelations from Allah: "Fight those who believe not in Allah nor the Last Day, nor hold that forbidden which hath been forbidden by Allah and His Messenger, nor acknowledge the religion of Truth, (even if they are) of the People of the Book, until they pay the Jizya [the tax on non-Muslims] with willing submission, and feel themselves subdued" (9:29).

MUHAMMAD THE GENERAL

Scholar Ibn Warraq, author of *Why I Am Not a Muslim* and editor of several collections of scholarly essays on the Qur'an and Muhammad, calls the Qur'an the most "gnomic, elusive, and allusive of holy scriptures"—

not least because people seem to be able to read it and come to diametrically opposite conclusions about what it says.[23]

So, with material praising both tolerance and intolerance, where does mainstream Islam draw the line? Very early in the history of Islam, Muslims noticed and began to grapple with how Muhammad's messages changed in character over the course of his prophetic career (610 to 632 A.D.). Muhammad's earliest biographer, a pious eighth-century Muslim named Muhammad Ibn Ishaq Ibn Yasar, explains that originally Muhammad "had not been given permission to fight or allowed to shed blood. . . . He had simply been ordered to call men to God and to endure insult and forgive the ignorant. The Quraysh [Muhammad's Arab tribe, who were pagans] had persecuted his followers, seducing some from their religion, and exiling others from their country. They had to choose whether to give up their religion, be maltreated at home, or to flee the country, some to Abyssinia, others to Medina."

As tensions increased between Muhammad and the Quraysh, the time for forgiveness ended:

When [the] Quraysh became insolent towards God and rejected His gracious purpose, accused His prophet of lying, and ill treated and exiled those who served Him and proclaimed His unity, believed in His prophet, and held fast to His religion, He gave permission to His apostle to fight and to protect himself against those who wronged them and treated them badly.[24]

Ibn Ishaq then explains the progression of Qur'anic revelation about warfare. First, he explains, Allah allowed Muslims to wage defensive warfare. Then once Muslims "are in the ascendant they will establish prayer, pay the poor-tax, enjoin kindness, and forbid iniquity, i.e., the Prophet and his companions all of them."[25] The key phrase here is "in the ascendant," which means they will establish an Islamic state. But that was not Allah's last word on the circumstances in which Muslims should fight: "Then God sent down to him: 'Fight them so that there be no more seduction,' i.e., until no believer is seduced from his religion. 'And the religion is God's,' i.e., until God alone is worshipped."[26]

The Qur'an verse Ibn Ishaq quotes here (2:193) commands much more than defensive warfare: Muslims must fight until "the religion is God's"—that is, until Allah alone is worshipped. Later Islamic law, based on this development in the doctrine of jihad warfare during Muhammad's career, would offer non-Muslims three options: conversion to Islam, subjugation as inferiors under Islamic law, or warfare. According to Sheikh 'Abdullah bin Muhammad bin Humaid, a former Saudi Arabian chief justice, "at first 'the fighting' was forbidden, then it was permitted and after that it was made obligatory." He also distinguishes two groups Muslims must fight: "(1) against them who start 'the fighting' against you (Muslims)...(2) and against all those who worship others along with Allah...as mentioned in *Surat Al-Baqarah* (II), *Al-Imran* (III) and *At-Taubah* (IX)...and other Surahs (Chapters of the Qur'an)."[27] (The Roman numerals after the names of the chapters of the Qur'an are the numbers of the suras: Sheikh 'Abdullah is referring to verses quoted above such as 2:216, 3:157–158, 9:5, and 9:29.)

This understanding of the Qur'an isn't limited to the Wahhabi sect of Saudi Arabia, to which Sheikh 'Abdullah belongs, and which many Western analysts imagine to have originated Islamic doctrines of warfare against unbelievers. Jihad theorist Sayyid Qutb, who was not a Wahhabi, subscribes to the same view of the Qur'an. In his jihad manifesto *Milestones*, he quotes at length from the great medieval scholar Ibn Qayyim to sum up "the nature of Islamic Jihad," which is, in Qutb's fair distillation of Ibn Qayyim, that in the course of Muhammad's prophetic career "Muslims were first restrained from fighting; then they were permitted to fight; then they were commanded to fight against the aggressors; and finally they were commanded to fight against all the polytheists."[28] He also quotes Ibn Qayyim to emphasize the need to wage war against and subjugate non-Muslims, particularly the Jewish and Christian "People of the Book":

After the command for Jihaad came, the non-believers were divided into three categories: one, those with whom there was peace; two, the people with whom the Muslims were at war; and three, the Dhimmies [those subjugated under Islamic rule and paying a special tax].... It was also explained that war should be declared against those from among the "People of the Book" who declare open enmity, until they agree to pay Jizyah [the dhimmi tax] or accept Islam. Concerning the polytheists and the hypocrites, it was commanded in this chapter that Jihaad be declared against them and that they be treated harshly.[29]

Qutb says that if someone rejects Islam, "then it is the duty of Islam to fight him until either he is killed or until he declares his submission."[30]

Related to Muhammad's evolving concept of jihad in the Qur'an is the Islamic doctrine of abrogation (*naskh*). In this theory, Allah's later revelations to Muhammad cancel out the earlier ones. According to this idea, the violent verses of the ninth sura, including the Verse of the Sword: (9:5) "slay the unbelievers wherever you find them," abrogate the peaceful verses, because they were revealed later in Muhammad's prophetic career: in fact, most Muslim authorities agree that the ninth sura was the very last section of the Qur'an revealed to Muhammad.

In line with this, some classical Islamic theologians asserted that the Verse of the Sword abrogates as many as 124 more peaceful and tolerant verses of the Qur'an.[31] *Tafsir al-Jalalayn*, a commentary on the Qur'an by the respected medieval imams Jalal al-Din Muhammad ibn Ahmad al-Mahalli and Jalal al-Din 'Abd al-Rahman ibn Abi Bakr al-Suyuti, asserts that the Qur'an's ninth sura "was sent down when security was removed by the sword."[32] Another mainstream and respected Qur'an commentator of that time, Isma'il bin 'Amr bin Kathir al Dimashqi, known popularly as Ibn Kathir, declares that sura 9:5 "abrogated every agreement of peace between the Prophet and any idolater, every treaty, and every term.... No idolater had any more treaty or promise of safety ever since Surah Bara'ah [the ninth sura] was revealed."[33] Ibn Juzayy, yet another Qur'an commentator whose works are still read in the Islamic world, agreed: the Verse of the Sword is "abrogating every peace treaty in the Qur'an."[34]

Ibn Kathir makes this clear in his commentary on another "tolerance verse": "And he [Muhammad] saith: O my Lord! Lo! these are a folk who believe not. Then bear with them, O Muhammad, and say: Peace. But they will come to know" (43:88–89). Ibn Kathir explains: "*Say Salam* (peace!) means, 'do not respond to them in the same evil manner in which they address you; but try to soften their hearts and forgive them in word and deed.'" However, that is not the end of the passage. Ibn Kathir then takes up the last part: *"But they will come to know.* This is a warning from Allah for them. His punishment, which cannot be warded off, struck them, and His religion and His word was supreme. Subsequently Jihad and striving were prescribed until the people entered the religion of Allah in crowds, and Islam spread throughout the east and the west."[35]

That work is not yet complete.

All this means that warfare against unbelievers until they either become Muslim or "pay the jizya with willing submission" (Qur'an 9:29) is the Qur'an's last word on jihad. Mainstream Islamic tradition has interpreted this as Allah's enduring marching orders to the human race: the Islamic *umma* (community) must exist in a state of perpetual war, punctuated only by temporary truces, with the non-Muslim world. These are very different from the marching orders Jesus gave His apostles in the "Great Commission" of the New Testament: "Therefore go and make disciples of all nations, baptizing them in the name of the Father and of the Son and of the Holy Spirit" (Matthew 28:19). The apostles hoped to win converts through the Holy Spirit; Muslims, given the final instructions of Allah to Muhammad, were to compel conversion or subjugation through holy war: jihad.

All four principal Sunni schools agree on the importance of jihad. Ibn Abi Zayd al-Qayrawani, a tenth-century Maliki jurist, declared:

> Jihad is a precept of Divine institution. Its performance by certain individuals may dispense others from it. We Malikis maintain that it is preferable not to begin hostilities with the enemy before having invited the latter to embrace the religion of Allah except where the enemy attacks first. They have the alternative of either converting to Islam or paying the poll tax (*jizya*), short of which war will be declared against them.[36]

According to Ibn Taymiyya, a fourteenth-century Hanbali jurist who is a favorite of Osama bin Laden and other modern-day jihadists:

Since lawful warfare is essentially jihad and since its aim is that the religion is God's entirely and God's word is uppermost, therefore according to all Muslims, those who stand in the way of this aim must be fought. As for those who cannot offer resistance or cannot fight, such as women, children, monks, old people, the blind, handicapped and their likes, they shall not be killed unless they actually fight with words (e.g., by propaganda) and acts (e.g., by spying or otherwise assisting in the warfare).[37]

The Hanafi school sounds the same notes:

It is not lawful to make war upon any people who have never before been called to the faith, without previously requiring them to embrace it, because the Prophet so instructed his commanders, directing them to call the infidels to the faith, and also because the people will hence perceive that they are attacked for the sake of religion, and not for the sake of taking their property, or making slaves of their children, and on this consideration it is possible that they may be induced to agree to the call, in order to save themselves from the troubles of war. . . . If the infidels, upon receiving the call, neither consent to it nor agree to pay capitation tax, it is then incumbent on the Muslims to call upon God for assistance, and to make war upon them . . . because God is the assistant of those who serve Him, and the destroyer of His enemies, the infidels, and it is necessary to implore His aid upon every occasion; the Prophet, moreover, commands us so to do.[38]

And so does the eleventh-century Shafi'i scholar Abu'l Hasan al-Mawardi, who echoed Muhammad's instructions to invite the unbelievers to accept Islam or fight them if they refuse:

The mushrikun [infidels] of Dar al-Harb (the arena of battle [which includes all areas outside of Islam]) are of two types: First, those whom the call of Islam has reached, but they have refused it and have taken up arms. The amir of the army has the option of fighting them ... in accordance with what he judges to be in the best interest of the Muslims and most harmful to the mushrikun. ... Second, those whom the invitation to Islam has not reached, although such persons are few nowadays since Allah has made manifest the call of his Messenger ... it is forbidden to ... begin an attack before explaining the invitation to Islam to them ... if they still refuse to accept after this, war is waged against them and they are treated as those whom the call has reached.[39]

NOT JUST OLD BOOKS

These are all extremely old authorities—such that one might reasonably assume that whatever they say couldn't possibly still be the consensus of the Islamic mainstream. The laws of the United States have evolved considerably since the adoption of the Constitution, which itself has been amended. So why shouldn't this be true of Islamic law as well? Many observers assume that it must be, and that al Qaeda's departure from mainstream Islam must be located in its preference for the writings of ancient jurists rather than modern ones. But in this, unfortunately, they fail to reckon with the implications of the closing of the gates of *ijtihad*.

Ijtihad is the process of arriving at a decision on a point of Islamic law through study of the Qur'an and Sunnah (records of Muhammad's words and deeds). From the beginning of Islam, the authoritative study of such sources was reserved to a select number of scholars who fulfilled certain qualifications, including a comprehensive knowledge of the Qur'an and Sunnah, as well as knowledge of the principle of analogical reasoning (*qiyas*) by which legal decisions are made; knowledge of the consensus (*ijma*) on any given question of Muhammad, his closest companions, and the scholars of the past; and more, including living a blameless life. The founders of the schools of Islamic jurisprudence are among the small number of scholars—*mujtahedin*—thus qualified to perform ijtihad. But they all lived very long ago; for many centuries, independent study of the Qur'an and Sunnah has been discouraged among Muslims, who are instead expected to adhere to the rulings of one of those established schools. Since the death of Ahmed ibn Hanbal, from whom the Hanbali school takes its name, in 855 A.D., no one has been recognized by the Sunni Muslim community as a mujtahid of the first class—that is, someone who is qualified to originate legislation of his own, based on the Qur'an and Sunnah. Islamic scholar Cyril Glassé notes that "'the door of ijtihad is closed' as of some nine hundred years, and since then the tendency of jurisprudence (*fiqh*) has been to produce only commentaries upon commentaries and marginalia."[40]

Shi'ite Muslims have never accepted that ijtihad is a thing of the past. Suffice it to say that Islam is divided between those who think that the closing of interpretation has led to intellectual stagnation in Islam and those who think that it is the guarantor of sharia law. One fact that is not open to dispute is that all Muslims, whether Shi'ite or Sunni, accept the necessity of jihad. Even Islamic apologist Karen Armstrong admits that "Muslim jurists...taught that, because there was only one God, the whole world should be united in one polity and it was the duty of all Muslims to engage in a continued struggle to make the world accept the divine principles and create a just society." Non-Muslims "should be made to surrender to God's rule. Until this had been achieved, Islam must engage in a perpetual warlike effort." But, she says, "this martial theology was laid aside in practice and became a dead letter once it was clear that the Islamic empire had reached the limits of its expansion about a hundred years after Muhammad's death."[41]

The problem is that however much of a dead letter it became in practice during times of weakness in the Islamic world, this doctrine of Islamic supremacism was never reformed or rejected. No one seems to have told the warriors of jihad who besieged Europe throughout the Dark Ages, the Middle Ages, the Renaissance, and up until the seventeenth century that the Islamic empire had already reached the limits of its expansion centuries before. No one seems to have told the modern-day warriors of Islam from Bosnia to the Philippines that jihad is a dead letter, and that Islam isn't doing any more expanding. Saudi sheikh Muhammad Saleh al-Munajjid, whose lectures and Islamic rulings (*fatawa*) circulate widely throughout the Islamic world, demonstrates this in a discussion of whether Muslims should force others to accept Islam. In considering Qur'an 2:256 ("There is no compulsion in religion"), the sheikh quotes Qur'an 9:29, as well as 8:39 ("And fight them until there is no more Fitnah (disbelief and polytheism, i.e., worshipping others besides Allaah), and the religion (worship) will all be for Allaah Alone [in the whole of the world]" and the Verse of the Sword. Of the latter, Sheikh Muhammad says simply: "This verse is known as Ayat al-Sayf (the Verse of the Sword). These and similar verses abrogate the verses which say that there is no compulsion to become Muslim."[42]

Underscoring the fact that none of this is of merely historical interest is another Shafi'i manual of Islamic law that in 1991 was certified by the highest authority in Sunni Islam, Cairo's Al-Azhar University, as conforming "to the practice and faith of the orthodox Sunni community."[43] This manual, *'Umdat al-Salik* (available in English as *Reliance of the Traveller*), spends a considerable amount of time explaining jihad as "war against non-Muslims."[44] It spells out the nature of this warfare in quite specific terms: "The caliph makes war upon Jews, Christians, and Zoroastrians . . . until they become Muslim or pay the non-Muslim poll tax." It adds a comment by a Jordanian jurist that corresponds to Muhammad's instructions to call the unbelievers to Islam before fighting them: the caliph wages this war only "provided that he has first invited [Jews, Christians, and Zoroastrians] to enter Islam in faith and practice, and if they will not, then invited them to enter the social *order* of Islam by paying the non-Muslim poll tax (jizya). . . while remaining in their ancestral religions."[45]

Also, if there is no caliph, Muslims must still wage jihad.[46] And there is something else also. In Islamic law, jihad warfare may be defensive or offensive. Jihad is ordinarily *fard kifaya*—an obligation on the Muslim community as a whole, from which some are freed if others take it up. Jihad becomes *fard ayn*, or obligatory on every individual Muslim to aid in any way he can, if a Muslim land is attacked. That is what jihadists argue today—that the American presence in Iraq and Afghanistan makes jihad *fard ayn*, or obligatory on every individual Muslim. But this is just jihad for the defense of Muslim lands, although the defensive aspect of jihad activity is often interpreted quite elastically. It is the province of the caliph, who for Sunni Muslims was the successor of Muhammad as the political, military, and religious leader of the Muslim community, to authorize the waging of offensive jihad to spread the rule of Islamic law into non-Muslim lands. The caliphate, however, was abolished by the secular Turkish government in 1924.

This is a primary reason why jihadists want to restore the caliphate. In 1996 the Taliban's Mullah Omar went to the shrine of the Respectable Cloak of Muhammad in Kandahar and stood on the roof of the shrine wrapped in the cloak. His followers proclaimed him *Emir al Momineen*, or leader of the believers—a title of the caliph.[47] So far, however, only a jihadist group in Algeria has joined the Taliban in accepting Mullah Omar as caliph.[48]

In any case, the desire to restore the caliphate ultimately highlights the expansionist, imperialist, totalitarian, and globalist aims of the jihad movement, even as today it presents itself as a defensive action against Western evils. That expansionism is based on Qur'anic passages such as 9:29 and the life and teachings of Muhammad. Pakistani brigadier S. K. Malik's 1979 book *The Qur'anic Concept of War* (a book that made its way to the American mujahedin Jeffrey Leon Battle and October Martinique Lewis, and which carried a glowing endorsement from future Pakistani president Muhammad Zia-ul-Haq), delineates the same stages in the Qur'anic teaching about jihad: "The Muslim migration to Medina brought in its wake events and decisions of far-reaching significance and consequence for them. While in Mecca, they had neither been proclaimed an Ummah [community] nor were they granted the permission to take up arms against their oppressors. In Medina, a divine revelation proclaimed them an 'Ummah' and granted them the permission to take up arms against their oppressors. The permission was soon afterwards converted into a divine command making war a religious obligation for the faithful."[49]

Muhammad Sa'id Ramadan al-Buti, a theology professor at Damascus University, echoes the classic Islamic legal tenet that Muslims can legitimately wage war against those who resist the proclamation of Islam in his book *Jihad in Islam: How to Understand and Practice It*.[50] He sees legitimate jihads as purely defensive, and claims that three of the four major Sunni schools of Islamic jurisprudence, the Hanafi, Maliki, and Hanbali, all agree. But the fourth major Sunni school school of jurisprudence, the Shafi'i, as well as the minor Zahiri school, favor offensive jihad. The Shafi'is and Zahiris, according to al-Buti, "proclaimed that the fundamental cause of Jihad is to terminate Paganism."[51]

Imran Ahsan Khan Nyazee, assistant professor on the faculty of Shari'ah and Law of the International Islamic University in Islamabad, quotes the twelfth-century Maliki jurist Abu al-Walid Muhammad ibn Ahmad Ibn Rushd in a 1994 book on Islamic law. Ibn Rushd reports that the consensus among Muslim scholars (in traditional Islamic legal terms, once a consensus is reached among scholars it cannot be modified) is "that the purpose of fighting with the People of the Book . . . is one of two things: it is either their conversion to Islam or the payment of *jizyah*." Nyazee concludes: "This leaves no doubt that the primary goal of the Muslim community, in the eyes of its jurists, is to spread the word of Allah through jihad, and the option of poll-tax [jizya] is to be exercised only after subjugation" of non-Muslims.[52]

But if this is so, why hasn't the worldwide Islamic community been waging jihad on a large scale up until relatively recently? Nyazee says it is only because they have not been able to do so: "The Muslim community may be considered to be passing through a period of truce. In its present state of weakness, there is nothing much it can do about it."[53]

In this view, then, the jihad must continue as long as there are unbelievers, and only falls into abeyance when Muslims do not have the military strength to press forward with it. Making war on unbelievers is one of the responsibilities of the Muslim *umma*. That this view can be found not only in the writings of contemporary Islamic jihadists but also in ancient Muslim scholars underscores its traditional character. Modern mujahedin do not believe they are "hijacking" Islam. They believe they are restoring its proper interpretation—and they are successfully convincing peaceful Muslims around the world that they are correct. And they will continue to do so for as long as peaceful Muslims fail to formulate new and non-literalist ways of interpreting the Qur'an and the words and deeds of Muhammad.

Of course, people will do evil in all kinds of circumstances, and will use all manner of justification for it, but the violent passages in the Bible are not equivalent to those in the Qur'an in content, in mainstream interpretation, or in the effect they have had on believers through the ages. This is why violence is more prevalent and harder to eradicate in Islam than it has ever been in Christianity. To try to deny this by an instinctive cultural relativism, as so many do, is specious and dangerously misleading.

MERCY VS. JUDGMENT

In Bertrand Russell's *Why I Am Not a Christian*, he takes issue with Jesus as a model of moral behavior on several grounds—notably because He preaches about hell. Russell says, "I do not myself feel that any person who is really profoundly humane can believe in everlasting punishment"—yet it is a simple matter of observation that many people who are indeed profoundly humane, from St. Francis of Assisi to Mother Teresa of Calcutta, have so believed.[54]

Russell also feels pangs of grief for the fig tree cursed by Jesus: "This is a very curious story, because it was not the right time of year for figs, and you really could not blame the tree."[55] Other critics of Jesus have taken issue with his apparent rudeness to the Syrophoenician woman who asks him to heal her daughter (Matthew 15:21–28), and to his harsh words for the Pharisees, to whom he says, "You are of your father the devil" (John 8:44). But these objections seem quaint if we compare them to what a reasonable person might object to regarding jihad and Islamic supremacism in the teachings of the Qur'an, Muhammad, and Islamic theologians. And no one can reasonably equate Jesus's command to "love your enemies" (Matthew 5:44) with the Qur'an's directive to the followers of Muhammad to be "ruthless to the unbelievers" (48:29).

The mercy that is so much a part of Christianity has virtually no home in Islam, contrary to its repeated invocations of Allah as *ar-Rahim*, "the merciful." An emblematic contrast is in the treatment within each religion of the Mosaic law's command to stone adulterers. In a celebrated incident in the Gospels, Jesus tells a group that has assembled to stone to death an adulterous woman: "Let the one among you who is without sin be the first to throw a stone at her." Then, after the crowd dispersed in shame, he said to the woman, "Neither do I condemn you. Go, and from now on do not sin any more" (John 7:53–8:11).

On the other hand, an adulterous couple was once brought to Muhammad, who used the occasion to challenge the Jewish leaders about their fidelity to the letter of their own law. "What do you find in the Torah," he asked them, "about the legal punishment of ar-Rajm (stoning)?" They answered, "We announce their crime and lash them," whereupon a former rabbi and convert to Islam, cried, "You are telling a lie. Torah contains the order of Rajm." One of the Jews then began to read from the Torah, but he skipped the verse mandating stoning for adultery, covering it with his hand.[56] The former rabbi commanded, "Lift your hand!" The verse duly read, Muhammad exclaimed, "Woe to you Jews! What has induced you to abandon the judgment of God which you hold in your hands?"[57] Muhammad ordered the couple to be stoned to death; another Muslim remembered, "I saw the man leaning over the woman to shelter her from the stones."[58]

Rabbinic Judaism ever since the destruction of the Temple had evolved non-literal ways to understand such commands, while in Islam literal interpretation is still very much alive.

Yet many people have a hard time believing that many Muslims accept the idea of jihad. We have all met Muslims who personally are gentle souls who profess to abhor religious violence, and who assure us that their religion is peaceful. Are they lying?

They may not be. In Islam, as in all religious traditions, there is a spectrum of belief, knowledge, and fervor. Many who call themselves Muslims know or care little about what the mainstream authorities of the religion actually teach. Some who are quite devout have only a glancing familiarity, at best, with the material outlined here about jihad warfare. Most Muslims worldwide today are not Arabs, and do not speak Arabic—especially the Qur'an's difficult seventh-century Arabic. Yet all the sects and schools of Islam mandate that prayers must be said and the Qur'an recited in Arabic—making this for many merely an exercise in formalism, involving the repetition of syllables they do not understand.

The Islamic ideology of jihad warfare has been deemphasized in modern times for a complex of historical reasons, but the result has been that many Muslims have heard little or nothing about it, at least until jihadist recruiters began appearing with texts entitled "Jihad: the Forgotten

Obligation" and the like.[59] In his memoir *The Caliph's House: A Year in Casablanca*, Tahir Shah recounts the arrival of jihadist recruiters in a Casablanca slum.[60] They parked a "well-built trailer" across the street from the mosque, and set about trying to win the local people to their virulent vision of Islam.

Jihadists today view the vast body of cultural Muslims as a huge recruiting field, and have often recruited them by calling them back to the full practice of their religion, where they expect they will be rewarded for their fidelity to the teachings of the Qur'an and Islamic tradition on jihad.

CHAPTER SIX

THE CROSS AND THE SWORD

CHRISTIAN FISH, MUSLIM SHARKS

"The Christians had the fish so we responded with the shark. If they want to portray themselves as weak fishes, okay. We are the strongest."

So said an Egyptian Muslim in response to a bumper-sticker war that broke out in Cairo in late 2003. When Coptic Christians began putting the Christian fish symbol, long popular with American evangelicals, on their cars, Muslims responded with their own bumper stickers depicting sharks. One Christian woman commented, "All I wanted to say is that I am a Christian, kind of expressing my Coptic identity. I think choosing a shark doesn't make sense, as if someone is saying, 'I am a violent, bloody creature, look at me.'"[1] The contrast resonates with implications.

A certain group of strict Christian literalists drives horses and buggies and eschews electricity because automobiles and incandescent lights aren't mentioned in the Bible. They and other Christian groups maintain a strict pacifism because Jesus said, "Do not resist one who is evil. But if any one strikes you on the right cheek, turn to him the other also" (Matthew 5:39) and "all who take the sword will perish by the sword" (Matthew 26:52). Recently a group of strict Muslim literalists, acting literally in a distinctively Islamic manner, threatened falafel vendors in Baghdad with death. One of the vendors, Abu Zeinab, tells the story: "I said I was just feeding the people, but they said there were no falafels in Muhammad the prophet's time, so we shouldn't have them either. I felt like telling them there were no Kalashnikovs in Mohammed's time either, but I wanted to keep my life."[2]

The contrast between these two forms of literalism couldn't be starker. And the contrasts don't stop there. The Qur'an directs Muslims to tell Jews and Christians that "our Allah and your Allah is One, and unto Him we surrender" (29:46)—and certainly the belief that Jews, Christians, and Muslims all worship the same God is not limited to Muslims. The Catholic Church affirmed at the Second Vatican Council that Muslims, "professing to hold the faith of Abraham, along with us adore the one and merciful God, who on the last day will judge mankind"—a cautiously worded statement that has often been misunderstood. It does not affirm that Islam is a divinely inspired religion.[3] And the ways in which Christians and Muslims envision that one and merciful God of Abraham differ markedly, beginning with the flat contradiction of "no one who denies the Son has the Father" (I John 2:23) and "He to whom belongs the dominion of the heavens and the earth: no son has He begotten, nor has He a partner in His dominion" (Qur'an 25:2).

One of the principal differences between Christianity and Islam is in the concept of martyrdom. In both Greek and Arabic, "martyr" means "witness," and in both Christianity and Islam one who gives his life for the faith is considered to have borne witness to the truth of the faith to the highest degree. But in Islam there is an aggressiveness to this concept that is lacking in Christianity. The Qur'an's only absolute guarantee of a place in Paradise is given to those who "slay and are slain" for Allah (9:111), whereas there is nothing in the Christian concept of martyrdom about martyrs receiving a reward for killing unbelievers. Even when Pope Urban II called the First Crusade in 1095, he said (according to one account of his speech at the Council of Clermont) that "all who die by the way, whether by land or by sea, or in battle against the pagans, shall have immediate remission of sins." Note that the pope said "all who die," not "all who kill."[4]

The different concepts of martyrdom, of course, proceed from vastly different core principles, as delineated by the founders of each religion. The Qur'an's denial of the crucifixion (4:157) is just one manifestation of the many ways in which Jesus scandalizes Muslims. Jesus the meek and mild, who gives himself up to the authorities, who endures humiliation and execution for our sake, makes no sense in an Islamic context. And the one who says of his tormentors, "Forgive them, Lord, for they know not what they do," whose kingdom is not of this world, who tells his followers to turn the other cheek and love their enemies, who instructs Peter to sheath his sword because those who live by the sword die by the sword, and who led no armed resistance movement against anyone nor sought to become a king on Earth is rather different from Muhammad, who leads armies, conquers territories, and promises a heavenly future of unlimited wine and women to those who die in battle.

It is hard to imagine a Christian preacher saying anything like what Ayatollah Khomeini said on the occasion of the prophet Muhammad's birthday in 1981:

> The real Day of God is the day that Amir al-Mo'menin [Ali, Shi'ite Islam's first Imam] drew his sword and slaughtered all the khavarej [a group that rejected Ali's leadership] and killed them from the first to the last.
>
> The Days of God are when Allah, the gracious, the almighty, causes an earthquake. It is when He slaps on the face. It is when he causes a hurricane. He whips this people to become humans.
>
> If the Amir al-Mo'menin wanted to be tolerant, he would not have drawn his sword killing 700 people in one go.
>
> In our prisons we have more of the same kind of people who are corrupt. If we do not kill them, each one of them that gets out will become a murderer! They don't become humans.
>
> Why do you mullahs only go after the ordinances of prayer and fasting? Why do you only read the Qur'anic verses of mercy and do not read the verses of killing?
>
> Qur'an says; kill, imprison!
>
> Why are you only clinging to the part that talks about mercy? Mercy is against God.
>
> Mehrab [the prayer niche in a mosque, in front of which the imam stands to lead prayers] means the place of war, the place of fighting. Out of the mehrabs, wars should proceed, just as all the wars of Islam used to proceed out of the mehrabs.

The prophet [had a] sword to kill people.

Our imams were quite military men. All of them were warriors. They used to wield swords; they used to kill people. We need a Khalifa [caliph] who would chop hands, cut throats, stone people. In the same way that the messenger of God used to chop hands, cut throats, and stone people. In the same way that he massacred the Jews of Bani Qurayza [a Jewish tribe of Medina massacred by Muhammad] because they were a bunch of discontent[ed] people. If the Prophet used to order to burn a house or exterminate a tribe, that was justice.

The lives of people must be secured through punishment. Because, the protection of the masses lies beneath these very punitive executions. With just a few years of imprisonment things don't get fixed. You must put aside this childish sentimentalism. We believe that the accused essentially does not have to be tried. He or she must just be killed. Only their identity is to be established and then they should be killed.[5]

Almost a thousand years earlier, when calling the First Crusade, Pope Urban is reported to have said: "I, or rather the Lord, beseech you as Christ's heralds to publish this everywhere and to persuade all people of whatever rank, foot-soldiers and knights, poor and rich, to carry aid promptly to those Christians and to destroy that vile race from the lands of our friends.... Moreover, Christ commands it."[6] So, yes, Christians have undoubtedly issued calls for violence too, and committed horrible atrocities. No one has a monopoly on evil. But since we have seen that the Christian scriptures do not teach anything comparable to the Qur'an's mandate to wage war against unbelievers, we ought to examine some of the principal historical crimes attributed to Christianity, and see how deeply rooted they are within it, and how likely they are to recur. And then we could do the same with Islam. Do the most notorious actions of Muslims align with Islamic principles, or do they transgress them?

"SLAVES, OBEY YOUR MASTERS"

One of the most common criticisms of Christianity centers on its posture toward slavery. Taken at face value, the Bible condones the practice. The apostle Paul says flatly: "Slaves, be obedient to those who are your earthly masters, with fear and trembling, in singleness of heart, as to Christ" (Ephesians 6:5). He wasn't saying anything remotely controversial for the times, and of course has been criticized for accepting the cultural status quo instead of challenging it. No culture on earth ever questioned the morality of slavery until relatively recent times—and then it was Christians who did the questioning.

The roots of abolitionism can be traced to the church's practice of baptizing slaves and treating them as human beings equal in dignity to all others. St. Isidore of Seville declared that "God has made no difference between the soul of the slave and that of the freedman."[7] His statement was rooted in what St. Paul told the slaveowner Onesimus about his runaway slave Philemon: "Perhaps this was why he was parted from you for a while, that you might have him back forever, no longer as a slave but as more than a slave, as a beloved brother."

In the year 649, Clovis II, king of the Franks, married a slave, who later began a campaign to halt the traffic in slaves. The Catholic Church now honors her as St. Bathilda.[8] Charlemagne and other Christian leaders in the so-called Dark Ages opposed slavery within the boundaries of Christendom. According to historian Rodney Stark, "slavery ended in medieval Europe only because the church extended its sacraments to all slaves and then managed to impose a ban on the enslavement of Christians (and of Jews). Within the context of medieval Europe, that prohibition was effectively a rule of universal abolition."[9] And in the New World, when the Spanish conquistadors were energetically enslaving South American Indians and importing black Africans as slaves, their chief opponent was a Catholic missionary and bishop, Bartolomé de Las Casas, who was instrumental in compelling the Spanish crown to enact a law in 1542 prohibiting enslavement of the Indians.

However, slavery persisted through the ages, and was at times even given ecclesiastical sanction. In the antebellum United States, there was no shortage of Southerners who used scripture to support the morality of slavery. But while such preachers could point to the existence and acceptance of slavery in the Old and New Testaments, the abolitionist movement was predicated upon the Christian principle of the dignity of all who are redeemed in Christ. Pioneering English abolitionists Thomas Clarkson and William Wilberforce were both motivated to work for an end to slavery by their deep Christian faith. So was American anti-slavery crusader William Lloyd Garrison, who remarked in a speech in Charleston, South Carolina, on the day Abraham Lincoln was shot: "Abolitionism, what is it? Liberty. What is liberty? Abolitionism. What are they both? Politically, one is the Declaration of Independence; religiously, the other is the Golden Rule of our Savior."[10]

Abraham Lincoln was himself much preoccupied with Genesis 3:19: "In the sweat of your face you shall eat bread." In May 1864 he wrote to a delegation of Baptists, "To read in the Bible, as the word of God himself, that 'In the sweat of thy face shalt thou eat bread,' and to preach therefrom that, 'In the sweat of other man's faces shalt thou eat bread,' to my mind can scarcely be reconciled with honest sincerity."[11] Later that same year he replied to the wife of a Confederate prisoner who had appealed to him for her husband's release: "You say your husband is a religious man; tell him when you meet him, that I say I am not much of a judge of religion, but that, in my opinion, the religion that sets men to rebel and fight against their government, because, as they think, that government does not sufficiently help some men to eat their bread on the sweat of other men's faces, is not the sort of religion upon which people can get to heaven!"[12]

Not only did anti-slavery views exist in the Christian world from the Dark Ages on, but it was also Christian ideas that brought about the global abolition of slavery.

ISLAMIC SLAVERY

In the Islamic world, however, the situation is very different. The prophet Muhammad owned slaves, and, as does the Bible, the Qur'an takes the existence of slavery for granted. According to the Qur'an, a slave can be freed, for instance, as penance for his master's broken oath, but the Qur'an goes much farther than the New Testament in tolerating slavery. It even gives a man permission to have sexual relations with his slave girls, which could include married women as well: "And all married women (are forbidden unto you) save those (captives) whom your right hands possess. It is a decree of Allah for you" (4:24).

Why should such passages be any more troubling than biblical passages such as Exodus 21:7–11, which gives regulations for selling one's daughter as a slave? Because in Islam there is no equivalent of the Golden Rule, as articulated by Jesus. The closest Islamic tradition comes to this is one hadith in which Muhammad says, "None of you will have faith till he likes for his (Muslim) brother what he likes for himself."[13] The parenthetical "Muslim" in that sentence was added by a Saudi translator and does not appear in the original Arabic; however, "brother" is generally used in Islamic tradition to refer to fellow Muslims. Also mitigating against a universal interpretation of this maxim is the sharp distinction between believers and unbelievers that runs throughout Islam. The Qur'an says that the followers of Muhammad are "ruthless to the unbelievers but merciful to one another" (48:29), and that the unbelievers are the "worst of created beings" (98:6). One may exercise the Golden Rule in relation to a fellow Muslim, but according to the laws of Islam, the same courtesy is not to be extended to unbelievers.

That is one principal reason why the primary source of slaves in the Islamic world has been non-Muslims, whether Jews, Christians, Hindus, or pagans. Most slaves were non-Muslims who had been captured during jihad warfare. The pioneering scholar of the treatment of non-Muslims in Islamic societies, Bat Ye'or, explains the system that developed out of jihad conquest:

> The jihad slave system included contingents of both sexes delivered annually in conformity with the treaties of submission by sovereigns who were tributaries of the caliph. When Amr conquered Tripoli (Libya) in 643, he forced the Jewish and Christian Berbers to give their wives and children as slaves to the Arab army as part of their *jizya*. From 652 until its conquest in 1276, Nubia was forced to send an annual contingent of slaves to Cairo. Treaties concluded with the towns of Transoxiana [Iranian central Asia], Sijistan [eastern Iran], Armenia, and Fezzan (Maghreb) under the Umayyads and Abbasids stipulated an annual dispatch of slaves from both sexes. However, the

main sources for the supply of slaves remained the regular raids on villages within the *dar-al-harb* [non-Islamic regions] and the military
expeditions which swept more deeply into the infidel lands, emptying
towns and provinces of their inhabitants.[14]

Historian Speros Vryonis observes that "since the beginning of the Arab
razzias [raids] into the land of Rum [the Byzantine Empire], human booty
had come to constitute a very important portion of the spoils." The Turks,
as they steadily conquered more and more of Anatolia, reduced many of
the Greeks and other non-Muslims there to slave status: "They enslaved
men, women, and children from all major urban centers and from the
countryside where the populations were defenseless."[15] Indian historian
K. S. Lal states that wherever jihadists conquered a territory, "there developed a system of slavery peculiar to the clime, terrain, and populace of the
place." When Muslim armies invaded India, "its people began to be
enslaved in droves to be sold in foreign lands or employed in various
capacities on menial and not-so-menial jobs within the country."[16]

Slaves faced pressure to convert to Islam. Patricia Crone, in an analysis of Islamic political theories, notes that after a jihad battle was concluded, "male captives might be killed or enslaved.... Dispersed in
Muslim households, slaves almost always converted, encouraged or pres-
surized by their masters, driven by a need to bond with others, or slowly,
becoming accustomed to seeing things through Muslim eyes even if they
tried to resist."[17] Thomas Pellow, an Englishman who was enslaved in
Morocco for twenty-three years after being captured as a cabin boy on a
small English vessel in 1716, was tortured until he accepted Islam. For
weeks he was beaten and starved, and finally gave in after his torturer
resorted to "burning my flesh off my bones by fire, which the tyrant did,
by frequent repetitions, after a most cruel manner."[18]

Slavery was taken for granted throughout Islamic history. Yet while the
European and American slave trades get lavish attention from historians
(as well as from mau-mauing reparations advocates and guilt-ridden politicians), the Islamic slave trade actually lasted longer and brought suffering
to a larger number of people. It is exceedingly ironic that Islam has been
presented to American blacks as the egalitarian alternative to the "white

man's slave religion" of Christianity, as Islamic slavery operated on a larger scale than did the Western slave trade, and lasted longer. While historians estimate that the transatlantic slave trade, which operated between the sixteenth and nineteenth centuries, involved around 10.5 million people, the Islamic slave trade in the Sahara, the Red Sea, and the Indian Ocean areas began in the seventh century and lasted into the nineteenth, and involved 17 million people.[19]

Nor was there a Muslim abolitionist movement, no Clarkson, Wilberforce, or Garrison. When the slave trade ended, it was ended not through Muslim efforts but through British military force.

Even so, there is evidence that slavery continues beneath the surface in some Muslim countries—notably Saudi Arabia, which only abolished slavery in 1962; Yemen and Oman, both of which ended legal slavery in 1970; and Niger, which didn't abolish slavery until 2004. In Niger, the ban is widely ignored, and as many as one million people remain in bondage. Slaves are bred, often raped, and generally treated like animals.[20]

There are even slavery cases involving Muslims in the United States. A Saudi named Homaidan al-Turki was sentenced in September 2006 to twenty-seven years to life in prison for keeping a woman as a slave in his Colorado home. For his part, al-Turki claimed that he was a victim of anti-Muslim bias. He told the judge, "Your honor, I am not here to apologize, for I cannot apologize for things I did not do and for crimes I did not commit. The state has criminalized these basic Muslim behaviors. Attacking traditional Muslim behaviors was the focal point of the prosecution."[21] The following month, an Egyptian couple living in Southern California received a fine and prison terms, to be followed by deportation, after pleading guilty to holding a ten-year-old girl as a slave.[22] And in January 2007, an attaché of the Kuwaiti embassy in Washington, Waleed al-Saleh, and his wife were charged with keeping three Christian domestic workers from India in slave-like conditions in their Virginia home. One of these women remarked, "I believed that I had no choice but to continue working for them even though they beat me and treated me worse than a slave."[23]

Slavery is still practiced openly today in two Muslim countries, Sudan and Mauritania. In line with historical practice, Muslim slavers in the

Sudan primarily enslave non-Muslims, chiefly Christians. According to the Coalition Against Slavery in Mauritania and Sudan (CASMAS), a human rights and abolitionist movement founded in 1995, "The current Khartoum government wants to bring the non-Muslim Black South in line with sharia law, laid down and interpreted by conservative Muslim clergy. The Black animist and Christian South remembers many years of slave raids by Arabs from the north and east and resists Muslim religious rule and the perceived economic, cultural, and religious expansion behind it."[24]

One modern-day Sudanese Christian slave, James Pareng Alier, was kidnapped and enslaved when he was twelve years old. Religion was a major element of his ordeal: "I was forced to learn the Koran and rebaptised Ahmed. They told me that Christianity was a bad religion. After a time we were given military training and they told us we would be sent to fight." Alier has no idea of his family's whereabouts.[25] The BBC reported in March 2007 that slave raids "were a common feature of Sudan's twenty-one-year north-south war, which ended in 2005. . . . According to a study by the Kenya-based Rift Valley Institute, some 11,000 young boys and girls were seized and taken across the internal border—many to the states of South Darfur and West Kordofan. . . . Most were forcibly converted to Islam, given Muslim names, and told not to speak their mother tongue."[26] Yet even today, while non-Muslims were enslaved and often forcibly converted to Islam, their conversion does not lead to their freedom. Mauritanian anti-slavery campaigner Boubacar Messaoud explains that "it's like having sheep or goats. If a woman is a slave, her descendants are slaves."[27]

Anti-slavery crusaders like Messaoud have great difficulty working against this attitude, because it is rooted in the Qur'an and in Muhammad's own example.

THOSE VIOLENT CHRISTIANS: THE CRUSADES

Proponents of the idea that all religions are equal in their capacity to inspire violence frequently invoke the Crusades, as if they were equivalent to contemporary Islamic jihad violence. And indeed, in the popular mind the Crusaders were bloodthirsty proto-imperialists, clutching Bible in one hand and sword in the other, drunk on religious dogma and bent on conquering Islamic land, slaughtering the populace indiscriminately, and forcing the terrified survivors to convert to Christianity.

Reality could hardly be more different. In fact, the Crusades were a late and small-scale response to Islamic jihad conquests that began 450 years before the First Crusade and overwhelmed what had been up to the time of these conquests over half of Christendom. Three of the five principal centers of early Christianity—Alexandria, Antioch, and Jerusalem—were conquered and Islamized before the First Crusade, and a fourth (Constantinople) would fall in 1453, 150 years after the Islamic conquest of the last Crusader kingdom.

The initial pace of these jihad conquests was breathtakingly fast. In 635, the jihadists took Damascus; in 636, al-Basrah in Iraq; in 637, Antioch; and in 638, Jerusalem, the birthplace of Christianity and the jewel of the Christian East.[28] As Sophronius, the patriarch of Jerusalem, handed over the city to the conquering caliph Umar, he recalled a Bible verse: "Behold the abomination of desolation, spoken of by Daniel the prophet."[29] The Muslims took Caesarea in 641 and Armenia in 643, and the conquest of Egypt took place in the same period. They also won decisive victories over the Byzantines at Sufetula in Tunisia in 647, opening up North Africa, and over the Persians at Nihavand in 642. By 709 they had complete control of North Africa; by 711 they had subdued Spain and were moving into France. Muslim forces first tried to take Constantinople in August 716, but the great city would not fall to them for another 700 years. Meanwhile, Sicily fell in 827. By 846 Rome was in danger of being captured by jihadists; repulsed, they "sacked the cathedrals of St. Peter beside the Vatican and of St. Paul outside the walls, and desecrated the graves of the pontiffs."[30]

The Byzantines and other Christians fought back and regained some territory, but most of these conquests were never reversed. Then, early in the eleventh century, conditions for Christians in the Holy Land rapidly deteriorated. In 1004, the Fatimid caliph Abu 'Ali al-Mansur al-Hakim ordered churches destroyed and church property seized. Over the next ten years thirty thousand churches were destroyed. Untold numbers of

Christians converted to Islam simply to save their lives. In 1009, al-Hakim commanded that the Church of the Holy Sepulcher, which marked the traditional site of Christ's burial in Jerusalem, be destroyed, along with several other churches (including the Church of the Resurrection). He also ordered Christians to wear heavy crosses around their necks (and Jews heavy blocks of wood in the shape of a calf). He piled on other humiliating decrees, culminating in the order that they accept Islam or leave his dominions.[31]

The erratic caliph ultimately relaxed his persecution, and in 1027 the Byzantines were allowed to rebuild the Church of the Holy Sepulcher. But the Christians in the Holy Land were not out of danger.[32] In 1056, Muslims expelled three hundred Christians from Jerusalem and forbade European Christians from entering the new Church of the Holy Sepulcher.[33] Then in 1071, the Seljuk Turks crushed the Byzantines in the Battle of Manzikert; they conquered Syria in 1076 and Jerusalem in 1077. It was against this backdrop that Byzantine emperor Alexius I Comnenus appealed to the pope for help. Ultimately, the First Crusade, called by Pope Urban II in 1095, came in response to that call.

The warriors of the First Crusade and some of the later Crusades committed atrocities that cannot be excused, including the notorious sack of Jerusalem in 1099, during which they set alight a synagogue full of Jews. Their behavior in this, as heinous as it was, wasn't the singular atrocity that later historians and polemicists have made it out to be; in fact, it was common practice at the time for invaders to deal harshly with cities that resisted siege and leniently with those that surrendered without a fight. Muslim armies frequently behaved in exactly the same way when entering a conquered city. This is not to excuse the crusaders' conduct by pointing to similar incidents and suggesting that "everybody does it," as Islamic apologists frequently do today when confronted with the realities of modern jihad terrorism. One atrocity does not excuse another, but it does illustrate that the Crusaders' behavior in Jerusalem was consistent with that of other armies of the period, as all states subscribed to the same notions of siege and resistance.

In 1148, Muslim commander Nur ed-Din ordered the killing of every Christian in Aleppo. In 1268, when the jihad forces of the Mamluk sultan Baybars took Antioch from the Crusaders, Baybars wrote a taunting letter to the Crusader ruler, Count Bohemond VI. If Bohemond had been in the city when the Muslims took it, Baybars wrote, "you would have seen your knights prostrate beneath the horses' hooves, your houses stormed by pillagers and ransacked by looters, your wealth weighed by the quintal, your women sold four at a time and bought for a dinar of your own money!...You would have seen your Muslim enemy trampling on the place where you celebrate the Mass, cutting the throats of monks, priests, and deacons upon the altars, bringing sudden death to the patriarchs and slavery to the royal princes."[34]

Most notorious of all may be the jihadists' entry into Constantinople on May 29, 1453, when they—like the crusaders in Jerusalem in 1099—finally broke through a prolonged resistance to their siege. Here again the rivers of blood ran, as historian Steven Runciman notes. The Muslim soldiers, "slew everyone that they met in the streets, men, women, and children without discrimination. The blood ran in rivers down the steep streets from the heights of Petra toward the Golden Horn. But soon the lust for slaughter was assuaged. The soldiers realized that captives and precious objects would bring them greater profit."[35]

The crusaders, for their part, never resorted to forced conversions or even extensive missionary efforts. Missionaries did join the Crusades, especially the later ones, but their efforts were never large, and were certainly not supplemented by force. The Spanish Muslim chronicler Ibn Jubayr even noted that some Muslims preferred to live in crusader territories rather than in the neighboring Muslim lands. "Upon leaving Tibnin (near Tyre)," he recounts, "we passed through an unbroken skein of farms and villages whose lands were efficiently cultivated. The inhabitants were all Muslims, but they live in comfort with the Franj [Franks, or crusaders]—may God preserve them from temptation! Their dwellings belong to them and their property is unmolested." Ibn Jubayr even says that when these men "compare their lot to that of their brothers living in Muslim territory," they find that "the latter suffer from the injustice of their coreligionists, whereas the Franj act with equity."[36]

In light of all this, historian Bernard Lewis finds contemporary Western embarrassment over the Crusades a bit excessive:

We have seen in our own day the extraordinary spectacle of a pope apologizing to the Muslims for the Crusades. I would not wish to defend the behavior of the Crusaders, which was in many respects atrocious. But let us have a little sense of proportion. We are now expected to believe that the Crusades were an unwarranted act of aggression against a peaceful Muslim world. Hardly. The first papal call for a crusade occurred in 846 C.E., when an Arab expedition from Sicily sailed up the Tiber and sacked St. Peter's in Rome. A synod in France issued an appeal to Christian sovereigns to rally against "the enemies of Christ," and the pope, Leo IV, offered a heavenly reward to those who died fighting the Muslims. A century and a half and many battles later, in 1096, the Crusaders actually arrived in the Middle East. The Crusades were a late, limited, and unsuccessful imitation of the jihad—an attempt to recover by holy war what had been lost by holy war. It failed, and it was not followed up.[37]

Thus here again, the imitation of Christ and the imitation of Muhammad are very different affairs. Large-scale Crusades haven't recurred in the Christian world over the last eight hundred years because there is no imperative in the teaching of Christ to justify warfare in the name of the religion. In contrast, while many millions of Muslims in many areas of the world have grown up for generations without hearing about the jihad imperative, the teachings of jihad have remained part of Islam, capable of being revived at any time by those with the means and determination to do so. If the Christian and post-Christian West has anything to apologize for in the Crusades, the Islamic world has a great deal more for which it should apologize in the jihad wars that began many centuries before the Crusades and still have not ended.

Such an apology, of course, is not forthcoming from Muslim leaders. Yet the world's moral indignation, as well as that of the West, is focused much more vocally and persistently upon the Crusades and other perceived sins of Christendom, with no corresponding attention paid at all either to historic or contemporary Islamic jihad violence. Tony Blair and other Western leaders apologize for slavery and even consider reparations for slave descendants, while no one at such high levels is similarly concerned about ongoing Islamic slavery in North Africa. These peculiar myopias once again manifest the self-loathing that the cultural Left has inculcated in the Western consciousness for decades. If it is not reversed, quickly and decisively, our very survival could be at stake.

DIDN'T CATHOLICS KILL HUNDREDS OF THOUSANDS IN THE INQUISITION?

For anti-Christian polemicists, the apotheosis of Christian violence was not the Crusades, but the Inquisition.

In the year 494 Pope Gelasius I wrote to the Roman emperor Anastasius: "There are two powers, august Emperor, by which this world is chiefly ruled, namely, the sacred authority of the priests and the royal power." Those two powers are, in this view, represented by the two swords mentioned in the Gospel of Luke: "And they said, 'Look, Lord, here are two swords.' And he said to them, 'It is enough.'" "Of these," continued Gelasius, "that of the priests is the more weighty, since they have to render an account for even the kings of men in the divine judgment. You are also aware, dear son, that while you are permitted honorably to rule over human kind, yet in things divine you bow your head humbly before the leaders of the clergy and await from their hands the means of your salvation. In the reception and proper disposition of the heavenly mysteries you recognize that you should be subordinate rather than superior to the religious order, and that in these matters you depend on their judgment rather than wish to force them to follow your will."[38]

In this Gelasius succinctly articulated an understanding of the relationship between the civil and the ecclesiastical power that had been evolving since the emperor Constantine legalized Christianity in 313, and the emperor Theodosius declared the faith of the Nicene Creed the official religion of the Roman Empire in 391. This understanding led to the prosecution of religious crimes by the civil authority, culminating in the notorious Spanish Inquisition, which by all accounts attempted to compel its victims to go against the dictates of their own conscience. This practice was not in harmony with the early Christian understanding of the freedom of conscience and religion. Among the early church fathers it was

taken for granted that true religion required a free conscience. Early in the
third century Tertullian wrote to a Roman pagan that "it is a fundamental
human right, a privilege of nature, that every man should worship according to his own convictions: one man's religion neither harms nor helps
another man. It is assuredly no part of religion to compel religion—to
which free will and not force should lead us."[39]

One of the most influential of the early church fathers, Origen, in line
with common Christian practice at that time, contrasted the tenets of
Christianity with the law of Moses. He pointed out that Christians "could
not slay their enemies, or condemn to be burned or stoned, as Moses commands, those who had broken the law, and were therefore condemned as
deserving of these punishments."[40] Lactantius declared that "religion cannot be imposed by force; the matter must be carried on by words rather
than by blows, that the will may be affected." In words that future Christian leaders would have done well to take to heart, he said:

> Oh with what an honorable inclination the wretched men go astray!
> For they are aware that there is nothing among men more excellent
> than religion, and that this ought to be defended with the whole of our
> power; but as they are deceived in the matter of religion itself, so also
> are they in the manner of its defense. For religion is to be defended,
> not by putting to death, but by dying; not by cruelty, but by patient
> endurance; not by guilt, but by good faith.... For if you wish to defend
> religion by bloodshed, and by tortures, and by guilt, it will no longer
> be defended, but will be polluted and profaned. For nothing is so
> much a matter of free will as religion; in which, if the mind of the wor-
> shipper is disinclined to it, religion is at once taken away, and ceases
> to exist.[41]

However, once Nicene Christianity became the official religion of the
Empire, the emperors began to enact a series of decrees that either
restricted the rights of non-orthodox Christians or exiled them. Fourth-
century bishop St. Optatus of Milevis was the first Christian writer to
break with the common tendency to contrast Christian freedom with the
law of Moses, invoking Old Testament examples to justify the state's use

of force against religious dissidents and professing wonder at those who disagreed, "As if no one at all ought ever to be killed in punishment of offences against God!"[42]

Yet even at this point there was no consensus. St. John Chrysostom, one of the most influential of all the fathers of the Eastern church, wrote that "it is not right to put a heretic to death, since an implacable war would be brought into the world."[43] Likewise St. Augustine of Hippo, the most influential Western theologian for nearly a millennium, wrote of heretics that "it is not their death, but their deliverance from error, that we seek."[44]

This picture began to change in the Middle Ages, when the idea that the state administered earthly punishments on behalf of the church became paramount. The Catharist movement spread so quickly through Western Europe that some civil leaders believed that the survival of Christian society itself was at stake, and instituted capital punishment for heresy—although some church leaders, including St. Bernard of Clairvaux and Peter Cantor, an influential French professor of theology, still urged against it. Nevertheless, in the thirteenth century a number of European polities began to enact laws mandating that heretics be burnt to death. It was in this context that the Inquisition was first established.

In 1252 Pope Innocent IV even authorized the use of torture, not as punishment but as a method of eliciting the truth: as long as the victim was not killed or dismembered, as long as it was used only once, and as long as the weight of evidence was against the suspect. St. Thomas Aquinas wrote that heretics "deserve not only to be separated from the church by excommunication, but also to be severed from the world by death."[45] While the distinction between spiritual and civil authority remained, by this time the church was enthusiastically abetting the state's use of the second sword against its enemies—although capital punishment was still not the norm, and sentences more often involved the prescription of various good works: pilgrimages, church-building, and so on.[46]

There were several distinct Inquisitions. The medieval Inquisition that began in the thirteenth century was not the inspiration for the Inquisition of myth, the ecclesiastical reign of terror that allegedly murdered millions of innocent people for the crime of not accepting Christianity. That honor belongs to the Spanish Inquisition, which was established in 1478 by the Catholic monarchs Ferdinand and Isabella with authorization from Pope Sixtus IV. But by 1482, Sixtus had received numerous reports of abuses, leading to his appointment of the infamous Dominican priest Tomás de Torquemada as grand inquisitor in 1483. While the church executed no one, but handed them over to the civil power for punishment, at this point the ecclesiastical and civil power were working as one in a way that they never had before and never would again. The Jews and Muslims who had converted to Christianity for social rather than religious reasons, and who continued to practice their former religions in secret, were considered enemies of the Catholic state and were treated as such. Estimates of how many people Torquemada had put to death during his fifteen years as grand inquisitor range from 2,000 to 8,800.[47] Torquemada was also a key supporter of the decree of Ferdinand and Isabella expelling the Jews from Spain in 1492.

The Spanish Inquisition continued until the early nineteenth century, although it was greatly diminished in its latter years. Juan Antonio Llorente, an Inquisition official in the late eighteenth century and a historian of the Spanish Inquisition, estimated that in all slightly fewer than 32,000 people were executed.[48] However, more recently several historians have found that number immensely exaggerated and suggest that the actual number is closer to 3,200.[49] As this covers a period of several hundred years, even the high number hardly amounts to genocidal proportions or comes remotely close to the millions massacred by the rapacious inquisitors of myth.

Ultimately, the precise number is unimportant because it is jarring that the church of Jesus Christ acceded to the execution of even one person. It is jarring because it manifests a spirit so completely at variance with what Christ taught and how he behaved. Whatever the political justifications of the Inquisition, the involvement of the church demonstrated that its leaders had forgotten or were ignoring Jesus's parable of the wheat and tares, in which Christ speaks of the "kingdom of heaven" as containing weeds among the wheat, and directs that the weeds not be uprooted, "lest in gathering the weeds you root up the wheat along with them. Let both grow together until the harvest." The testimony of the earlier church fathers against capital punishment for heretics was more in line with this, as is the general understanding among Catholics, Protestants, and Eastern Orthodox Christians today.

The execution of heretics thus represents an aberration in the life of the church, at variance with the teachings of Christ and the early Christian thinkers. The contrast with Islamic apostasy law is sharp and unmistakable. While in the Islamic state as traditionally conceived, Jews and Christians have the right to practice their religions—with certain severe restrictions—the same relative generosity is not applied to Muslims who wish to leave Islam. Muhammad said, "Whoever changed his Islamic religion, then kill him,"[50] and that remains normative for Islam. A modern manual of Islamic law stipulates that "when a person who has reached puberty and is sane voluntarily apostasizes from Islam, he deserves to be killed."[51] This principle isn't easily susceptible to reform because it is founded on a statement of Muhammad that Muslims generally consider to be authentic.

The spirit of Torquemada is still alive in the world today, but not among Christians. Rather, it can be found only among the Muslims who demanded that Abdul Rahman be put on trial for his life in Afghanistan in 2006.

BUT WAIT A MINUTE: WHAT ABOUT TIMOTHY MCVEIGH?

Karen Armstrong, who has written a history of Islam and two biographies of Muhammad, said in 2004, "When the IRA was bombing Britain, we didn't call them 'Christian terrorists.'" Nor were the Orthodox Christian Serbs who fought Muslims in 1995 called "Christian terrorists." Said Armstrong, "We recognized them as people who had lost their moral bearings."[52]

The same point has been made again and again about Timothy McVeigh, the 1995 Oklahoma City bomber. Louis Farrakhan said in 2001, "Timothy McVeigh was from a Christian nation . . . and nobody said the Christian Timothy McVeigh, they said Timothy McVeigh." Boxer Mike Tyson said piously, "Religion can't be defined from one single person's action. Timothy McVeigh was a Christian." In this vein, Muslims have insisted that just because Mohamed Atta was a Muslim, all Muslims shouldn't be under suspicion. Abdulwahab Alkebsi of the Center for the Study of Islam and Democracy said after September 11, "Let's call bin Laden what he is: He is a terrorist. It has nothing to do with Islam—just as much as you don't want to call Timothy McVeigh a Christian terrorist or a Christian killer."[53]

However, there is one problem with this attitude: McVeigh wasn't a Christian at all, but was an agnostic at the time of the bombing. He told friends, "Science is my religion."[54]

Moreover, Armstrong and the others gloss over the fact that Osama bin Laden and other Islamic terrorists routinely invoke Islamic teachings to justify their actions, and explain them with copious Qur'an quotes and examples from the life of Muhammad. So the sobriquet "Islamic terrorism" is not simply an unfair conflation of two unrelated things, capitalizing on the coincidental and irrelevant fact that a certain group of terrorists has a Muslim background. In fact, these terrorists have explained again and again that Islam is their primary motivation. The IRA, by contrast, was fighting a political dispute, which was settled through political means. Numerous peace settlements, meanwhile, have been scuttled in Israel by the unwillingness of the jihadists to compromise on their religious goals, which involve the destruction of Israel for religious reasons.

Finally, there is the Lord's Resistance Army (LRA) in Uganda, a group that is probably better known outside Uganda than within it owing to its usefulness to the advocates of moral equivalence between Christianity and Islam. The LRA, we're told, wants to institute religious law in Uganda, making the Ten Commandments the law of the land. Is this just like the jihadists and their dreams of sharia? Well, no. Unlike the jihadists, who are operating according to the canons of defensive jihad as delineated by all the schools of Islamic jurisprudence, the LRA reflects the theological teaching of no Christian sect. It is backed by no clerics, and its teachings are not and cannot be founded upon the Bible. Even writer and professed atheist Christopher Hitchens, who has no love for Christianity, acknowledges that the LRA's leader, Joseph Kony, is "obviously far away from the Christian 'mainstream.'" In fact, "his paymasters and armorers are the cynical Muslims of the Sudanese regime, who use him to make trouble for the government of Uganda, which has in turn supported rebel groups in Sudan. In an apparent reward for this support, Kony at one stage began denouncing the keeping and feeding of pigs"—hardly orthodox Christian behavior.[55]

The fact is, there is simply no group anywhere in the world today that is committing violent acts and justifying them by quoting the Bible and invoking Christianity. But there are many, many groups committing violent acts and justifying them by quoting the Qur'an and invoking Islam.

CHAPTER SEVEN

CHRISTIAN ANTI-SEMITISM VS. ISLAMIC "APES AND PIGS"

The persistent myth of a tolerant, pluralistic Muslim Spain (which finally gave way to the fanatical Catholic regime of Ferdinand and Isabella) and a tolerant, pluralistic Ottoman Empire (which took in the Jews whom Ferdinand and Isabella expelled) both depend upon the Inquisition, as grand inquisitor Torquemada was instrumental in Spain's expulsion of the Jews. Yet at the same time, Christian anti-Semitism and anti-Semitism in general is much older than the Spanish Inquisition, and the Inquisition can perhaps only be fully understood with reference to it.

Christian anti-Semitism was long based on a cluster of New Testament passages that seemed to establish that the Jews as a people bore responsibility for the death of Jesus, and were consequently accursed. When the Roman procurator Pontius Pilate washed his hands before the crowd of Jews who were calling for the death of Jesus, he said, "I am innocent of this man's blood; see to it yourselves." The crowd responded, "His blood be on us and on our children!" (Matthew 27:24–25) St. Paul reminds the church in Thessalonica that "you suffered the same things from your own countrymen as they did from the Jews, who killed both the Lord Jesus and the prophets, and drove us out, and displease God and oppose all men by hindering us from speaking to the Gentiles that they may be saved—so as always to fill up the measure of their sins. But God's wrath has come upon them at last!" (I Thessalonians 2:14–16) And Jesus Himself replies to those who identify themselves as "children of Abraham" by saying, "You

are of your father the devil, and your will is to do your father's desires"
(John 8:44). He goes on to say that the devil is a murderer and a liar.

Yet historian Malcolm Hay points out that "although the popular tradition that 'the Jews' crucified Christ goes back to the beginnings of the
Christian Church, no justification can be found for it in the New Testament. St. Matthew, St. Mark, and St. Luke all took special care to impress
upon their readers the fact that the Jewish people, their own people, were
not responsible for, and were for the most part ignorant of, the events which
led up to the apprehension, the trial and the condemnation of Christ."[1]
Luke, of course, was a Gentile, but all the other New Testament writers
were indeed Jews. Hay notes that Matthew "states quite clearly in his
twenty-sixth chapter that 'the Jews' had nothing to do with the plot against
Christ. He explains who the conspirators were, and why they had to do
their work in secret. 'Then were gathered together the Chief Priests and the
Ancients of the people into the court of the High Priest who is called
Caiaphas. And they consulted together that by subtlety they might appre-
hend Jesus and put him to death.' Secrecy was essential to the plans of the
plotters because they 'feared the multitude' (Matthew 21:46). They were
afraid that 'the Jews' might find out what was brewing and start a riot."[2]

Hay also observes that those who were plotting to kill Jesus "were
engaged upon an enterprise which they knew would not meet with popular approval. They had no mandate from the Jewish people for what they
were about to do. They did not represent the two or three million Jews
who at that time lived in Palestine, or another million who lived in Egypt,
or the millions more who were scattered all over the Roman Empire. . . .
The conspirators did not even represent the wishes of the Jewish population in and around Jerusalem."[3]

What, then, of the three passages above, which seem to affirm that the
Jews killed Jesus, bear responsibility for shedding His blood, and are the
devil's children? St. Paul, a Jew himself, in speaking of those who
"killed . . . the Lord Jesus" was referring to the same small circle of leaders
who are seen plotting in Matthew's Gospel; Jesus is addressing the same
group. And as for the exclamation "His blood be upon us and on our children!" in light of such affirmations that "we are now justified by his blood"
(Romans 5:9) and that the saints have "washed their robes and made them

white in the blood of the Lamb" (Revelation 7:14), this is just as likely, if not more likely, to be an assertion of salvation rather than of guilt.

However, as the church grew and the Jewish presence within it diminished, these distinctions were lost. Where St. John and St. Paul speak of "the Jews" in referring to the chief priests and elders who plotted against Jesus, Christians became accustomed to understanding them as referring to all Jews. Jews became a focus of Christian polemic as those who had rejected their messiah and His salvation. Early Christian apologist St. Justin Martyr, in his *Dialogue with Trypho the Jew*, quotes a passage from the prophet Isaiah and remarks, "This same law [of God] you have despised, and His new holy covenant you have slighted; and now you neither receive it, nor repent of your evil deeds."[4]

The idea that the Jews had killed Jesus and despised God found one of its most vehement and unbridled expressions in a series of homilies preached by John Chrysostom, who was patriarch of Constantinople from 398 to 404. In 386 Chrysostom, then a priest in Antioch, was deeply concerned about Christians who went to synagogues and participated in services there, and devoted these sermons to trying to end this practice. Of course, the fact that Christian attendance in synagogues was widespread in late fourth-century Antioch indicates that neither anti-Semitism nor anti-Judaism were dominant among Christians at the time, many of whom obviously understood that there was a bond between Christianity and Judaism. (Islam, by contrast, has from the beginning mounted its challenge to the legitimacy of both faiths from the outside.)

This bond was just what Chrysostom was challenging. At one point he quotes Amos 5:21: "I hate, I despise your feasts, and I take no delight in your solemn assemblies." Then he asks: "Does God hate their festivals and do you share in them? He did not say this or that festival, but all of them together.... Is not the place also an abomination? Before they committed the crime of crimes, before they killed their Master, before the cross, before the slaying of Christ, it was an abomination. Is it not now all the more an abomination?"

Not content with accusing Jews of deicide, Chrysostom also dehumanizes them: "Christ was speaking to the Canaanite woman when He called the Jews children and the Gentiles dogs. But see how thereafter the order was changed about: they became dogs, and we became the children. . . . Another prophet hinted at this when he said: 'Israel is as obstinate as a stubborn heifer.' And still another called the Jews 'an untamed calf.' Although such beasts are unfit for work, they are fit for killing. And this is what happened to the Jews: while they were making themselves unfit for work, they grew fit for slaughter."

He applies Jesus's polemic against the Jewish leaders to all the Jews: "No Jew adores God! Who say so? The Son of God says so. For he said: 'If you were to know my Father, you would also know me. But you neither know me nor do you know my Father.' Could I produce a witness more trustworthy than the Son of God? If, then, the Jews fail to know the Father, if they crucified the Son, if they thrust off the help of the Spirit, who should not make bold to declare plainly that the synagogue is a dwelling of demons?"[5]

Chrysostom made his own sentiments abundantly clear: "I hate the synagogue and abhor it. . . . And so it is that we must hate both them and their synagogue. . . . I hate the Jews."[6]

Chrysostom's sermons were so thick with scriptural allusions, and so suffused with righteous indignation, that it is disconcerting that he seems to have neglected utterly the obligation to "love your neighbor as yourself" and even to "love your enemies." Yet the church has never considered its saints infallible, and Chrysostom's enduring place in it stems not from his attacks on Jews and Judaism, but from his liturgical, dogmatic, and spiritual writings, in which he often displays an awareness of God's mercy that he was unwilling to extend to the Jewish community of Antioch. In any case, the attitudes toward Jews that he expressed in these sermons became widespread among Christians in Europe, and not a few have seen in his polemic and in the words and deeds of other Christians of antiquity and the Middle Ages the seeds of the Nazi genocide.[7] Historian Daniel Jonah Goldenhagen minces no words: "The main responsibility for producing the all-time leading Western hatred [of Jews] lies with Christianity. More specifically, with the Catholic Church."[8]

However, Rabbi David G. Dalin, a historian of the Catholic Church's relations with the Jews, says this is "bad history and bad scholarship."[9] Malcolm Hay, who chronicles in searing detail the mistreatment Jews suffered in Europe at the hands of Christians, notes also that the most basic right, the right to live, was "one which no Pope, no Catholic theologian, has ever denied to the Jews—a right which no ruler in Christendom ever denied to them until the advent of Adolf Hitler."[10] Clearly, however, the Nazis sought justification for their actions from Christian anti-Semitism. Nazi propagandist Julius Streicher applied Jesus's words in John 8:44 to all Jews, calling for "the extermination of that people whose father is the devil," and the Nazis reprinted John Chrysostom's words in support of their activities.[11] There is nevertheless a large gulf between the anti-Judaism of Chrysostom and other Christian leaders, and that of the Nazis, who were for the most part anti-Christian and certainly anti-Catholic. Their anti-Semitism was rooted in Darwinian racial theories that posited the Aryans as the master race and the Jews as *untermenschen*.

Still, there is no doubt that the history of Jews in Christian Europe is largely marked by mistreatment, abuse, discrimination, and worse. A 1998 Vatican document on the Holocaust noted that "the history of relations between Jews and Christians is a tormented one. His Holiness Pope John Paul II has recognized this fact in his repeated appeals to Catholics to see where we stand with regard to our relations with the Jewish people. In effect, the balance of these relations over two thousand years has been quite negative."[12] Some of that negativity came from John Paul's medieval predecessors. Pope St. Zachary reaffirmed a prohibition on intermarriage.[13] Leo VII directed the archbishop of Mainz to expel Jews who refused to convert to Christianity from cities within his diocese.[14] St. Gregory VII forbade Jews to hold authority over Christians.[15]

The Fourth Lateran Council decreed in 1215 that Jews must wear distinctive garb—a directive initially emphasized, then suspended, then insisted upon again by Pope Honorius III.[16] Gregory IX led a campaign against Jewish books that led to a massive book-burning in Paris.[17] Nicholas III required Jews to assemble to hear proselytizing sermons and ordered that those who had been baptized but then returned to Judaism be "turned over to the secular power"—which meant almost certain execution.[18] Honorius IV wrote a letter to the English bishops warning them about Jewish efforts to convert Christians—which ultimately led to the expulsion of the Jews from England.[19] John XXII resumed the campaign against Jewish books, ordering the Talmud suppressed.[20] Centuries later, in 1858, police of the Papal States seized a six-year-old Jewish boy,

Edgardo Mortara, from his family because a Catholic servant girl who worked for the family had baptized him. Pope Pius IX refused numerous entreaties to return the boy to his family. Mortara became a Catholic priest and died in 1940.[21] Many consider the incident one of the chief obstacles to the canonization of Pius IX.

But as Dalin illustrates, the papal record is not monochromatic: "The historical fact is that popes have often spoken out in defense of the Jews, have protected them during times of persecution and pogroms, and have protected their right to worship freely in their synagogues. Popes have traditionally defended Jews from wild anti-Semitic allegations. Popes regularly condemned anti-Semites who sought to incite violence against Jews."[22]

This is not, as some might think, a strictly modern phenomenon. For instance, Pope St. Gregory I, who wrote harshly, in Chrysostom's vein, of the Jews' rejection of Christ, nevertheless issued an edict dictating that Jews "should have no infringement of their rights.... We forbid to vilify the Jews. We allow them to live as Romans and to have full authority over their possessions."[23] When a bishop in Palermo seized a synagogue and converted it into a church, the building could not be returned to its former owners because it had now been consecrated; however, Gregory ordered the bishop to pay the owners a fair price, so that the Jews "should in no way appear to be oppressed, or to suffer an injustice."[24] He also forbade forced conversion of Jews, a prohibition later repeated by Gregory IV.[25]

Pope St. Gregory I's directives formed the basis of the Jews' status in Western Europe for a considerable time thereafter. Pope Alexander II commended bishops in Narbonne and Spain for protecting Jews from attacks by Christians.[26] When would-be Crusaders massacred Jews in Speyer, Worms, Mainz, Cologne, and elsewhere before the First Crusade, it is noteworthy that local bishops often acted to end these slaughters.[27] Pope Calixtus II thereafter reaffirmed Gregory's prohibition of attacks on Jews, and also forbade forced conversion and attacks on synagogues.[28] Still, however, such attacks continued during the Second Crusade. St. Bernard of Clairvaux declared that "whoever touches a Jew so as to lay hands on his life, does something as sinful as if he laid hands on the Lord himself!"[29] Yet in 1147, Crusaders attacked the Jews of Wurzburg not long after St. Bernard had left the area.[30]

Such attacks were fueled by Christian polemics, such as that of French diplomat and theologian Peter of Blois, whose *Against the Perfidious Jews* depicted the Jews as thoroughly debased and dehumanized.[31] Even St. Bernard and other Christian notables preached sermons in which the Jews were depicted as savage, subhuman beasts.[32] Bishop of Lincoln Robert Grosseteste was no innovator when he wrote: "As murderers of the Lord, as still blaspheming Christ, and mocking his passion, [Jews] were to be in captivity to the princes of the earth." Yet he added a backhanded affirmation of the unlawfulness of killing them: "As they have the brand of Cain, and are condemned to wander over the face of the earth, so were they to have the privilege of Cain, that no one was to kill them."[33]

The popes also held fast against forced conversions and attacks on the Jews. Pope Innocent III, although he condemned Jews as "the sons of the crucifiers, against whom to this day the blood cries to the Father's ears," stated:

> For we make the law that no Christian compel them, unwilling or refusing, by violence to come to baptism.
>
> Too, no Christian ought to presume . . . wickedly to injure their persons, or with violence to take away their property, or to change the good customs which they have had until now in whatever region they inhabit.
>
> Besides, in the celebration of their own festivals, no one ought to disturb them in any way, with clubs or stones, nor ought any one try to require from them or to extort from them services they do not owe, except for those they have been accustomed from times past to perform.
>
> In addition to these, We decree . . . that no one ought to dare to mutilate or diminish a Jewish cemetery, nor, in order to get money, to exhume bodies once they have been buried.[34]

Those who dared transgress these prohibitions were threatened with excommunication. Innocent also noted that Calixtus and four other popes had extended the same protections to the Jews. According to Dalin, "Calixtus's defense of the Jews, with its promise of continuing papal protection, was reissued at least twenty-two times by successive popes between the twelfth and fifteenth centuries."[35]

Of course, this reissuing wouldn't have been necessary if Jews were not continually being attacked in Europe. Many of these attacks centered around the "blood libel," the contention that Jews killed Christian children and mixed their blood into their Passover matzoh. Pope Innocent IV issued a strong denial of the blood libel, as did Gregory X, Martin V, and Sixtus IV. Paul III denounced those who "pretend, in order to despoil them of their goods, that the Jews kill little children and drink their blood."[36] That this had to be repeated over several centuries testifies to the persistence of the libel in Christian Europe, but nevertheless, excommunication was consistently the penalty for those who spread such stories or victimized Jews on such a basis. And while many popes affirmed that the Jews must be protected, the crowned kings of Catholic Europe often took just the opposite view. A twelfth-century chronicler says of King Phillip of France: "He hated the Jews, and had heard many accusations against them, of blaspheming the name of Jesus Christ."[37]

Gregory X also affirmed the validity of Jewish testimony, declaring, "An accusation against Jews based solely on the testimony of Christians was invalid; Jewish witnesses must also appear." Clement VI defended Jews from charges that they were responsible for the Black Death; Boniface IX granted full Roman citizenship to Jews; Martin V directed that "every Christian treat the Jews with a humane kindness" and forbade preachers "to preach against the Jews, to attempt to interrupt their normal relations with their neighbors, to infringe upon their religious rights, or to exclude them from normal activities (including attendance at universities)." He also reaffirmed the repudiation of the blood libel.

Leo X ordered the entire Talmud to be printed by a Christian printer in Rome so as to discourage anti-Semitic rumors about its contents.[38] Clement VII commissioned a new translation of the Old Testament from Hebrew into Latin, to be completed by six Christians and six Jews working together.[39]

The catechism of the Council of Trent, which was first published in 1566, denies that the Jews bear responsibility for the crucifixion of Christ:

> Christ not only suffered for sinners, but even for those who were the very authors and ministers of all the torments He endured.... In this

guilt are involved all those who fall frequently into sin; for, as our sins consigned Christ the Lord to the death of the cross.... This guilt seems more enormous in us than in the Jews, since according to the testimony of the same apostle: *If they had known it, they would never have crucified the Lord of glory*; while we, on the contrary, professing to know Him, yet denying Him by our actions, seem in some sort to lay violent hands on Him.... Furthermore men of all ranks and conditions were gathered together against the Lord, and against His Christ. Gentiles and Jews were the advisers, the authors, the ministers of His Passion: Judas betrayed Him, Peter denied Him, all the rest deserted Him.[40]

Innocent X and Benedict XIV both worked to end the blood libel and the persecution of Jews in Poland.[41] Leo XIII spoke out in defense of Alfred Dreyfus, a French military officer wrongly accused of treason in a notorious case.[42] St. Pius X and Benedict XV acted against anti-Semitism in Italian politics and media.[43]

It was thus not without justification that Pius XI was able to write in 1928: "Moved by this Christian charity, the Holy See has always protected this people [the Jews] against unjust vexations, and just as it reprobates all rancour and conflicts between peoples, it particularly condemns unreservedly hatred against the people once chosen by God: the hatred that commonly goes by the name of anti-Semitism."[44] Pius XI used his encyclical letter *Mit Brennender Sorge*—pointedly written in German instead of Latin, and directed to the German bishops—to condemn the anti-Semitism of the Nazi regime. The Nazis, in response, forbade its publication in Germany and denounced Pius XI as half-Jewish.[45] That encyclical, drafted by Cardinal Eugenio Pacelli, who two years later became Pope Pius XII, declared:

Whoever exalts race, or the people, or the State, or a particular form of State, or the depositories of power, or any other fundamental value of the human community—however necessary and honorable be their function in worldly things—whoever raises these notions above their standard value and divinizes them to an idolatrous level, distorts and perverts an order of the world planned and created by God; he is far from the true faith in God and from the concept of life which that faith upholds.[46]

When Vienna's Cardinal Innitzer rang the city's church bells to celebrate Hitler's entry into the city after the Anchluss in 1938, Pius called Innitzer to Rome and rebuked him—and, according to historian Michael Phayer, had the rebuke "communicated through diplomatic channels to the United States so that world governments would know where the Vatican stood regarding Hitler's Germany."[47] On September 6, 1938, he told a group of pilgrims from Belgium that "anti-Semitism is inadmissible; spiritually, we are all Semites."[48]

Then in 1965, the Second Vatican Council definitively rejected the idea that the Jews were responsible for the death of Christ, and all anti-Semitism:

> True, the Jewish authorities and those who followed their lead pressed for the death of Christ; still, what happened in His passion cannot be charged against all the Jews, without distinction, then alive, nor against the Jews of today. Although the Church is the new people of God, the Jews should not be presented as rejected or accursed by God, as if this followed from the Holy Scriptures.
>
> Furthermore, in her rejection of every persecution against any man, the Church, mindful of the patrimony she shares with the Jews and moved not by political reasons but by the Gospel's spiritual love, decries hatred, persecutions, displays of anti-Semitism, directed against Jews at any time and by anyone.[49]

Pope John Paul II likewise said in 2000: "We hope that the Jewish people will acknowledge that the Church utterly condemns anti-Semitism and every form of racism as being altogether opposed to the principles of Christianity. We must work together to build a future in which there will be no more anti-Judaism among Christians or anti-Christian sentiment among Jews."[50] When he became pope in 2005 Benedict XVI extended greetings to his "brothers and sisters of the Jewish people, to whom we are joined by a great spiritual heritage, rooted in God's irrevocable promises."[51]

Noting that anti-Semitic attitudes still linger today among Orthodox Christians, in April 2007 a group of twelve priests led by Fr. Innokenty Pavlov of the Biblical Theological Institute in Moscow called for liturgical reform and renunciation of the idea that Christians have replaced Jews as God's chosen people—in defiance of St. Paul's statement that "the gifts and the call of God are irrevocable" (Romans 11:29). While some of the foremost Orthodox thinkers of the nineteenth and twentieth centuries, notably Vladimir Soloviev and Sergiy Bulgakov, loved and respected Jews, anti-Semitism still exists among Orthodox Christians. Said Pavlov, "We came to the firm belief that it is high time for the Orthodox Church to correct its attitude toward Jews and Judaism."[52]

While Christian anti-Semitism has been minimized, it still exists, particularly in the Middle East where some Christians have absorbed the anti-Semitism of the Islamic culture that surrounds them. But the record of history, the official teaching of the Catholic Church (as seen in the Second Vatican Council and other documents and papal statements), and the actions of Christians around the world today all illustrate that anti-Semitism is not intrinsic to Christianity.

BUT WHAT ABOUT HITLER AND HIS POPE?

Adolf Hitler was baptized a Catholic, but repudiated his Catholic faith early in life. His desire to annihilate the Jews was motivated not by Christian principles, but by the race-based social Darwinism undergirding the National Socialist regime.

Hitler publicly worked to co-opt the Christian churches, but privately despised Christianity, saying that Catholicism was "humbug."[53] He saw himself as a rationalist and believed that "Christianity is an invention of sick brains: one could imagine nothing more senseless, nor any more indecent way of turning the idea of the Godhead into a mockery."[54] He thought that Christianity's influence on the world had been largely negative: "Christianity is the worst of the regressions that mankind can ever have undergone.... One cannot succeed in conceiving how much cruelty, ignominy and falsehood the intrusion of Christianity has spelt for this world of ours."[55] He sneeringly likened it to Communism: "The heaviest blow that ever struck humanity was the coming of Christianity. Bolshevism is Christianity's illegitimate child. Both are inventions of the Jew. The deliberate lie in the matter of religion was introduced into the world by Christianity.... Pure Christianity—the Christianity of the catacombs—is concerned with translating the Christian doctrine into facts. It leads quite simply to the annihilation of mankind. It is merely whole-hearted Bolshevism, under a tinsel of metaphysics."[56]

Hitler also complained on many occasions about the harm Christianity had brought to the German people: "The catastrophe, for us, is that of being tied to a religion that rebels against all the joys of the senses."[57] The harm came not just from asceticism, but from the Christian spirit of charity and forgiveness, which he contrasted unfavorably with Japanese Shintoism and Islam: "You see, it's been our misfortune to have the wrong religion. Why didn't we have the religion of the Japanese, who regard sacrifice for the Fatherland as the highest good? The Mohammedan religion too would have been much more compatible to us than Christianity. Why did it have to be Christianity with its meekness and flabbiness?"[58] He expressed regret that Islamic jihadists had not won the Battle of Tours in 732, and spread Islam over Europe: the Arabs, he speculated, would not have been able to stand Europe's climate, and the Germans would have become the leaders of a great Islamic empire. "Had Charles Martel not been victorious at Poitiers— already, you see, the world had fallen into the hands of the Jews, so gutless a thing was Christianity!—then we should in all probability have been converted to Mohammedanism, that cult which glorifies heroism and which opens the seventh heaven to the bold warrior alone. Then the Germanic races would have conquered the world. Christianity alone prevented them from doing so."[59] For "Christianity is a rebellion against natural law, a protest against nature. Taken to its logical extreme, Christianity would mean the systematic cultivation of the human failure."[60]

Ultimately, Hitler planned to eradicate Christianity: "When National Socialism has ruled long enough, it will no longer be possible to conceive of a form of life different from ours. In the long run, National Socialism and religion will no longer be able to exist together."[61] And indeed, "our epoch will certainly see the end of the disease of Christianity."[62] When he took power, he made life difficult for churchmen who opposed him, arresting hundreds of priests and other Christian leaders. Adolf Wagner, the Nazi minister of state, said in 1935, "In the days that lie immediately ahead of us the fight will not be either against Communists or Marxists, but against Catholicism. Everyone will find himself faced with the serious question: German or Catholic? This struggle will not be easy."[63] Hitler strove to empty Christianity of its content, replacing it with his own Nietzschean perspective: a Nazi Christmas card issued in 1944 bore this quotation from Hitler: "All nature is a gigantic struggle between strength and weakness, an eternal victory of the strong over the weak."[64] Not quite in the spirit of the season.

But as Hitler privately looked forward to the end of Christianity, did he not have Pope Pius XII as his willing dupe?

Christopher Hitchens, in his amusingly written atheist tract *God Is Not Great*, attacks the notion of divine providence by writing of Catholics:

> Believers are supposed to hold that the pope is the vicar of Christ on earth, and the keeper of the keys of Saint Peter. They are of course free to believe this, and to believe that god decides when to end the tenure of one pope or (more important) to inaugurate the tenure of another. This would involve believing in the death of an anti-Nazi pope, and the accession of a pro-Nazi one, as a matter of divine will, a few months before Hitler's invasion of Poland and the opening of the Second World War.[65]

Hitchens's assumption that Pope Pius XII was "pro-Nazi" has of course become embedded in popular consciousness ever since the first publication of Rolf Hochhuth's play *The Deputy* in 1963, which first alleged that Pius was sympathetic to the Nazis. The notion was given a scholarly patina by John Cornwell's *Hitler's Pope* in 1999. Yet *Newsweek*'s Kenneth Woodward noted about Cornwell's book, "errors of fact and ignorance of context appear on almost every page.... This is bogus scholarship."[66] Several historians, including David Dalin, Ronald Rychlak, and the Jesuit Pierre Blet, have marshaled an impressive array of evidence to establish that Pius was anything but a supporter of Hitler. Pius XII, says Dalin, "was not 'Hitler's pope' but a protector and friend of the Jewish people at a moment in history when it mattered most."[67]

But wasn't Pius silent in the face of Nazi atrocities against the Jews? When Pius died in 1958, Golda Meir, who was at that time the Israeli foreign minister, said, "The life of our times was enriched by a voice speaking out about great moral truths above the tumult of daily conflict. We mourn a great servant of peace."[68] The *Jerusalem Post* declared: "Jews will recall the sympathetic references to their sufferings contained in many of his pronouncements, the refuge from Nazi terror which he gave to many in the Vatican during the last war, and the very cordial way he received his Jewish visitors." The *Jewish Post* of Winnipeg asserted in November 1958 that no one did more "to help the Jews in their hour of greatest tragedy, during the Nazi occupation of Europe, than the late pope."[69]

Did these people and others only imagine that Pius spoke out against Hitler, when in fact he really sympathized with the Nazi dictator? On Christmas day 1942 the *New York Times* called the pope "a lonely voice crying out of the silence of a continent."[70] But was he crying out about the plight of the Jews? In January 1940, Boston's *Jewish Advocate* stated: "The Vatican radio this week broadcast an outspoken denunciation of German atrocities and persecution in Nazi [occupied] Poland, declaring they affronted the moral conscience of mankind." The broadcast gave details of atrocities committed not just against Catholics, but against Jews also.

In June 1942, Hitler congratulated himself for the failure of his earlier attempt to create a Lutheran "bishop of the Reich." He asked, "Who, indeed, is prepared to give me a guarantee that one fine day the Protestant bishop of the Reich will not make common cause against me with the pope!"[71] A strange remark for someone to make if he had the pope in his pocket. The *Times* reported in August 1942 that Pius was working to save the Jews in Vichy France.[72] In response to those efforts, the *California Jewish Voice* called the pope the Jews' "spiritual ally." In April 1943, Cardinal Pierre Gerlier of Lyons, France, stated that Pius XII had ordered him to oppose anti-Semitic actions by the Vichy government. The Vatican protested to the German government against the persecution of Italian Jews in late 1943.[73] In 1944, Nazis occupying Rome began to search churches for hidden Jews, and bombed Castel Gandolfo, the pope's summer residence, when Pius protested.[74]

Moved by the pope's acts on behalf of the Jewish people, many of which he witnessed personally, the chief rabbi of Rome, Israel Zolli, converted to Catholicism after the war and adopted the name Eugenio to honor Pius XII, whose given name was Eugenio Pacelli.[75] Late in 1945, the World Jewish Congress gave a financial gift to the Vatican in recognition of its efforts to rescue Jews from the Nazis.[76] The Jewish historian Sir Martin Gilbert, author of several books on the Holocaust, has stated that "hundreds of thousands of Jews [were] saved by the Catholic Church, under the leadership and with the support of Pope Pius XII."[77] Another Jewish historian, Pinchas Lapide, estimates that as many as 800,000 Jews were saved through Pius XII's efforts.[78] It is a pity that these real achievements have been obscured by a mountain of propaganda.

It is also worth nothing that while Hitler may not have had a pope, he did have a mufti: Haj Amin al-Husseini, the mufti of Jerusalem, met with Hitler and made plans to work with the Germans to exterminate the Jews in the Holy Land. He also worked during World War II to form Waffen SS units among Muslims in the Balkans.[79]

CHRISTIAN ANTI-SEMITISM, MUSLIM ANTI-SEMITISM

Anti-Semitism in the Islamic world has often been attributed to the baneful influence of Christianity. Many analysts assert that the Islamic designation of Jews (as well as Christians) as "People of the Book" indicates a higher level of respect for them than was manifested by Christians who derided Jews as bestial "Christ-killers." Journalist Lawrence Wright asserts in this vein in *The Looming Tower: Al-Qaeda and the Road to 9/11*:

Until the end of World War II...Jews lived safely—although submissively—under Muslim rule for 1,200 years, enjoying full religious freedom; but in the 1930s, Nazi propaganda on Arabic-language shortwave radio, coupled with slanders by Christian missionaries in the region, infected the area with this ancient Western prejudice [anti-Semitism]. After the war, Cairo became a sanctuary for Nazis, who advised the military and the government. The rise of the Islamist movement coincided with the decline of fascism, but they overlapped in Egypt, and the germ passed into a new carrier.[80]

This is a common view, but in reality there is a strong native strain of anti-Semitism in Islam, which is rooted in the Qur'an. The Muslim holy book contains a great deal of material that forms the foundation for a hatred of Jews that exists independently of the Christian variety. It is also, in many ways, more virulent and harder to eradicate. The Qur'an portrays the Jews as the craftiest, most persistent, and most implacable enemies of the Muslims—and there is no Muslim equivalent of the Second Vatican Council to mitigate against destructive interpretations. The Qur'anic material on the Jews remains the prism through which far too many Muslims see the Israeli-Palestinian conflict—and Jews in general—to this day.

A vivid illustration of this came in 2004 from Islam Online, a website founded by, among others, the internationally influential Sheikh Yusuf al-Qaradawi in 1997. Although al-Qaradawi has won praise from Islamic scholar John Esposito for engaging in a "reformist interpretation of Islam and its relationship to democracy, pluralism, and human rights," that "reformist" impulse doesn't seem to carry over to his view of Jews (he has justified suicide bombings against Israeli civilians), or the view of them he has allowed to be published on Islam Online.[81] In 2004 the site posted an article titled "Jews as Depicted in the Qur'an," in which Sheikh 'Atiyyah Saqr, the former head of the Fatwa Committee at the most respected institution in Sunni Islam, Al-Azhar University in Cairo, depicts Jews in a chillingly negative light, illustrated with abundant quotations from the Qur'an. Among other charges he levels at the Jews, Saqr says that they "used to fabricate things and falsely ascribe them to Allah"; they "love to listen to lies"; they disobey Allah and ignore his commands; they wish "evil for people" and try to "mislead them"; and they "feel pain to see others in happiness and are gleeful when others are afflicted with a calamity." He adds that "it is easy for them to slay people and kill innocents," for "they are merciless and heartless." And each charge he follows with Qur'anic citations.[82]

Though he offers many examples of the alleged evil traits of the Jews supported by the Qur'an, Saqr doesn't mention the notorious Qur'anic passages that depict an angry Allah transforming Jews into apes and pigs: 2:63–66, 5:59–60, and 7:166. The first of those passages depicts Allah telling the Jews who "profaned the Sabbath": "Be as apes despicable!" It goes on to say that these accursed ones serve "as a warning example for their time and for all times to come." The second has Allah directing Muhammad to remind the "People of the Book" about "those who incurred the curse of Allah and His wrath, those of whom some He transformed into apes and swine, those who worshipped evil." The third essentially repeats this, saying of the Sabbath-breaking Jews that when "in their insolence they transgressed (all) prohibitions," Allah said to them, "Be ye apes, despised and rejected."

In traditional Islamic theology these passages have not been considered to apply to all Jews. The classic Qur'anic commentator Isma'il bin 'Amr bin Kathir al Dimashqi (Ibn Kathir), whose commentary is widely distributed and respected among Muslims today, quotes earlier authorities saying that "those who violated the sanctity of the Sabbath were turned into monkeys, then they perished without offspring," and that they "only lived on the earth for three days, for no transformed person ever lives more than three days."[83] While parts of the Qur'an are hostile to the Jews, Muhammad's curse, in this case, was limited to these Sabbath-breakers, not to all Jews.

However, that hasn't stopped contemporary jihadists from frequently referring to Jews as the "descendants of apes and swine." The implication is that today's Jews are bestial in character and are the enemies of Allah, just as the Sabbath-breakers were. The grand sheikh of Al-Azhar, Muhammad Sayyid Tantawi, the most respected cleric in the world among Sunni Muslims today, has called Jews "the enemies of Allah, descendants of apes and pigs." Saudi sheikh Abd al-Rahman al-Sudayyis, imam of the principal mosque in the holiest city in Islam, Mecca, said in a sermon that Jews are "the scum of the human race, the rats of the world, the violators of pacts and agreements, the murderers of the prophets, and the offspring of apes and pigs."

Another Saudi sheikh, Ba'd bin Abdallah al-Ajameh al-Ghamidi, made the connection explicit: "The current behavior of the brothers of apes and pigs, their treachery, violation of agreements, and defiling of holy places . . . is connected with the deeds of their forefathers during the early period of Islam—which proves the great similarity between all the Jews living today and the Jews who lived at the dawn of Islam." A 1996 Hamas publication says that today's Jews are bestial in spirit, and this is a manifestation of the punishment of their forefathers.[84] In January 2007, Palestinian Authority president Mahmoud Abbas stated, "The sons of Israel are mentioned as those who are corrupting humanity on earth," referring to Qur'an 5:64.[85]

All this shows that leading Muslim authorities approach the Qur'an not as a document rooted in history, but as a blueprint for understanding the world today. Likewise, Sheikh 'Atiyyah Saqr describes the Qur'anic teachings that because Jews "revolted against the Divine ordinances . . . they found no warm reception in all countries where they tried to reside. Rather, they would either be driven out or live in isolation." Moreover, "Almighty Allah told us that He'd send to them people who'd pour on them rain of severe punishment that would last till the Day of Resurrection." Then comes a threat: "All this gives us glad tidings of the coming victory of Muslims over them once Muslims stick to strong faith and belief in Allah and adopt the modern means of technology."[86] The "rain of severe punishment" resulting from adoption of the "modern means of technology" may come to fruition in Iranian president Mahmoud Ahmadinejad's nuclear ambitions and implacable hostility to Israel. In January 2007 he warned that the "demise" of the "Zionist regime" is "imminent."[87] Does he plan to bring about that demise with a nuclear "rain of severe punishment"?

In the 1970s Sheikh Tantawi wrote a 700-page treatise, *Jews in the Qur'an and the Traditions*, in which he concluded:

[The] Qur'an describes the Jews with their own particular degenerate characteristics, i.e., killing the prophets of Allah, corrupting His words by putting them in the wrong places, consuming the people's wealth frivolously, refusal to distance themselves from the evil they do, and other ugly characteristics caused by their deep-rooted lasciviousness . . .

only a minority of the Jews keep their word. . . . [A]ll Jews are not the same. The good ones become Muslims, the bad ones do not.[88]

Nor is this just a modern view. The classic Qur'anic commentators do not mitigate the Qur'an's words against Jews, but only add fuel to the fire. Ibn Kathir explained Qur'an 2:61 ("They were covered with humiliation and misery; they drew on themselves the wrath of Allah") this way: "This Ayah [verse] indicates that the Children of Israel were plagued with humiliation, and that this will continue, meaning that it will never cease. They will continue to suffer humiliation at the hands of all who interact with them, along with the disgrace that they feel inwardly."[89] Another Middle Ages commentator of lingering influence, 'Abdallah ibn 'Umar al-Baidawi, explains the same verse this way: "The Jews are mostly humiliated and wretched either of their own accord, or out of coercion of the fear of having their *jizya* [punitive tax] doubled."[90]

Ibn Kathir notes Islamic traditions that predict that at the end of the world, "the Jews will support the Dajjal (False Messiah), and the Muslims, along with 'Isa [Jesus], son of Mary, will kill the Jews."[91] The idea in Islam that the end times will be marked by Muslims killing Jews comes from the prophet Muhammad himself, who said, "The Hour will not be established until you fight with the Jews, and the stone behind which a Jew will be hiding will say, 'O Muslim! There is a Jew hiding behind me, so kill him.'"[92] This is, not unexpectedly, a favorite motif among contemporary jihadists. On March 30, 2007, a spokesman for Hamas, Dr. Ismail Radwan, said on Palestinian Authority television:

> The Hour [Resurrection] will not take place until the Muslims fight the Jews and the Muslims kill them, and the rock and the tree will say: "Oh, Muslim, servant of Allah, there is a Jew behind me, kill him!"
>
> We must remind our Arab and Muslim nation, its leaders and people, its scholars and students, remind them that Palestine and the Al Aqsa mosque will not be liberated through summits nor by international resolutions, but it will be liberated through the rifle. It will not be liberated through negotiations, but through the rifle, since this occupation knows no language but the language of force. . . . O Allah,

strengthen Islam and Muslims, and bring victory to your Jihad-fighting worshipers, in Palestine and everywhere.... Allah take the oppressor Jews and Americans and their supporters![93]

HOW ISLAMIC ANTI-SEMITISM
PLAYED OUT IN HISTORY

The history of Jews who lived under Muslim rule is a more or less unbroken record of theologically sanctioned humiliation and wretchedness. Although, like the Christians, Jews were allowed to practice their religion within restrictions, they were seldom allowed to forget their humiliation. Although the strictness with which the laws of dhimmitude (the subservient status of Jews and Christians) were enforced varied, they were never abolished, and during times of relaxation the subject populations always lived in fear that they would be enforced with new stringency. Muslim rulers did not forget that the Qur'an mandates that both Jews and Christians must "feel themselves subdued." One notable instance is recounted by Arab historian Philip Hitti: "The caliph al-Mutawakkil in 850 and 854 decreed that Christians and Jews should affix wooden images of devils to their houses, level their graves even with the ground, wear outer garments of honey color, i.e., yellow, put two honey-colored patches on the clothes of their slaves, ... and ride only on mules and asses with wooden saddles marked by two pomegranate-like balls on the cantle."[94] A millennium later, in 1888, little had changed. A Tunisian Jew noted:

> The Jew is prohibited in this country to wear the same clothes as a Muslim and may not wear a red tarbush. He can be seen to bow down with his whole body to a Muslim child and permit him the traditional privilege of striking him in the face, a gesture that can prove to be of the gravest consequence. Indeed, the present writer has received such blows. In such matters the offenders act with complete impunity, for this has been the custom from time immemorial.[95]

In 1291 Isaac ben Samuel, a noted Kabbalist and Palestinian Jew, sought refuge in a Christian-controlled area of Spain after the collapse of the last Crusader kingdom in the Levant. He explained, "For, in the eyes of the

Muslims, the children of Israel are as open to abuse as an unprotected field. Even in their law and statutes they rule that the testimony of a Muslim is always to be believed against that of a Jew. For this reason our rabbis of blessed memory have said, 'Rather beneath the yoke of Edom [Christendom] than that of Ishmael [Islam]. They [the rabbis] plead for mercy before the Holy One, Blessed be He, saying, 'Master of the World, either let us live beneath Thy shadow or else beneath that of the children of Edom' (Talmud, Gittin 17a)."[96]

Ben Samuel's choice of Christian Spain is paradoxical, as Muslim Spain was supposed to have been a famous exception to the oppression of Jews that prevailed elsewhere among both Muslims and Christians. Islamic apologist Karen Armstrong enunciates the common wisdom when she says that "until 1492, Jews and Christians lived peaceably and productively together in Muslim Spain—a coexistence that was impossible elsewhere in Europe."[97] Even the U.S. State Department has proclaimed that "during the Islamic period in Spain, Jews, Christians, and Muslims lived together in peace and mutual respect, creating a diverse society in which vibrant exchanges of ideas took place."[98]

Yet the philosopher Maimonides, a Jew who lived for a time in Muslim Spain and then fled that supposedly tolerant and pluralistic land, remarked, "You know, my brethren, that on account of our sins God has cast us into the midst of this people, the nation of Ishmael, who persecute us severely, and who devise ways to harm us and to debase us.... No nation has ever done more harm to Israel. None has matched it in debasing and humiliating us. None has been able to reduce us as they have.... We have borne their imposed degradation, their lies, and absurdities, which are beyond human power to bear."

Notably, Maimonides directed that Jews could teach rabbinic law to Christians, but not to Muslims. For Muslims, he said, will interpret what they are taught "according to their erroneous principles and they will oppress us. [F]or this reason...they hate all [non-Muslims] who live among them." But the Christians, he said, "admit that the text of the Torah, such as we have it, is intact"—as opposed to the Islamic view that the Jews and Christians have corrupted their scriptures. Christians, continued Maimonides, "do not find in their religious law any contradiction with ours."[99]

Even María Rosa Menocal, in her romantic and fantastic hagiography of Muslim Spain, *The Ornament of the World*, acknowledges the second-class status to which Jews and Christians were relegated there. "In return for this freedom of religious conscience the Peoples of the Book (pagans had no such privilege) were required to pay a special tax—no Muslims paid taxes—and to observe a number of restrictive regulations: Christians and Jews were prohibited from attempting to proselytize Muslims, from building new places of worship, from displaying crosses or ringing bells. In sum, they were forbidden most public displays of their religious rituals."[100]

According to historian Richard Fletcher, "Moorish Spain was not a tolerant and enlightened society even in its most cultivated epoch."[101] On December 30, 1066, about four thousand Jews in Granada were murdered by rioting Muslim mobs—more than would be killed in the Crusaders' infamous Rhineland pogroms of the mid-twelfth century.[102] What enraged the Granadan Muslims was the political power of the Jewish vizier Samuel ibn Naghrila and his son Joseph: the mob resented the fact that these men had authority over Muslims, which they saw as a "breach of sharia."[103] The mob was incited to kill the Jews by a poem composed by Muslim jurist Abu Ishaq: "I myself arrived in Granada and saw that these Jews were meddling in its affairs.... So hasten to slaughter them as a good work whereby you will earn God's favor, and offer them up in sacrifice, a well-fattened ram."[104] The mob heeded his call. A Muslim chronicler (and later sultan of Granada), 'Abd Allah, said that "both the common people and the nobles were disgusted by the cunning of the Jews, the notorious changes they had brought in the order of things, and the positions they occupied in violation of their pact [of second-class status]." He recounted that the mob "put every Jew in the city to the sword and took vast quantities of their property."[105]

In *The Legacy of Islamic Antisemitism* Andrew Bostom amasses an enormous amount of documentary evidence establishing the degradations the Jews suffered at the hands of Muslims throughout Islamic history. Bostom notes that jihadist designation of Jews as "apes and pigs," in accord with the Qur'an, has ample historical precedent. Muhammad himself used it before ordering that every adult male of the Banu Qurayza, a Jewish tribe, be killed, calling the Jews "you brothers of monkeys."[106] The poem that inspired the Muslims to massacre the Jews in Granada in 1066 included the line, "Many a pious Muslim is in awe of the vilest infidel ape" (referring to the Jewish vizier). Zaynu'd-Din 'Ali b. Said praised the anti-Jewish riots and massacres in Baghdad in 1291 (which spread widely in the region), saying, "These apish Jews are done away and shent [ruined]." Bostom mentions another slaughter:

> Referring to the Jews as "brothers of apes," who repeatedly blas-phemed the prophet Muhammad, and whose overall conduct reflected their hatred of Muslims, the Moroccan cleric al-Maghili (d. 1505) fomented, and then personally led, a Muslim pogrom (in ~1490) against the Jews of the southern Moroccan oasis of Touat, plundering and killing Jews en masse, and destroying their synagogue in neigh-boring Tamantit. Al-Maghili's virulent Islamic antisemitism was per-haps captured best in a line from a verse diatribe he composed: "Love of the Prophet requires hatred of the Jews."[107]

Nevertheless, historian Bernard Lewis asserts that overall, Jews had it bet-ter in the Islamic world than they did in Catholic Europe. "There is noth-ing in Islamic history," he says, "to compare with the Spanish expulsion of Jews and Muslims, the Inquisition, the *autos-da-fé*, the wars of religion, not to speak of more recent crimes of commission and acquiescence. There were occasional persecutions, but they were rare, and usually of brief duration, related to local and specific circumstances."[108] Dinesh D'Souza has made much of this in his recent attempts to portray Islam and Christianity as equally likely to give rise to violent impulses.[109]

However, such judgments betray less about the historical data than they do about Westerners judging Christians more severely than Muslims. This is a venerable tradition, going back, as the Islamic scholar Ibn War-raq points out, to Voltaire and Edward Gibbon:

> Gibbon, like Voltaire, painted Islam in as favorable a light as possible to better contrast it with Christianity. The English historian empha-sized Muhammad's humanity as a means of indirectly criticizing the Christian doctrine of the divinity of Christ. Gibbon's anticlericalism

led him to underline Islam's supposed freedom from that accursed class, the priesthood. Indeed, the familiar pattern is reemerging— Islam is being used as a weapon against Christianity. Gibbon's deistic view of Islam as a rational, priest-free religion, with Muhammad as a wise and tolerant lawgiver, enormously influenced the way all Europeans perceived their sister religion for years to come. Indeed, it established myths that are still accepted totally uncritically by scholars and laymen alike. Both Voltaire and Gibbon subscribed to the myth of Muslim tolerance, which to them meant Turkish tolerance.[110]

Yet a question that is much more important than the respective awarding of historical points or demerits is whether Christian or Islamic anti-Semitism is likely to recur. Europe has in recent years grown hostile to Jews to an extent not seen since Nazism's heyday, but the anti-Semites today are principally not native European Christians, but Muslim immigrants (and Muslims, by mid-century, could be the majority population of several European states).

In Britain, there were three times more anti-Semitic incidents in 2007 than there were in 1997.[111] A December 2006 study, according to the *Telegraph*, determined that "in London and Manchester, where Muslims outnumber Jews by four to one, anti-Semitic offenses exceeded anti-Muslim offenses." One rabbi was attacked in July 2006 by seven Pakistani Muslim teenagers, who shouted, "We are Pakistani, you are Jewish. We are going to kill you."[112] In Belgium in November 2006, according to *Flanders News*, "a group of young Turkish immigrants in the Limburg municipality of Beringen attacked a group of Jewish school children by throwing stones at them, shouting anti-Semitic slogans."[113] In summer 2006, after a Jewish man was assaulted in Oslo, Norwegian Jews were warned not to wear kippahs on the street, for fear they would be physically attacked.[114]

And these are just a few recent examples of a long and ever lengthening string of such incidents. The European Union commissioned a report about the new rise of anti-Semitism in Europe in 2003, but buried it when its findings showed that anti-Semitic acts were largely the province of young Muslims. After an outcry, the report was released in 2004, but journalist Ambrose Evans-Pritchard noted that the results "had been consistently massaged by the EU watchdog to play down the role of North African youth."[115]

As time goes by, however, these new realities will be harder and harder to ignore.

The ultimate question regarding Christian and Islamic anti-Semitism is: given the choice, would Jews today prefer to live in a Christian or in an Islamic country?

CHAPTER EIGHT

THE WEST CALLS FOR DIALOGUE; ISLAM CALLS FOR JIHAD

Fourteenth-century Byzantine emperor Manuel II Paleologus gained worldwide exposure in 2006 after Pope Benedict XVI quoted him in his Regensburg speech on reason and faith. The quoted passages read: "Show me just what Mohammed brought that was new, and there you will find things only evil and inhuman, such as his command to spread by the sword the faith he preached. . . . God is not pleased by blood—and not acting reasonably is contrary to God's nature. Faith is born of the soul, not the body. Whoever would lead someone to faith needs the ability to speak well and to reason properly, without violence and threats. . . . To convince a reasonable soul, one does not need a strong arm, or weapons of any kind, or any other means of threatening a person with death." The pope's remarks touched off worldwide Islamic riots, illustrating that many Muslims take a different view, and are not interested in dialogue of any kind.

"CAN'T WE TALK ABOUT THIS?"

On November 2, 2004, Dutch filmmaker Theo van Gogh met one such Muslim. Van Gogh was bicycling through the streets of Amsterdam when Mohammed Bouyeri, a Muslim wearing traditional Islamic clothing, started shooting at him. After van Gogh fell off his bike, Bouyeri ran up to him and began slitting his throat, attempting to behead him. In his agony, van Gogh pleaded with his killer, "Can't we talk about this?"[1] Bouyeri replied by stabbing van Gogh repeatedly. He left a note attached to the knife that he plunged into van Gogh's body. The note contained verses from the Qur'an and threats to other Dutch public figures who opposed the flood of Muslim immigrants into the Netherlands.[2]

Bouyeri killed van Gogh because of the filmmaker's twelve-minute video *Submission*, which had aired on Dutch television a few weeks before the murder. A collaboration between van Gogh and a Somali ex-Muslim woman, Ayaan Hirsi Ali, who was then a member of the Dutch parliament, *Submission* decried the mistreatment of Muslim women. It featured images of battered women wearing transparent robes that exposed their breasts, with verses from the Qur'an written on their bodies.

At his trial, Bouyeri was unrepentant—and absolutely clear about why he murdered van Gogh. "I did what I did purely out of my beliefs," he explained, Qur'an in hand. "I want you to know that I acted out of conviction and not that I took his life because he was Dutch or because I was Moroccan and felt insulted. . . . If I ever get free, I would do it again."[3] He was, he said, acting in accord with Islamic law: "What moved me to do what I did was purely my faith. I was motivated by the law that commands me to cut off the head of anyone who insults Allah and his prophet."[4]

"Can't we talk about this?" and "I was motivated by the law that commands me to cut off the head of anyone who insults Allah and his prophet" sum up in a nutshell the postures of the West and the Islamic world today. On the one side there is a determination to talk, to negotiate, to accommodate—no matter what the provocation. On the other are fury, intransigence, and absolute conviction. Moreover, pervasive in the West is the assumption that everyone wants peace and is willing to compromise and negotiate, regardless of whatever evidence to the contrary. After the terrorist group Hamas won 57 percent of the vote in Palestinian Authority elections, Secretary of State Condoleezza Rice said: "The Palestinian people have apparently voted for change, but we believe that their aspirations for peace and a peaceful life remain unchanged."[5] Rice clung to this hope despite the unequivocal words of Hamas's Mahmoud Zahar: "We have no peace process. We are not going to mislead our people to tell them we are waiting, meeting, for a peace process that is nothing."[6]

POPE CALLS FOR DIALOGUE...
AND GETS RIOTS

This dichotomy was epitomized by the Muslim reaction to the speech Pope Benedict delivered at the University of Regensburg in Germany on September 12, 2006. The pope's somewhat recondite address gained international notoriety for his quotation of Manuel II Paleologus. Ironically, in light of its aftermath, the pope had intended his speech to inspire "that genuine dialogue of cultures and religions so urgently needed today," by highlighting the importance of reason to faith (and vice versa).

For any dialogue to succeed, however, there needs to be some degree of mutual respect and broad agreement about the parameters of the discussion. In his address, Pope Benedict argued that "not to act in accordance with reason is contrary to God's nature," and that reason must be the basis for any fruitful dialogue. He noted, however, that Manuel II's Persian interlocutor believes that to speak of reason in such a way would be tantamount to limiting the divine power. He recounts that after the emperor characterizes Muhammad's innovations as "evil and inhuman," he "goes on to explain in detail the reasons why spreading the faith through violence is something unreasonable. Violence is incompatible with the nature of God and the nature of the soul."

In contrast, Pope Benedict continued, "for Muslim teaching, God is absolutely transcendent. His will is not bound up with any of our categories, even that of rationality." Medieval Islamic philosopher Ibn Hazm, he says, "went so far as to state that God is not bound even by his own word, and that nothing would oblige him to reveal the truth to us. Were it God's will, we would even have to practise idolatry."[7] The pope asked, however, whether "the conviction that acting unreasonably contradicts

God's nature" is not "merely a Greek idea," or a Christian one, but is "always and intrinsically true"—and spends the rest of the address explaining his affirmative answer.

A DIALOGUE, INDEED...BUT NOT QUITE AS REASONABLE AS HE HAD HOPED

The pope's address was a carefully reasoned and respectful invitation to dialogue. The initial response to it from the Islamic world, however, was not as generous and open-minded as he had perhaps hoped. Instead of responding to his call for reasonable dialogue, Muslim spokesmen focused on his quotation about Muhammad, and to a lesser degree on his observations about rationality and the nature of God. The spokeswoman for Pakistan's foreign office, Taslim Aslam, asserted that the pope misunderstood Islam.[8] That was perhaps the mildest immediate response. Turkey's leading Muslim cleric, Ali Bardakoglu, who heads that country's Religious Affairs Directorate, called the Regensburg address "extraordinarily worrying, saddening, and unfortunate." He pointed to the sins of Christianity: "The church and the Western public, because they saw Islam as the enemy, went on crusades. They occupied Istanbul, they killed thousands of people. Orthodox Christians and Jews were killed and tortured."

Bardakoglu even claimed that religious warfare was a Christian, not a Muslim phenomenon. The Christians at the time of the Crusades, he asserted, "saw war against those outside the Christian world as a holy duty. That's why the Western clerics always have in the back of their minds a crusade mentality and the idea of holy war." Religious strife in the West could be laid at the feet not of restive and growing Muslim populations in Europe, but of the church: "If there's a religious antagonism in the West, it's the responsibility of the logic-ignoring Christian church."[9] When the pope visited Turkey in November 2006, Bardakoglu was hardly more conciliatory, scolding those who attempted to "demonstrate the superiority of their own beliefs."[10]

Even Islamic jihadists, who hate the pope anyway and who certainly don't repudiate violence, were angry. Mohamed Mahdi Akef, leader of the Muslim Brotherhood, the first modern Islamic terror organization (whence sprang Hamas and al Qaeda), said the pope "aroused the anger of the whole Islamic world and strengthened the argument of those who say that the West is hostile to everything Islamic."[11] Grand Ayatollah Mohammed Hussein Fadlallah, Lebanon's leading Shi'ite cleric, asked that the pope "apologize for this false reading of Islam.... We do not accept the excuse of the Vatican that the pope was not targeting Islam and had not intended to engage in a detailed study of jihad."[12]

Fadlallah himself, however, had shortly before praised the terror group Hizballah for waging "a new battle of Khaybar" against Israel.[13] So he certainly was not an opponent of jihad violence. As for his reference to "Khaybar," it was, in Muhammad's time, an Arabian oasis inhabited by Jews—many of whom the prophet had previously exiled from the Islamic city of Medina. "The apostle," reported Muhammad's first biographer, Ibn Ishaq, "seized the property piece by piece and conquered the forts one by one as he came to them." Muhammad ordered one of the Jewish leaders tortured in order to force him to reveal the location of the community's treasure. The wretched man refused to talk and was ultimately beheaded; Muhammad claimed his wife as a war prize and hastily arranged a wedding ceremony. Later that night, he halted the Muslims' caravan out of Khaybar in order to consummate the marriage. Muhammad agreed to let the people of Khaybar to go into exile as long as they left behind all their gold and silver.[14] This, then, was the aggressive campaign of conquest and exile Fadlallah was invoking.

On the Friday after the pope's remarks, Muslims all over the world heard sermons denouncing Benedict. They streamed out of the mosques to hold furious demonstrations. The Associated Press reported that "Pakistan's legislature unanimously condemned Pope Benedict XVI. Lebanon's top Shi'ite cleric demanded an apology. And in Turkey, the ruling party likened the pontiff to Hitler and Mussolini and accused him of reviving the mentality of the Crusades."[15]

In the Arabic-language London newspaper *al-Sharq al-Awsat*, columnist Hussein Shabakshy wrote, "It is clear that such remarks only contribute to the fueling of the fire raging between Islam and the West. There is no difference between Osama bin Laden and Ayman al-Zawahiri speaking from their caves in Tora Bora and the stage of an important Christian saint. Both parties contribute to the world verbal weapons for mass destruction."[16] Shabakshy failed to note that the pope had not master-minded any bombings or suicide attacks. Meanwhile, an Iraqi Shi'ite cleric, Sheikh Abdul-Kareem al-Ghazi, criticized the pope for departing from Christianity, which he, like Rosie O'Donnell, likened to Islam: "The pope and Vatican proved to be Zionists," he opined, "and they are far from Christianity, which does not differ from Islam. Both religions call for forgiveness, love, and brotherhood."[17]

However, not much forgiveness, love, and brotherhood were in the offing from the Islamic world. During Friday prayers in Mogadishu several days after the Regensburg address, Somali cleric Sheikh Abubukar Hassan Malin called on Muslims to kill the pope: "We urge you Muslims wherever you are to hunt down the pope for his barbaric statements as you have pursued Salman Rushdie, the enemy of Allah who offended our religion. Whoever offends our Prophet Mohammed should be killed on the spot by the nearest Muslim."[18] The same day, Syed Ahmed Bukhari, the principal cleric of the largest mosque in India, called upon Muslims to "respond in a manner which forces the pope to apologize."[19]

The violence started soon afterward. In the West Bank, a jihad group called the Army of Guidance issued a leaflet warning that it would "target all Crusaders in the Gaza Strip until the pope issues an official apology.... All centers belonging to Crusaders, including churches and institutions, will from now on be targeted. We will even attack the Crusaders as they sit intoxicated in their homes." Six churches in the West Bank were bombed or set on fire, and one in Gaza was fired upon.[20] An Iraqi jihadist group calling itself the Mujahedeen Army, addressing Pope Benedict as "you dog of Rome," threatened to send suicide bombers to the Vatican, in order to "shake your thrones and break your crosses in your home.... We swear to God to send you people who adore death as much as you adore life."[21] Another Iraqi jihad group, the Mujahideen Shura Council, issued a similar threat: "We tell the worshipper of the cross (the pope) that you and the West will be defeated, as is the case in Iraq, Afghanistan, Chechnya. We shall break the cross and spill the wine.... God will (help) Muslims to conquer Rome.... God enable us to slit their throats, and make their money and descendants the bounty of the mujahideen."[22]

An Iraqi jihadist group with the improbable name of Islamic Salafist Boy Scout Battalions threatened to kill every Christian in Iraq unless the pope apologized.[23] A month after the Regensburg speech, the *New York Times* reported: "Several extremist groups threatened to kill all Christians unless the pope apologized. Sunni and Shiite clerics united in the condemnation, calling the comments an insult to Islam and the Prophet Muhammad. In Baghdad, many churches canceled services after receiving threats. Some have not met since."[24] On the Sunday after the pope's remarks, a nun was shot dead in Somalia as she went about her work in a Mogadishu hospital.[25]

In London that same day, Muslim demonstrators outside London's Westminster Cathedral held signs openly threatening the pope: "Pope Benedict go to Hell," "Pope Benedict you will pay, the Muja Hadeen [warriors of jihad] are coming your way," "Pope Benedict watch your back," and the like.[26] One of the leaders of the demonstration, Islamic hard-liner Anjem Choudary, echoed the call for the pope's death: "The Muslims take their religion very seriously and non-Muslims must appreciate that and they must also understand that there may be serious consequences if you insult Islam and the prophet. Whoever insults the message of Mohammed is going to be subject to capital punishment. . . . I think that warning needs to be understood by all people who want to insult Islam and want to insult the prophet of Islam."[27]

In late November 2006, Islamic jihadists in Iraq murdered a sixty-nine-year-old Presbyterian church elder, after calling his family on a cell phone to say: "We have him, and we will kill him. We will cut his throat. We will take revenge for the pope's words. We will take revenge on all of you. We will kill all the Christians, and we will start with him."[28]

A group of Muslim clerics in the Gaza Strip called upon the pope to convert to Islam. The clerics said, "We want to use the words of the Prophet Muhammad and tell the pope: '*Aslim Taslam*'"—that is, embrace Islam and you will be safe.[29] This echoed a series of letters Muhammad wrote to the rulers of the nations surrounding Arabia, calling them to his new faith. His letter to Heraclius, the Eastern Roman emperor in Constantinople, is typical of the series: "Now then, I invite you to Islam (i.e., surrender to Allah), embrace Islam and you will be safe; embrace Islam and Allah will bestow on you a double reward. But if you reject this invitation of Islam, you shall be responsible for misguiding the peasants (i.e., your nation)."[30]

There is, of course, an implied threat in this: if you do not embrace Islam, you will not be safe. And in light of the death threats that Pope Benedict received after his remarks, it would be reasonable to assume that the implied threats were also part of his own "invitation" to Islam.

The post-Regensburg fallout continued for many months—even after the pope issued repeated (albeit carefully worded) apologies, assuring Muslims that Manuel II Paleologus's opinion was not his own. He also met with Islamic leaders in the Vatican. In late March 2007, the most influential cleric in Sunni Islam, the grand sheikh of Cairo's Al-Azhar University, Mohammed Sayyed Tantawi, canceled a scheduled meeting with the pope in Rome after pressure from many Muslim clerics still angry over the Regensburg address.[31]

There could have been no more dramatic illustration of the pope's observations that "for Muslim teaching, God is absolutely transcendent" and is "not bound up with any of our categories, even that of rationality," as opposed to the Christian view that "acting unreasonably contradicts God's nature," than the irrational and murderous rage that marked the Muslim response to his address. The Muslim mobs that shouted for the pope's blood were not interested in acting reasonably. They were only interested in protecting, as they saw it, the absolutely transcendent God from what they saw as an intolerable insult. The contrast was vivid and unmistakable.

UNFORTUNATELY, THIS IS NOTHING NEW

The international riots and killings that followed Pope Benedict's address in Regensburg were not the first such incident. Islamic scholar Daniel Pipes lists five others that have occurred in recent years, noting that they are happening with increasing frequency. The first four:

- 1989—Salman Rushdie's novel *The Satanic Verses* prompted Ayatollah Khomeini to issue a death edict against him and his publishers, on the grounds that the book "is against Islam, the

Prophet, and the Koran." Subsequent rioting led to more than twenty deaths, mostly in India.

- 1997—The U.S. Supreme Court refused to remove a 1930s frieze showing Muhammad as lawgiver that decorates the main court chamber. The Council on American-Islamic Relations made an issue of this, leading to riots and injuries in India.
- 2002—American evangelical leader Jerry Falwell calls Muhammad a "terrorist," leading to church burnings and at least ten deaths in India.
- 2005—An incorrect story in *Newsweek*, reporting that American interrogators at Guantanamo Bay, "in an attempt to rattle suspects, flushed a Qur'an down a toilet," is picked up by the famous Pakistani cricketer Imran Khan and prompts protests around the Muslim world, leading to at least fifteen deaths.[32]

The fifth incident began in late 2005 and erupted worldwide in early 2006. These were the riots and killings over cartoons of Muhammad in a Danish newspaper. The Organization of the Islamic Conference decided at its meeting in Mecca in December 2005 to use the cartoons as an object lesson in the perils of Western secularism. Muslim cartoon rage was not spontaneous, but it spread quickly all across the Muslim world.[33] At least 139 people were killed and 823 were injured in the international cartoon riots, and the cartoonists now live under death threats.[34]

In reality, however, the cartoons themselves were inoffensive. Nine were entirely innocuous, while three made a connection between Islam and violence. The one that became the most notorious depicted Muhammad with a bomb in his turban—but the Muslims driven to murderous rage by this incident were never driven to such paroxysms by the alleged "hijacking" of their religion by Osama bin Laden and other Islamic jihadists who (at least in modern times) made the equation between Muhammad and violence in the first place. The "crisis," as silly as it was, provoked diplomatic responses, official United Nations discussions, international boycotts, and the threatening of utterly innocent businesspeople and embassy personnel. In January 2006 gunmen seized an EU office in Gaza, demanding apologies from Denmark and Norway (where another publication later reprinted the cartoons).[35] The following day, demonstrators chanted "War on Denmark, death to Denmark" as they burned Danish flags.[36] Arab interior ministers, meeting in Tunis, declared, "We ask the Danish authorities to take the necessary measures to punish those responsible for this harm and to take action to avoid a repeat."[37] Libya and Saudi Arabia recalled their ambassadors from Copenhagen, and several Muslim organizations complained to the United Nations.

As it grew into an international cause célèbre, the cartoon controversy indicated the gulf between the Islamic world and the West in matters of freedom of speech and expression. Freedom of speech encompasses precisely the freedom to annoy, to ridicule, and to offend. Islamic organizations around the world tried to use the cartoon controversy to place Islam off-limits not just for ridicule, but for discussion of those elements within it that encourage violence and oppression. The entire cartoon incident was a dispiriting reminder of the Islamic world's very different idea of what constitutes reasonable debate, and its determination to silence anyone it considers to have offended Islam.

ONE NONVIOLENT RESPONSE

However, in contrast to both the cartoon incident and the most publicized aftermath of the pope's Regensburg address, the Muslim response to the pope was not uniformly violent or threatening. A group of one hundred eminent Islamic authorities issued an open letter to Pope Benedict, in which they (mostly) gently remonstrated with him for his, in their view, ignorance of Islam. Signers included two authors of popular books on Islam, Seyyed Hossein Nasr of George Washington University and Akbar Ahmed of American University; the prominent American Muslim Hamza Yusuf Hanson, founder and director of the Zaytuna Institute in California; Sheikh Muhammad Sa'id Ramadan al-Buti of the University of Damascus; Sheikh Nuh Ha Mim Keller, a convert from Catholicism to Islam and senior fellow of the Aal al-Bayt Institute for Islamic Thought in Jordan; as well as the muftis of Egypt, Syria, Jordan, Lebanon, Oman, Istanbul, Bosnia and Herzegovina, Kosovo, Russia, Uzbekistan, Croatia, Slovenia, and Sanjak (a region of Serbia), along with Islamic authorities from Saudi Arabia, Iran, Kuwait, Morocco, Bahrain, Malaysia, Indonesia, Britain, France, Belgium, the United States, and elsewhere.[38]

In this document, weighty with the approval of so many authorities, the writers admonished Pope Benedict with the Qur'an verse "there is no compulsion in religion" (2:256), which they quote no fewer than six times, and tell him that "the notion that Muslims are commanded to spread their faith 'by the sword' or that Islam was in fact largely spread 'by the sword' does not hold up to scrutiny." They also engage in an exercise of moral equivalence that would do Chris Hedges proud, attempting to refute the proposition that violence goes against God's nature by asserting that "Christ himself used violence against the money-changers in the temple and said 'Do not think that I came to bring peace on the earth; I did not come to bring peace, but a sword' (Matthew 10:34–36)."[39]

While apparently implying that Jesus somehow sanctioned religious violence, however, the Muslim writers do rhetorical violence to the context of Jesus's words, as well as to the totality of those of Muhammad and the Qur'an. The full quote from Matthew depicts Jesus saying: "Do not think that I have come to bring peace on earth; I have not come to bring peace, but a sword. For I have come to set a man against his father, and a daughter against her mother, and a daughter-in-law against her mother-in-law; and a man's foes will be those of his own household." Christians of all sects throughout history have understood this as referring to the fact that one who is committed to Christ will often face opposition even from his own family; it has never been invoked as justifying physical war or been invoked by Christians who were waging war.

Nor do the Islamic writers mention the many statements of the Qur'an and Muhammad on waging religious warfare, even to dismiss them or explain them away. It is rather jarring that Jesus's "sword verse" about family conflict is quoted, while the Qur'an's famous Verse of the Sword goes unmentioned. Nor are any of the other Qur'anic verses that Islamic jurists have used to construct a theology of warfare against unbelievers even mentioned. Likewise passed over in silence are key mainstream traditions, accepted as authentic by the overwhelming majority of Muslims around the world, in which Muhammad delineates three choices that Muslims are to offer to non-Muslims:

Fight in the name of Allah and in the way of Allah. Fight against those who disbelieve in Allah. Make a holy war.... When you meet your enemies who are polytheists, invite them to three courses of action. If they respond to any one of these, you also accept it and withhold yourself from doing them any harm. Invite them to accept Islam; if they respond to you, accept it from them and desist from fighting against them.... If they refuse to accept Islam, demand from them the Jizya. If they agree to pay, accept it from them and hold off your hands. If they refuse to pay the tax, seek Allah's help and fight them.[40]

The choices for unbelievers are thus either conversion, subjugation as inferiors with the obligation of paying the tax and submitting to inferior status under the rule of Islamic law, or war. "Peaceful coexistence as equals in a pluralistic society" is not an option.

In another hadith that is repeated several times in the collection of traditions that Muslims consider most reliable, Muhammad says, "I have been ordered (by Allah) to fight against the people until they testify that none has the right to be worshipped but Allah and that Muhammad is the Messenger of Allah, and perform *As-Salat* (prayers) and give *Zakat* [obligatory charity], so if they perform all that, then they save their lives and properties from me except for Islamic laws, and their reckoning (accounts) will be with (done by) Allah."[41]

It might be that many Islamic leaders do not accept these traditions, or do not consider them valid for today. Very well. Then it is incumbent upon them, especially in light of the way jihadists use these traditions and others, to say so. None of the signers of the open letter to Pope Benedict XVI did; instead they ignored this material altogether while bringing up other material of dubious relevance.

MARGINAL AND MAINSTREAM THINKERS

The open letter scolded the pope for quoting Ibn Hazm, whom the writers dismiss as "a worthy but very marginal figure, who belonged to the Zahiri school of jurisprudence which is followed by no one in the Islamic world today." They recommend instead as "more influential and more representative of Islamic belief" the great eleventh-century Sufi philosopher and theologian Abu Hamid al-Ghazali for a better understanding of "classical formulations of the doctrine of transcendence." The choice of al-Ghazali is ironic for several reasons. No doubt he was a pivotal figure in Islamic intellectual history, and one who still wields considerable influence. But he was also, particularly with his classic work *The Incoherence of the Philosophers*, the single figure in Islamic history who bears the most responsibility for the marginalization of philosophy and reason in Islam and the victory of a dogmatic Qur'anic orthodoxy—precisely the point the pope addressed at Regensburg about the necessity of philosophy, reason, and faith informing each other.

For al-Ghazali, most philosophy was a veil for heresy. Because philosophers taught their own ideas rather than those of the Qur'an, they were simply blasphemers.[42] Al-Ghazali charged that the teachings of the principal Muslim philosophers (especially al-Farabi and Avicenna) "challenge the [very] principles of religion."[43]

Al-Ghazali, according to scholar Tilman Nagel, "was inspired by a notion that we frequently see in Islam's intellectual history: the notion that everything human beings can possibly know is already contained in the Koran and the hadith."[44] With unswerving fidelity to Islamic law, al-Ghazali at the end of *The Incoherence of the Philosophers* poses himself a final question: "If someone says: 'You have explained the doctrines of these [philosophers]; do you then say conclusively that they are infidels and *that the killing of those who uphold their beliefs is obligatory?*'"[45] He answers: "Pronouncing them infidels is necessary in three questions," and goes on to explain three areas in which they have deviated from Islamic orthodoxy. And thus they must be killed.

The writers of the open letter to Pope Benedict XVI do not mention any of this. Nor do they bring up the fact that al-Ghazali was an open proponent of the doctrine that Muslims must wage war against unbelievers:

> [O]ne must go on jihad (i.e., warlike *razzias* or raids) at least once a year.... One may use a catapult against them [non-Muslims] when they are in a fortress, even if among them are women and children. One may set fire to them and/or drown them.... If a person of the *ahl*

al-kitab [People of the Book] is enslaved, his marriage is [automati-
cally] revoked.... One may cut down their trees.... One must destroy
their useless books. Jihadists may take as booty whatever they
decide.... They may steal as much food as they need.

Al-Ghazali was just as firm on the need for the People of the Book under
Muslim rule—the dhimmis—to "feel themselves subdued" by the Muslims, in accord with Qur'an 9:29:

> [T]he *dhimmi* is obliged not to mention Allah or His Apostle.... Jews,
> Christians, and Majians must pay the *jizya*...on offering up the *jizya*,
> the *dhimmi* must hang his head while the official takes hold of his
> beard and hits [the dhimmi] on the protuberant bone beneath his ear
> [i.e., the mandible].... They are not permitted to ostentatiously dis-
> play their wine or church bells...their houses may not be higher than
> the Muslims', no matter how low that is. The *dhimmi* may not ride an
> elegant horse or mule; he may ride a donkey only if the saddle[-work]
> is of wood. He may not walk on the good part of the road. They [the
> dhimmis] have to wear [an identifying] patch [on their clothing], even
> women, and even in the [public] baths...[dhimmis] must hold their
> tongue.[46]

The open letter writers also omit any mention that *all* the existing schools
of Islamic jurisprudence teach the legitimacy of warfare against unbelievers in order to establish the hegemony of Islamic law. They purport to lay
out the "authoritative and traditional Islamic rules of war," but never mention what their own source al-Ghazali says: Muslims must make war
"upon Jews, Christians, and Zoroastrians...until they become Muslim or
pay the non-Muslim poll tax."[47] Instead, the writers note only that "non-
combatants are not permitted or legitimate targets"; "religious belief alone
does not make anyone the object of attack"; and "Muslims can and should
live peacefully with their neighbors." However, "this does not exclude
legitimate self-defense and maintenance of sovereignty." Of course, in
Islamic jurisprudence "self-defense and maintenance of sovereignty" can
mean something different than it does in the West, as professor Imran

Ahsan Khan Nyazee of Islamabad's International Islamic University points out when he says there is "no doubt that the primary goal of the Muslim community, in the eyes of its jurists, is to spread the word of Allah through jihad, and the option of poll-tax is to be exercised only after subjugation" of non-Muslims.[48] Whether the writers of the open letter to Pope Benedict XVI meant a pro forma affirmation of self-defense, as we in the West know it, or as Islamic law traditionally has it is an open question.

And that's the problem. Today jihadists are making recruits among peaceful Muslims worldwide by appealing to the teachings of the Qur'an and Muhammad, and on that basis portraying themselves as the exponents of "pure Islam." They claim they have rediscovered, as a popular jihadist pamphlet termed it, "the forgotten obligation" of jihad. If Islamic scholars and authorities, such as those who wrote to Pope Benedict, want to combat this, they need to address it. If they do not, if they simply ignore traditional Islamic teachings, such as are embraced by the jihadists, they open themselves to the suspicion that they are being disingenuous at best.

To defeat the jihadists, we don't need Islamic scholars to lecture the pope; we need them to lecture Muslims about why traditional Islamic teaching and jurisprudence on jihad must be reformed. There is a difference between reform and deception. If the Protestant Reformers had indignantly denied that the Catholic Church taught transubstantiation and the sacramental priesthood, instead of arguing that such doctrines should be discarded, they would not have been reformers, but obfuscators. There is little hope for the "can't we talk about this" approach when the pope calls for dialogue and the Islamic reaction is violence on one hand and disingenuousness on the other.

CHAPTER NINE

FAITH AND UNREASON

Friedrich Nietzsche once noted that "there is no such thing as science 'without any presuppositions.'... A philosophy, a 'faith,' must always be there first, so that science can acquire from it a direction, a meaning, a limit, a method, a right to exist."[1]

It may be jarring to those who believe that faith and reason are at odds, and that religions are all the same, but it is nevertheless a historical fact that modern science took its presuppositions from Christianity, and that Islam gave modern science no impetus at all.

At Regensburg, Pope Benedict XVI observed that "for Muslim teaching, God is absolutely transcendent. His will is not bound up with any of our categories, even that of rationality."[2] The one hundred Muslim authorities who wrote an open letter to the pope replied that this was an oversimplification, and that it is wrong "to conclude that Muslims believe in a capricious God who might...command us to evil."

But the pope was not saying that Allah would command his people to do evil, but that Allah *might change the concepts of good and evil*. In other words, Allah might always enjoin justice and kindness, but justice and kindness might have very different meanings.

The reason why this is so important for science is that Muslims believe that Allah's hand is unfettered—he can do anything. The Qur'an explicitly refutes the Judeo-Christian view of God as a God of reason when it says: "The Jews say: Allah's hand is fettered. Their hands are fettered and they are accursed for saying so" (5:64). In other words, it is heresy to say that God operates by certain natural laws that we can understand through reason. This argument was played out throughout Islamic history.

Muslim theologians argued during the long controversy with the Mu'-tazilite sect, which exalted human reason, that Allah was not bound to govern the universe according to consistent and observable laws. "He cannot be questioned concerning what He does" (Qur'an 21:23).

Accordingly, observations of the physical world had no value; there was no reason to expect that any pattern to its workings would be consistent, or even discernable. If Allah could not be counted on to be consistent, why waste time observing the order of things? It could change tomorrow. Stanley Jaki, a Catholic priest and physicist, explains that it was al-Ghazali, the philosopher recommended by the authors of the open letter to the pope, who "denounced natural laws, the very objective of science, as a blasphemous constraint upon the free will of Allah."[3] He adds that "Muslim mystics decried the notion of scientific law (as formulated by Aristotle) as blasphemous and irrational, depriving as it does the Creator of his freedom."[4] Social scientist Rodney Stark adds that Islam does not have "a conception of God appropriate to underwrite the rise of science.... Allah is not presented as a lawful creator but is conceived of as an extremely active God who intrudes in the world as he deems it appropriate. This prompted the formation of a major theological bloc within Islam that condemns all efforts to formulate natural laws as blasphemy in that they deny Allah's freedom to act."[5]

The great twelfth-century Jewish philosopher Moses Maimonides explained orthodox Islamic cosmology in these terms:

Human intellect does not perceive any reason why a body should be in a certain place instead of being in another. In the same manner they say that reason admits the possibility that an existing being should be larger or smaller than it really is, or that it should be different in form and position from what it really is; e.g., a man might have the height of a mountain, might have several heads, and fly in the air; or an elephant might be as small as an insect, or an insect as huge as an elephant.

This method of admitting possibilities is applied to the whole Universe. Whenever they affirm that a thing belongs to this class of admitted possibilities, they say that it can have this form and that it is also possible that it be found differently, and that the one form is not more possible than the other; but they do not ask whether the reality confirms their assumption. . . .

[They say] fire causes heat, water causes cold, in accordance with a certain habit; but it is logically not impossible that a deviation from this habit should occur, namely, that fire should cause cold, move downward, and still be fire; that the water should cause heat, move upward, and still be water. On this foundation their whole [intellectual] fabric is constructed.[6]

This fantastical cosmology comes from the Islamic conviction of the absolute sovereignty of Allah. Relatively early in its history, therefore, science in the Islamic world was deprived of the philosophical foundation it needed in order to flourish. Consequently, Professor Jaki observes, "the improvements brought by Muslim scientists to the Greek scientific corpus were never substantial."[7] The consequences of this have been far-reaching. Jaki details some of them:

More than two hundred years after the construction of the famed Blue Mosque, W. Eton, for many years a resident in Turkey and Russia, found that Turkish architects still could not calculate the lateral pressures of curves. Nor could they understand why the catenary curve, so useful in building ships, could also be useful in drawing blueprints for cupolas. The reign of Suleiman the Magnificent may be memorable for its wealth of gorgeously illustrated manuscripts and princely paraphernalia, but for no items worth mentioning from the viewpoint of science and technology. At the Battle of Lepanto the Turkish navy lacked improvements long in use on French and Italian vessels. Two hundred years later, Turkish artillery was primitive by Western standards. Worse, while in Western Europe the dangers of the use of lead had for some time been clearly realized, lead was still a heavy ingredient in kitchenware used in Turkish lands.[8]

These technological differences abetted the Catholic victory at the Battle of Lepanto on October 7, 1571. The Holy League, comprised of the Papal States, the Republic of Venice, Spain, Genoa, and others, defeated the Ottoman Turks in a decisive sea battle that the jihadists hoped would bring Europe within their grasp. Stark explains, "The European galleys not only had far more and far better cannons than did the Turks, but they no longer had their forward fire zone blocked by a high ramming beak—since they meant to blow the Turks out of the water, not ram into them. Firing powerful forward volleys, the Europeans annihilated Ottoman galleys while still rowing toward them; the Turks had to stop and turn sideways to fire, presenting much larger targets."[9]

In contrast to the dogmatic stagnation of the Islamic world, science was able to flourish in Christian Europe during the same period because Christian scientists were working from assumptions derived from the Bible, which were very different from those of the Qur'an. The Bible assumes that God's laws of creation are natural laws, a stable and unchanging reality—a sine qua non of scientific investigation.

Christian mathematicians and astronomers believed they could establish mathematical and scientific truths because they believed that God had established the universe according to certain laws—laws that could be discovered through observation and study. St. Thomas Aquinas even goes so far as to assert that "since the principles of certain sciences—of logic, geometry, and arithmetic, for instance—are derived exclusively from the formal principals of things, upon which their essence depends, it follows that God *cannot* make the contraries of these principles; He *cannot* make the genus not to be predictable of the species, nor lines drawn from a circle's center to its circumference not to be equal, nor the three angles of a rectilinear triangle not to be equal to two right angles." (Emphasis added)[10]

This is a far cry from Maimonides' depiction of Muslim philosophers envisioning elephants becoming snakes and fire turning cool. And to be sure, to a pious Muslim of Aquinas's day, such Christian ideas of an inviolable ordered universe was blasphemy, implying that "Allah's hand was fettered." But Christians did not consider it blasphemous in the least. "The rise of science," Stark explains, "was not an extension of classical learning. It was the natural outgrowth of Christian doctrine: nature exists because it was created by God. In order to love and honor God, it is necessary to fully appreciate the wonders of his handiwork. Because God is perfect, that handiwork functions in accord with *immutable principles*. By the full use of our God-given powers of reason and observation, it ought to be possible to discover those principles.... These were the crucial ideas that explain why science arose in Christian Europe and nowhere else."[11]

WAIT A MINUTE: DIDN'T MODERN SCIENCE ORIGINATE IN THE ISLAMIC WORLD?

Readers who received a modern education in a Western country may find Stark's statement implausible. After all, didn't modern science begin in the Islamic world? Didn't Muslims invent algebra, the astrolabe, and the zero? Didn't Muslims preserve the classics of ancient Greek philosophy while Europe was blinded by a narrow Christian dogmatism? Weren't the great Islamic empires of the past the bright lights of civilization, while Christian Europe was comparatively barbaric and primitive? "For while [the caliphs] al-Rashid and al-Mamun were delving into Greek and Persian philosophy," according to historian Philip Hitti, "their contemporaries in the West, Charlemagne and his lords, were reportedly dabbling in the art of writing their names.... No people in the early Middle Ages contributed to human progress as much as did the Arabs."[12]

In fact, much of this alleged history about Europe's ignorance and Islam's civilization is actually myth—and interestingly, a myth fostered by jihad, by Muslim conquests. The astrolabe was developed, if not perfected, long before Muhammad was born. The zero, which is often attributed to Muslims, and what we know today as "Arabic numerals" did not originate in Arabia, but in pre-Islamic India. Aristotle's work was preserved in Arabic not initially by Muslims, but by Christians like the fifth-century priest Probus of Antioch, who introduced Aristotle to the Arabic-speaking world.[13] Another Christian, Hunayn ibn-Ishaq, translated many works by Aristotle, Galen, Plato, and Hippocrates into Syriac. His son then translated them into Arabic.[14] Syrian Christian Yahya ibn 'Adi also translated works of philosophy into Arabic, and wrote one of his own, *The Reformation of Morals*. His student, another Christian named Abu 'Ali 'Isa ibn

Zur'a, also translated Aristotle and others from Syriac into Arabic. The first Arabic-language medical treatise was written by a Christian priest and translated into Arabic by a Jewish doctor in 683. The first hospital was founded in Baghdad during the Abbasid caliphate—not by a Muslim, but by a Nestorian Christian.[15] A pioneering medical school was founded at Gundeshapur in Persia by Assyrian Christians.

In sum, there was a time when it was indeed true that Islamic culture was more advanced than that of Europeans, but that superiority corresponds exactly to the period when Muslims were able to take the achievements of the Byzantines and others that they conquered. But after the Muslim overlords had stripped Jewish and Christian communities of their material and intellectual wealth, Islam went into a period of intellectual decline from which it has not yet recovered.

Certainly Muslims have innovated at high levels. Civilized people owe a debt to Muslim believers like Abu Ja'far Muhammad ibn Musa al-Khwarizmi, whose pioneering seventh-century treatise on algebra, *Al-Jabr wa-al-Muqabilah,* gave algebra its name and enjoyed wide influence in Europe. (Al-Khwarizmi, of course, was following in the pioneering footsteps of Diophantus of Alexandria, who died late in the third Christian century.) Abu Raihan al-Biruni did groundbreaking work on calculating longitude and latitude.[16] The caliph Harun al-Rashid's son Abu Jafar al-Ma'mun, who became caliph in 813, established professional standards for physicians and pharmacists.[17] Abu Bakr al-Razi, or Rhazes, wrote lengthy treatises on medicine and alchemy that influenced the development of medical science and chemistry in medieval Europe. The famous Muslim philosopher Avicenna (Ibn Sina) wrote a medical textbook that was preeminent among European doctors for five centuries—until the 1600s.[18] Prolific scholar Abu 'Uthman 'Amr ibn Bahr al-Jahiz wrote more than two hundred books on a multitude of subjects: from politics (*The Institution of the Caliphate*) and zoology (the seven-volume *Book of Animals*) to cuisine (*Arab Food*) and day-to-day living (*Sobriety and Mirth; The Art of Keeping One's Mouth Shut*).[19] Mathematician Abu Ali al-Hasan ibn al-Haytham did early and influential work in optics.[20]

But in almost every case, the Islamic scholars were building on what had been established by Jews, Christians, or others. And, as Rodney Stark points out, "Islamic scholars achieved significant progress only in terms of specific knowledge, such as certain aspects of astronomy and medicine, which did not require any general theoretical basis. And as time passed, even this sort of progress ceased."[21]

MUSLIMS INNOVATE, CHRISTIANS IMPROVE THE INNOVATIONS

1001 Inventions describes itself as "a unique UK-based educational project that reveals the rich heritage that the Muslim community share with other communities in the UK and Europe." It says that it is "a non-religious and non-political project seeking to allow the positive aspects of progress in science and technology to act as a bridge in understanding the interdependence of communities throughout human history"—and it does this by highlighting 1,001 inventions that Muslims are supposed to have brought to the world. This exhibit is designed for maximum popular appeal: "1001 Inventions consists of a UK-wide travelling exhibition, a colourful easy to read book, a dedicated website, and a themed collection of educational posters complementing a secondary school teachers' pack." It invites participants to "Discover Muslim Heritage in our World in seven conveniently organised zones: home, school, market, hospital, town, world, and universe."[22]

Many of these 1,001 inventions involve things on the order of "the world's first soft drink," and the perspective of this enterprise's organizers becomes clear from a section detailing astronomical revelations found in the Qur'an. In a manner reminiscent of Khruschev-era Soviet propaganda about how Russia invented everything from baseball to zoology, 1001 Inventions frequently asserts that innovations and discoveries usually attributed to Westerners actually originated in the Islamic world. "Abbas ibn Firnas," we're told, "was the first person to make a real attempt to construct a flying machine and fly. His first flight took place in 852 in Cordoba when he wrapped himself in a loose cloak stiffened with wooden struts and jumped from the minaret of the Great Mosque of Cordoba. Though this attempt was unsuccessful, he continued working on improving his design." And a bit more seriously, "The Polish scholar and inventor

Copernicus is credited as the founder of modern astronomy. Historians have recently established that most of his theories were based on those of Nasir al-Din al-Tusi and Ibn al-Shatir. Ibn al-Shatir's planetary theory and models are exactly mathematically identical to those prepared by Copernicus over a century after him, which raised the issue of how Copernicus acquired such elements of information. The line of transmission lies in Italy where Greek and Latin materials that made use of al-Tusi's device were circulating in Italy at about the time Copernicus studied there."

Such assertions only highlight the discomfiture of those who make them. For if Muslims really did make innovations in aerodynamics, astronomy, and other fields long before Europeans did, what happened then? Why were the Europeans the ones who made use of these discoveries for technological advancement? Even if Copernicus (who came from a devout Catholic family and may have been a priest himself) was influenced by Ibn al-Shatir, which is not universally accepted, why didn't Muslims make use of his insights the way Copernicus did?[23] Al-Shatir died in 1375, just under a hundred years before Copernicus was born in 1473. Yet in that century, and in the centuries thereafter, Islamic astronomers did nothing significant with their coreligionist's discoveries. If Islam contained the seeds of the high level of cultural attainment that the Islamic world enjoyed at its apex, why has it been unable to reverse its precipitous decline from those heights? Many Muslim and non-Muslim writers today answer this by blaming the West, but this just once again avoids the problem—for if Islam contains the means by which civilization can advance beyond anything the non-Muslim world has to offer, one would think that Muslims would be able to devise ways to circumvent the West's deleterious influence.

Directly opposed to Islam's repression of invention and innovations is Christianity's—especially Catholicism's—cultivation of learning and exploration. Few European or American students recognize, for example, the Catholic Church's pivotal role in the development of the university, science, free market economics, charitable institutions, and even secular legal codes.[24] Rodney Stark writes that medieval Europe's advances in production methods, navigation, and war technology "can be traced to the unique Christian conviction that progress was a God-given obligation, entailed in the gift of reason. That new technologies and techniques would always be forthcoming was a fundamental article of Christian faith. Hence, no bishops or theologians denounced clocks or sailing ships—although both were condemned on religious grounds in various non-Western societies."[25] While medieval Catholic Europe invented and made use of clocks, in 1560, Ogier Ghiselin de Busbecq, the Austrian ambassador to the Ottoman Empire, wrote that his hosts had "never been able to bring themselves to print books and set up public clocks. They hold that their scriptures, that is, their sacred books, would no longer be scriptures if they were printed; and if they established public clocks, they think that the authority of their muezzins and their ancient rites would suffer diminution."[26] It was not until the mid-nineteenth century, when Islamic norms were in retreat, that the first public clock was installed in Constantinople. This may have been the first public clock erected in any Islamic country.[27]

The effects of Christianity's openness to innovation and Islam's resistance to it reverberate through many fields. Even in medicine, while the Islamic world points proudly to many early physicians and medical theorists, it was not a Muslim, but Belgian physician and researcher Andreas Vesalius who paved the way for modern medical advances when he published the first accurate description of human internal organs, *De Humani Corporis Fabrica* (*On the Fabric of the Human Body*) in 1543. Why wasn't a Muslim able to do this? Because Vesalius was able to fill his book with detailed anatomical drawings—forbidden in Islam are artistic representations of the human body. Muslims, however, did allow themselves to benefit from Western creativity. In the late fifteenth century, Persian mystical poet Nur ad-Din Abd ar-Rahman Jami noted that his vision, which had become extremely poor, was saved "with the aid of Frankish glasses."[28]

BUT WHAT ABOUT GALILEO?

Professor Rodney Stark's reference to "the unique Christian conviction that progress was a God-given obligation" may strike some as odd given that the Catholic Church condemned Galileo Galilei, the "father of science" himself, as a heretic for saying that the Earth moved around the sun. Galileo and the Scopes "monkey trial" generally form the Catholic and Protestant bookends of the case that Christianity is anti-science. However, historian Thomas Woods notes of the former: "The one-sided version of the Galileo affair with which most people are familiar is very largely to blame for the widespread belief that the church has obstructed the advance of scientific inquiry. But even if the Galileo incident had been every bit as bad as people think it was, John Henry Cardinal Newman, the celebrated nineteenth-century convert from Anglicanism, found it revealing that this is practically the only example that ever comes to mind."[29]

As the story goes, an obscurantist church, blinded by dogma, hounded and condemned Galileo because church officials could not square the idea that the Earth moved around the sun with such scriptural declarations as "Thou didst set the Earth on its foundations, so that it should never be shaken." Reality was not quite so pat. In fact, Jesuit astronomers were among Galileo's earliest and most enthusiastic supporters. When Galileo first published supporting evidence for the Copernican heliocentric theory, Cardinal Maffeo Barberini sent him a letter of congratulations. When Galileo visited Rome in 1624, Cardinal Barberini had become Pope Urban VIII. The pope welcomed the scientist, gave him gifts, and assured him that the church would never declare heliocentrism heretical. In fact, the pope and other churchmen, according to historian Jerome Langford, "believed that Galileo might be right, but they had to wait for more proof."[30]

As Cardinal Robert Bellarmine explained, "If there were a real proof...that the sun does not go round the Earth but the Earth round the sun, then we should have to proceed with great circumspection in explaining passages of scripture which appear to teach the contrary, and rather admit that we did not understand them than declare an opinion to be false which is proved to be true. But as for myself, I shall not believe that there are such proofs until they are shown to me."[31] And that was the ultimate source of Galileo's conflict with the church: he was teaching as fact what still at that time had only the status of theory. When church officials asked Galileo in 1616 to teach heliocentrism as theory rather than as fact, he agreed; however, in 1632 he published a new work, *Dialogue on the Great World Systems*, in which he presented heliocentrism as fact again.

That was why Galileo was put on trial for suspected heresy and placed under house arrest. Historian J. L. Heilbron notes that from the beginning the controversy was not understood the way it has been presented by many critics of the church since then. The condemnation of Galileo, says Heilbron, "had no general or theological significance. Gassendi, in 1642, observed that the decision of the cardinals [who condemned Galileo], though important for the faithful, did not amount to an article of faith; Riccioli, in 1651, that heliocentrism was not a heresy; Mengeli, in 1675, that interpretations of scripture can only bind Catholics if agreed to at a general council; and Baldigiani, in 1678, that everyone knew all that."[32]

Speaking about the Galileo case in 1992, Pope John Paul II remarked:

> The Galileo case has been a sort of "myth," in which the image fabricated out of the events was quite far removed from reality. In this perspective, the Galileo case was the symbol of the church's supposed rejection of scientific progress, or of "dogmatic" obscurantism opposed to the free search for truth. This myth has played a considerable cultural role. It has helped to anchor a number of scientists of good faith in the idea that there was an incompatibility between the spirit of science and its rules of research on the one hand and the Christian faith on the other. A tragic mutual incomprehension has been interpreted as the reflection of a fundamental opposition between science and faith. The clarifications furnished by recent historical studies enable us to state that this sad misunderstanding now belongs to the past.

John Paul also reaffirmed the fundamentally Christian foundations of modern science: "Those who engage in scientific and technological research admit as the premise of its progress, that the world is not a chaos but a 'cosmos'—that is to say, that there exist order and natural laws which can be grasped and examined, and which, for this reason, have a certain affinity with the spirit."[33] In a 2000 address to the Pontifical Academy of Sciences, he observed that "the man of science...feels a special responsibility in relation to the advancement of mankind, not understood in generic or ideal terms, but as the advancement of the whole man and of everything that is authentically human. Science conceived in this way can encounter the church without difficulty and engage in a fruitful dialogue with her, because it is precisely man who is 'the primary and fundamental way for the church' (*Redemptor hominis*, n. 14)."[34]

When modern science was in its infancy, openness to such exploration was common only in Christian Europe, and was conspicuously lacking in the Islamic world.

CHAPTER TEN

DEMOCRACY, WHISKEY, SEXY

In the heady early days of America's incursion into Iraq, when Saddam Hussein's military machine collapsed and it seemed as if the Bush administration's democracy project would achieve quick and easy success, a man in Najaf summed up what he expected the Americans would bring to Iraq: "Democracy. Whiskey. And sexy!"[1]

Four years later, all three of these expected boons had fallen on hard times. Iraqi jihad groups, intent on replacing Saddam's relatively secular regime with an Islamic state, have murdered liquor store owners; Islamic law forbids Muslims to drink alcohol and likewise bans Christians from "openly displaying" it.[2] So much for whiskey. And sexy? Jihad groups have also threatened to kill women who venture outside with heads uncovered—including Christian women, who technically should be exempt from this sharia prohibition.[3] Democracy has fared little better, with Sunnis and Shi'ites unwilling to "overcome" (as Condoleezza Rice has exhorted them) their 1,400-year-old differences and grievances.[4]

The central problem of the democracy project in Iraq is Islam. Islam has always had a political and social character, including a full program for government. In fact, the first year of the Islamic calendar does not mark the birth or death of Muhammad, or the beginning of his prophetic ministry. It marks Muhammad's flight from Mecca to Medina, where he became a political and military leader and Islam became a state.

Islam assumes that its faith must be the ruling ideology of the state. And because Islamic law mandates discrimination against religious minorities (as well as women), it rules out the idea that all citizens enjoy equality of dignity and rights before the law.

So can Islamic countries be democratic? Some commentators think so. Dinesh D'Souza scolded conservatives in 2007 for "holding silly seminars on whether Islam is compatible with democracy. In reality, a majority of the world's Muslims today live under democratic governments—in Indonesia, Malaysia, India, Bangladesh, Nigeria, and Turkey, not to mention Muslims living in Western countries. There is nothing in the Koran or the Islamic tradition that forbids democracy."[5]

And of course there is no shortage of people who insist that Islam not only does not forbid, but in fact also actively fosters democracy. Abdulwahab Alkebsi of the Center for the Study of Islam and Democracy, for instance, has declared that the essentials of democracy are "consistent with Islam's clarion call for justice, equality, and human dignity.... According to the Qur'an, one of the explicit purposes of God's messengers is to offer mankind liberty, justice, and equality." Islam, he said, "lays the ground for the values of freedom, justice, and equality that are essential to democracy, more so than any other religion or dogma."[6]

Not only as much as any other religion or dogma, but more so. Can this really be true? Iranian journalist Amir Taheri thinks not. Arguing in favor of the proposition that Islam is incompatible with democracy during a debate in 2004, he directly contradicted the assertions D'Souza would make three years later: "There are fifty-seven nations in the Organisation of the Islamic Conference (OIC). Not one is yet a democracy. The more Islamic the regime in place the less democratic it is." He concluded, "Islam is incompatible with democracy."[7]

The fundamental problem, according to Taheri, is Islam's rejection of the idea that all people have equal dignity, a Christian idea that was central to abolishing slavery. But in Islam, it's a very different story. The very idea of equality, Taheri declared, "is unacceptable to Islam." He explained:

For the non-believer cannot be the equal of the believer. Even among the believers only those who subscribe to the three so-called Abrahamic religions: Judaism, Christianity and Islam (*Ahl el-Kitab*) are regarded as fully human. Here is the hierarchy of human worth in Islam: At the summit are free male Muslims. Next come Muslim male slaves. Then come free Muslim women. Next come Muslim slave women. Then come free Jewish and/or Christian men. Then come slave Jewish and/or Christian men. Then come slave Jewish and/or Christian women.

Each category has rights that must be respected. The People of the Book have always been protected and relatively well-treated by Muslim rulers, but often in the context of a form of apartheid known as dhimmitude. The status of the rest of humanity, those whose faiths are not recognised by Islam or who have no faith at all, has never been spelled out although wherever Muslim rulers faced such communities they often treated them with a certain measure of tolerance and respect (as in the case of Hindus under the Muslim dynasties of India.) Non-Muslims can, and have often been, treated with decency, but never as equals.[8]

Even today, although the fullness of Islamic law is not enforced anywhere in the Islamic world except Saudi Arabia and Iran, these fundamental ideas of the inequality of Muslims and non-Muslims remain rooted in Islamic cultures. In no country anywhere in the Islamic world do non-Muslims enjoy full equality of rights with Muslims.

Iran's UN delegate, Sa'id Raja'i-Khorassani, declared in 1985 that "the very concept of human rights was 'a Judeo-Christian invention' and inadmissible in Islam."[9] An Iranian Sufi leader, Sheikh Sultanhussein Tabandeh, wrote *A Muslim Commentary on the Universal Declaration of Human Rights* in 1970. While arguing for capital punishment if a Muslim is killed, Tabandeh argues against it if the murderer is Muslim and the victim non-Muslim: "Since Islam regards non-Muslims as on a lower level of belief and conviction, if a Muslim kills a non-Muslim . . . then his punishment must not be the retaliatory death, since the faith and conviction he possesses is loftier than that of the man slain. A fine only may be exacted from him."[10]

These principles run within both Shi'ite and Sunni Islam and explain why Taheri is right and D'Souza is wrong. Of the countries D'Souza cites to prove the compatibility of Islam with democracy, one—India—does not have a Muslim majority, and another—Nigeria—only has a Muslim major- ity in certain areas, with Muslims making up about half of the total pop- ulation. The others—Indonesia, Malaysia, Bangladesh, and Turkey—have overwhelming Muslim majorities, and they all discriminate against non- Muslims to various degrees; they also face challenges to their democratic principles from Muslim hard-liners. Democratic they may be in terms of head-counting, but if by democracy we mean respect for the sort of free- doms enshrined in our Constitution and Bill of Rights, they are not demo- cratic. In Bangladesh, a democratic state according to D'Souza, the government charged journalist Salah Uddin Shoaib Choudhury with sedi- tion, a capital crime, for criticizing Islamic jihad and calling for Bangla- desh to establish closer ties with Israel.[11] And in the other countries D'Souza lists, the situation is even worse.

INDONESIA: USING DEMOCRACY
TO DESTROY DEMOCRACY

"For years," reported the German newspaper Der Spiegel in April 2007, "radical Islamists have taken advantage of the democracy gained after the 1998 ouster of former Indonesian dictator Suharto to question that very democracy, all in the name of piety."

Much of this takes the form of enforcing sharia penalties, such as the public (and even televised) lashing of those caught with alcohol, and the public caning of couples caught kissing in public.[12] But it has also meant discrimination against Christians. When three Indonesian jihadists beheaded three Christian high school girls in October 2005, they received sentences ranging from fourteen to twenty years in prison; however, in September 2006 three Christians were executed for allegedly inciting vio- lence against Muslims during unrest between Muslims and Christians in Central Sulawesi six years previously. It was never definitively established that the three, Fabianus Tibo, Marinus Riwu, and Dominggus da Silva, killed anyone or exhorted anyone else to do so, but they were executed nonetheless. No Muslims were prosecuted for their role in the riots, although the violence was by no means one-sided.[13] Pope Benedict XVI called the executions of Tibo, Riwu, and da Silva "a defeat for humanity."[14]

Meanwhile, Muslims have burnt down well over a thousand churches in Indonesia since the late 1960s, and virtually none of the perpetrators have faced punishment.[15] In September 2006, a Muslim mob burned down a church in Indonesia's Aceh province after a Muslim forged and circulated a letter inviting Muslims to a revival service there. The mob was enraged by the Christians' apparent disregard of the sharia prohibition of proselytizing by non-Muslims. Local police knew of the forger's actions, but did nothing to stop him.[16]

"If they want sharia," says Dinesh D'Souza, "let them have it."[17] But that's just the problem: Indonesian Muslims have been letting Christians have it. With Christians living such a precarious existence, often with official sanction, it can hardly be said that the principle of equality is operative in Indonesia, however superficially democratic its government may appear.

MAY I PLEASE LEAVE ISLAM, SIR?

In another state widely lauded for its Islamic moderation, Malaysia, religious minorities are running increasingly afoul of government pressure to convert to Islam. Several large Hindu temples, some a hundred years old, have in recent years been classified as "illegal structures"—without explanation—and demolished.[18] In June 2006, the Malaysian state of Kelantan even went so far as to offer 10,000 ringgits (approximately $2,750) to any Muslim preacher who married a woman of the Orang Asli, the Malaysian aborigines, and converted her to Islam.[19] And in early 2007 the Malaysian government ordered human rights activist Malik Imtiaz Sarwar to disband his group dedicated to protecting religious freedom.

But the need for such an organization is clear: in April 2005, Malaysian police arrested two Americans for the crime of passing out Christian religious tracts.[20] Nor are Malaysian citizens in the clear: Lina Joy, a Malaysian Muslim who converted to Christianity, spent years battling authorities for permission to marry a Christian and to register as a Christian herself.[21]

In March 2007 the Islamic Religious Department in the Malaysian state of Malacca seized the fifteen-month-old daughter of Revathi Masoosai, a Muslim woman who had converted to Hinduism. Masoosai herself, according to the Associated Press, was committed to a "rehabilitation center run by Islamic authorities for her religious transgression."[22]

That same month, a woman's application to renounce Islam was denied by a sharia high court.[23] Zulhaidi Omar, a young Muslim who discovered that he was ethnically Chinese and had been switched to different parents at birth, likewise faced obstacles in renouncing the religion in which he had been raised.[24] And in April 2005, a government minister, Datuk Seri Mohammed Nazri Abdul Aziz Nazri, announced that Bibles in the Malaysian language were banned.[25]

Malaysian Christians have also gone without Christmas. In a nice coalescence between the aims of jihadists and Western secularists, Malaysian officials announced in 2004 that in order to "protect Muslim sensibilities," public Christmas celebrations attended by King Syed Sirajuddin and Prime Minister Abdullah Badawi would include no reference to Jesus.[26]

"If they want sharia, let them have it," says D'Souza. But unfortunately, when a Muslim majority gets sharia, non-Muslims get it too, even against their will. When British deputy prime minister John Prescott praised Malaysia's "tolerance" and said that Britain should learn from it, he was widely derided for ignoring Malaysia's increasingly poor record in dealing with its Christian, Buddhist, and Hindu minorities.[27]

TURKEY: A SECULAR STATE SLIDING TOWARD SHARIA

As World War I drew to a close, Mustafa Kemal Ataturk emerged from the ashes of the Ottoman Empire to establish the first Western-style republic in a majority-Muslim country. Ataturk was quite open about his goals. He said, "The civilized world is far ahead of us. We have no choice but to catch up. It is time to stop nonsense, such as 'should we or should we not wear hats?' We shall adopt hats along with all other works of Western civilization. Uncivilized people are doomed to be trodden under the feet of civilized people."[28] Ataturk preferred Western hats because their brims interfered with the frequent prostrations of Islamic prayer. And this was just one of many "anti-Islamic" measures he instituted in an effort to constrain political Islam. To this day, Muslim preachers in Turkish mosques must read a sermon issued by the state religion ministry, rather than deliver their own.

There was always resistance. Many Turks, according to Ataturk's biographer Andrew Mango, believed that "misery was the fruit of impiety, prosperity the reward of obedience to the law of Islam."[29] Religious uprisings have been a feature of the Turkish secular state virtually since its inception, and over the decades those desiring to restore Islam to centrality in public life have made steady gains. Politician Necmettin Erbakan led pro-Islamic forces against the Kemalist regime for three decades. Although forthrightly anti-Kemalist, he served as prime minister of the Kemalist state briefly in the 1990s; during his tenure, U.S. secretary of state Madeleine Albright spoke disapprovingly about the "drift of Turkey away from secularism."[30]

But that drift has only continued since then. Recep Tayyip Erdogan, a former member of Erbakan's now-disbanded National Salvation Party (which was outlawed for threatening the Turkish state's secular constitution), became Turkey's prime minister in March 2003. Erdogan was the front-runner to become president in the May 2007 elections until he withdrew because of public protests. The protesters feared Erdogan would destroy the Turkish secular state and restore Islamic rule.[31]

For many non-Muslims, however, Turkey is already less than a secular state. After his visit to Turkey in November 2006, Pope Benedict XVI asked the Turkish government to give legal status to the Catholic Church, which Turkey has refused to grant—even more than seven decades after the creation of the "secular" republic and a constitutional promise of religious freedom.[32] Christians face other discrimination as well. While the Turkish secular state does not enforce the traditional Islamic death penalty for apostasy, converts from Islam face various forms of harassment. In November 2006, two converts to Christianity, Hakan Tastan and Turan Topal, were put on trial for "insulting 'Turkishness.'"[33] The same week, a Protestant church was firebombed. Before that, it had been

stoned for months, with no interference by the police.[34] And the ecu-
menical patriarch of Constantinople faces ongoing low-level harassment
that leaves him with a dwindling, demoralized community and scant hope
for the future.[35]

Democracy? Perhaps. But not equality of rights. And that means that
democratic principles will in the course of time be undermined, whether
by Erdogan or one of his successors.

CHRISTIANITY AND DEMOCRACY

It was Christianity that gave the world the idea of separation of church
and state and of equality of rights before the law. Philosopher and cultural
analyst Roger Scruton observes that Christ's "Render therefore to Caesar
the things that are Caesar's; and unto God the things that are God's" "contrasts radically with the vision set before us in the Koran, according to
which sovereignty rests with God and His Prophet, and legal order is
founded in divine command."[36] And when those divine commands are
understood as denying equality of rights to non-Muslims (cf. Qur'an 9:29),
then it is exceedingly difficult, if not impossible, for states constituted
according to Islamic law to guarantee the same rights to all their citizens.

From a Muslim perspective, this is a virtue. Seyyed Hossein Nasr, a
professor at George Washington University and author of many books
about Islam, suggests that Christianity was incomplete because, unlike
Islam, it offered no comprehensive system for governance. Nasr asserts
that because Christianity "had no divine legislation of its own, it had to
absorb Roman law in order to become the religion of a civilization." Therefore "in Christian civilization law governing human society did not enjoy
the same divine sanction as the teachings of Christ. In fact this lack of a
divine law in Christianity had no small role to play in the secularization
that took place in the West during the Renaissance." By contrast, "Islam
never gave unto Caesar what was Caesar's. Rather, it tried to integrate the
domain of Caesar itself, namely, political, social, and economic life, into
an encompassing religious worldview."[37]

Jihadist Sayyid Qutb stated this idea more bluntly in 1948. After criticizing both the Communist world and the West for their materialism, he

continues, "But Christianity... cannot be reckoned as a real force in opposition to the philosophies of the new materialism; it is an individualist, isolationist, negative faith. It has no power to make life grow under its influence in any permanent or positive way.... Christianity is unable, except by intrigue, to compete with the social and economic systems that are ever developing, because it has no essential philosophy of actual, practical life. On the other hand, Islam is a perfectly practicable social system in itself.... It offers to mankind a perfectly comprehensive theory of the universe, life, and mankind."[38] In short, Islam offers a totalitarian, theocratic vision—which might be quite attractive to true believers like Qutb, but remains less appealing to dissenters.

Scruton notes that in contrast to this theocratic framework within Islam, "the fifth-century Pope Gelasius I made the separation of church and state into doctrinal orthodoxy, arguing that God granted 'two swords' for earthly government: that of the church for the government of men's souls, and that of the imperial power for the regulation of temporal affairs."[39] While the understanding of the relationship between the two has been the source of a great deal of controversy, "throughout the course of Christian civilization we find a recognition that conflicts must be resolved and social order maintained by political rather than religious jurisdiction."[40] One reason why this is so important is for the protection of minorities and dissenters—freedom of conscience, Scruton says, "requires secular government."[41]

Scruton, of course, is not referring to the aggressively anti-religious secularism that has dominated the public discourse on religion in the United States for several decades now, but simply to an established division between religious and political authority, such as has been traditional in the West. Even where state churches exist—as in the Church of England and in some Scandinavian states—the division of authority is clear, and discrimination against religious minorities has long ago been lifted (and lifted on grounds of Christian conscience). And of course in America, Protestants, Catholics, and Jews were guaranteed complete freedom to practice their religions, as a constitutional right, and to help build a polity based on the values they shared in common—from biblical and traditional teachings about the equality and dignity of all people before God.

Traditional Islam, however, does not allow for this. Islamic regimes invoke the death penalty for apostasy because that is what Muhammad commanded. And the very idea of any separation of religion and state is rejected in traditional Islam. Never until modern times were Muslim states ever ruled by anything other than Islamic law—though it wasn't always applied with equal vigor. In the nineteenth and twentieth centuries, Western colonialists brought their legal codes with them, such that many majority-Muslim countries today are ruled by amalgamations of Islamic and Western law.

And that is precisely what the jihadists see as abominable. Tunisian Muslim journalist and theorist Mohamed Elhachmi Hamdi has asserted that "no Islamic state can be legitimate in the eyes of its subjects without obeying the main teachings of the sharia."[42] Hamdi continues: "A secular government might coerce obedience, but Muslims will not abandon their belief that state affairs should be supervised by the just teachings of the holy law."[43] Influential Pakistani writer and political leader Sayyid Abul A'la Maududi taught the same thing, declaring that "the purpose of Islam is to set up a state on the basis of its own ideology and programme."[44]

Hamas, the Islamic resistance movement that is pursuing a relentless jihad against Israel, likewise affirms that establishing rule by Islamic law is a core element of its program: "Secular thought is diametrically opposed to religious thought. . . . For the Islamic nature of Palestine is part of our religion, and anyone who neglects his religion is bound to lose."[45] In April 2007, an al Qaeda–affiliated group in Iraq took credit for a suicide attack on the Iraqi parliament building that killed one and wounded twenty-three. It said the parliamentarians were legitimate targets because they were "apostates," and "the right to legislate belongs to God alone, and whoever disputes that is an apostate. The members of parliament deserve only death."[46]

Fawaz Turki, then a columnist for Saudi Arabia's *Arab News*, late in 2003 criticized the Bush administration's democracy project in the Middle East in milder language, but from essentially the same principles: "President Bush in effect wants Arabs, along with folks elsewhere in the Muslim world, to weld these habits of vision to an idiom appropriated from Jefferson, Locke and Montesquieu. Well, it ain't gonna happen, fellow, not only because the whole enterprise is degrading for its ethnocentric bias, but because that's not the way social systems organically evolve and transform."[47]

The democracy project "degrading for its ethnocentric bias"? If Bush administration officials saw Turki's column, it might have puzzled them, since they were working from the assumption that they were acting to protect and expand the scope of human rights. But the ideas of human rights and representative government that prevail in the West are rooted in Judeo-Christian assumptions not shared by many Muslims. The idea that Islamic law must rule the state is widespread among Muslims—as is amply demonstrated by the election results in the Palestinian Authority, Egypt, and elsewhere, and by the sharia provisions in the new Iraqi and Afghani constitutions. In fact, Muslims have never accepted any alternative to Islamic law except when it has been imposed by force (which is true even in secular Turkey, where the army keeps a lid on political Islam).

JUDEO-CHRISTIAN-ISLAMIC VALUES?

Most Americans aren't aware of it, but they're living in the land of Judeo-Christian-Islamic values. That hyper-hyphenated phrase began to be bandied about by Muslim advocacy groups, including the Council on American-Islamic Relations (CAIR), the Muslim American Society, and the American Muslim Council in 2003, as part of the large-scale public relations initiative they began in order to burnish Islam's image after September 11. Agha Saeed of the American Muslim Alliance recommended that the unwieldy phrase begin to trip off tongues "in all venues where we normally talk about Judeo-Christian values, starting with the media, academia, statements by politicians and comments made in churches, synagogues, and other places."[48]

But unfortunately for Saeed and the other boosters of this concept, the phrase "Judeo-Christian values" has real historical content, while the tripartite phrase does not. The American republic was founded upon values that were derived ultimately from the heritage of the Old and New Testaments. Most of the Founding Fathers were Christians, and those who were deists were strongly influenced by the Christian milieu in which they lived and were educated. Even Thomas Jefferson, the most famous non-Christian among the Founders, once wrote: "The philosophy of Jesus is the most sublime and benevolent code of morals ever offered to man. A more beautiful or precious morsel of ethics I have never seen."[49] Enlightenment thinkers such as John Locke, who laid the groundwork for the concept of non-establishment, also worked within a profoundly Christian cultural and intellectual context; in fact, Locke wrote a book titled *The Reasonableness of Christianity*. Jews have participated in American politics in important ways since the Revolutionary War, seeing in the principles of the Revolution and the burgeoning American republic nothing that contradicted their cherished beliefs. And of course the United States of America, founded by dissenters and refugees from Europe's religious wars, became a state more welcoming to Jews than practically any other in history.

If the American Revolution was in favor of expanding a liberty the colonists already took for granted as their birthright, many Muslims have a very different idea of what constitutes a just revolution. Jihad theorist Sayyid Qutb affirms that Muslims must "strike hard at all those political powers which force people to bow before them and which rule over them, unmindful of the commandments of God, and which prevent people from listening to the preaching and accepting the belief if they wish to do so. After annihilating the tyrannical force, whether it be in a political or a racial form, or in the form of class distinctions within the same race, Islam establishes a new social, economic, and political system, in which the concept of the freedom of man is applied in practice."[50]

"The freedom of man." That does sound like a Judeo-Christian value—until one realizes that he's talking about stoning for adultery, amputation for theft, polygamy, concubinage, the subjugation of women, and the other stipulations of the sharia, all of which he stoutly defended in his voluminous writings. Jihad, Qutb explains, "should leave every individual free to accept or reject [Islam], and if someone wants to accept it, it should not prevent him or fight against him. If someone does this [rejects Islam], then it is the duty of Islam to fight him until either he is killed or until he declares his submission."[51] For Qutb, the "freedom of man" meant freedom for Muslims to force everyone to live under Islamic law. For people with Judeo-Christian values, freedom means something else entirely.

THE QUR'AN: THE HIGHEST AUTHORITY IN AMERICA?

In light of all this, it was not so surprising that CAIR's board chairman, Omar Ahmad, would have said in 1998 that "Islam isn't in America to be equal to any other faith, but to become dominant. The Qur'an should be the highest authority in America, and Islam the only accepted religion on earth." Ahmad denies having said this, and even says he doesn't believe it: "It is not my stance, it is not what I believe in," Ahmad insisted. "The year before [the 1998 event] I was a commissioner for my city and took an oath on the Constitution and never had a problem. It doesn't make sense for me to think that way. I was shocked to hear somebody reported that." However, the original reporter stands by her story.[52] And as CAIR is a spin-off of a Hamas front group, the Islamic Association for Palestine, it would be more surprising if Ahmad, who co-founded CAIR in 1994 with Nihad Awad (who openly declared his support for Hamas that same year), did not hold to the same ideology as that held by Hamas.[53] CAIR spokesman Ibrahim Hooper told the *Minneapolis Star-Tribune* something very similar in 1993: "I wouldn't want to create the impression that I wouldn't like the government of the United States to be Islamic sometime in the future."[54]

Muslim groups have announced their intentions to become more active in American politics, and the election of the first Muslim congressman, Keith Ellison, indicates that these efforts are bearing fruit. But Ellison, who has accepted money from CAIR, has left a great many important questions unanswered.[55] During his campaign Ellison never explained his perspective on the relationship between the sharia and the U.S. Constitution. Whenever his Islamic faith came up, it was clear that he regarded such questions as insulting. Yet when he was faced with similar questions about his Catholicism in 1960, John Kennedy didn't take them as insults. He knew that there were plenty of anti-Catholic bigots, but he also knew that there were plenty of non-bigots with genuine questions, and he was prepared to answer them and affirm that his political decisions would not be dictated by the pope.

The fact is that Islam is the only religion in the world that has a set of detailed legal directives for the ordering of societies, and Muslims around the globe are pressing hard in numerous countries to put those directives into practice.

We cannot assume, in the teeth of centuries of evidence, that Islam will suddenly change its character and become compatible with democratic society as we understand it in the West. Such a transformation might be remotely possible, but only if Muslims explicitly reject sharia and the Islamic view of the state. So far they have not done so in any significant numbers.

CHAPTER ELEVEN

WOMEN IN THE WEST VS. BURQAS AND BEATINGS

Western feminists dislike many things about Christianity; they allege that it forces women into subservience, that it is traditionally anti-abortion, anti-divorce, and anti-sexual freedom. Moreover, the Catholic and Orthodox Churches don't allow female clergy members.

And certainly some of this true. Christianity traditionally does teach that the sanctity of life includes unborn children, that chastity is a virtue, and that divorce is tearing asunder what God has joined—though in the ancient world these Christian propositions were seen as liberating women from being treated as sexual chattel. One can also find passages in the Bible and in the teachings of early church fathers that imply or state a subordinate role for women.

For feminists, St. Paul is one of the prime offenders. But feminists usually neglect the balance that Paul provides, as in Ephesians 5:21–33: "Be subordinate to one another out of reverence for Christ. Wives should be subordinate to their husbands as to the Lord. For the husband is head of his wife just as Christ is head of the church, he himself the savior of the body. As the church is subordinate to Christ, so wives should be subordinate to their husbands in everything." So, yes, St. Paul says that women should be subordinate to their husbands. But he also says that husbands and wives should be "subordinate to one another" and goes on to say, "Husbands, love your wives, even as Christ loved the church. . . . So (also) husbands should love their wives as their own bodies. He who loves his wife loves himself. For no one hates his own flesh but rather nourishes and cherishes it, even as Christ does the church, because we are members of his body.... In any case, each one of you should love his wife as himself, and the wife should respect her husband."

This idea of how man and woman become one body, of how they complement one another, goes even deeper for Paul in the context of what it means to be a Christian: "For as many of you as were baptized into Christ have put on Christ. There is neither Jew nor Greek, there is neither slave nor free, there is neither male nor female; for you are all one in Christ Jesus. And if you are Christ's, then you are Abraham's offspring, heirs according to promise" (Galatians 3:27–29). This is a statement of equality of the sexes that one will not find in Islam.

In the Islamic world, there are advocates for women's rights, but obviously the status of women in Islamic societies is nothing like what it is in the West. And yet some feminists are so full of hatred for Christianity and the West that they have not hesitated to ally with the forces of global jihad. The most outrageous example of this is leftist lawyer Lynne Stewart, who was convicted in February 2005 of smuggling messages for jailed sheikh Omar Abdel Rahman, the mastermind of the 1993 World Trade Center bombing. She explained that she did it because she saw Sheikh Omar as an ally in the larger struggle: "To rid ourselves of the entrenched, voracious type of capitalism that is in this country that perpetuates sexism and racism, I don't think that can come nonviolently."[1]

JIHADISTS CRITIQUE THE TREATMENT OF WOMEN IN THE WEST

How did Stewart get the idea that Omar Abdel Rahman, a traditionalist Muslim who no doubt believes that women exist to serve men and that disobedient ones should be beaten (as per Qur'an 4:34), was a champion of the fight against sexism and racism?

She may have imbibed the Islamic jihadist critique of the status of women in the West today; jihadists often criticize the West for its materialistic, consumerist society that objectifies and degrades women. In his October 6, 2002, letter to the American people, Osama bin Laden touched on these themes: "You are a nation that exploits women like con-sumer products or advertising tools calling upon customers to purchase them. You use women to serve passengers, visitors, and strangers to increase your profit margins. You then rant that you support the liberation of women.... You are a nation that practices the trade of sex in all its forms, directly and indirectly. Giant corporations and establishments are established on this, under the name of art, entertainment, tourism, and freedom, and other deceptive names you attribute to it."[2]

As an alternative to this, Muslim critics of the West posit Islam as offering a vision of morality that respects the dignity of women. The Mus-lim Women's League, an American organization based in Los Angeles, even states that "spiritual equality, responsibility, and accountability for both men and women is a well-developed theme in the Qur'an. Spiritual equality between men and women in the sight of God is not limited to purely spiritual, religious issues, but is the basis for equality in all tempo-ral aspects of human endeavor."[3] These are venerable themes. As long ago as 1948, jihadist theorist Sayyid Qutb noted that France had recently granted women the right to administer their own property, and wrote acidly: "Islam has for fourteen centuries granted to women privileges which France had only just granted them. It has always granted them the right to work and the right to earn, which Communism now grants them."[4] A Muslim women's advocate in Egypt, Dr. Nawal El-Saadawi (who has suffered for her Islamic heterodoxy), recently insisted, "Our Islamic reli-gion has given women more rights than any other religion has, and has guaranteed her honour and pride."[5]

The case for this rests chiefly on several verses of the Qur'an. "Men," commands the Muslim holy book, "have fear of your Lord, who created you from a single soul. From that soul He created its mate, and through them He bestrewed the earth with countless men and women" (4:1). Allah adds, "I will deny no man or woman among you the reward of their labours. You are the offspring of one another" (3:195). Also, "Be they men or women, those that embrace the Faith and do what is right We shall surely grant a happy life; We shall reward them according to their noblest deeds" (16:97). It would seem, then, that Allah favors neither men nor women, but gives each individual what he or she deserves.

Muslim feminists and their allies assert that any oppression of women in Muslim countries occurs in spite of Islam, not because of it, and that the genuine Islamic attitude toward women is one of unstinting respect. The *hijab*, an Islamic head scarf, is an alleged example of this because it protects women from the lustful looks of men.

But the undeniable reality is that the condition and status of women in the Islamic world today is far worse than anything women have ever endured in the West. When women in the Islamic world live according to Western norms, it is only because of Western influence—which is targeted, often violently, by Islamic hard-liners. And the situation is getting worse. While the great majority of women in cities like Cairo and Damascus ventured outside with their heads uncovered a generation ago (when Western influence was stronger), today the great majority of women wear headscarves, and even non-Muslim women are sometimes pressured to wear them.[6] This is one element of the worldwide movement to restore what is seen as the purity of Islamic law. Another was the Taliban in Afghanistan, with its requirements that women wear stifling *burqas*, long gowns that cover their bodies entirely, even their faces; that women be denied schooling; and that they not venture outdoors unaccompanied. The Taliban, of course, repeatedly and insistently invoked Islamic law to justify these measures.

Such measures are not incidental to Islam—they are fundamental to it. Muhammad's favorite wife, Aisha, once proclaimed, "I have not seen any woman suffering as much as the believing women,"[7] i.e., the Muslim women. And there is abundant evidence to support this view. Women are subservient in the Islamic world to a degree that few in the West realize—in accord with Aisha's words of warning to her sister Muslims: "O womenfolk, if you knew the rights that your husbands have over you, every one of you would wipe the dust from her husband's feet with her face."[8]

Unfortunately for women, sharia law, rooted in seventh-century directives of the Qur'an and the prophet Muhammad, does not envision women as equal members of society. On the contrary, they are regarded as veritable possessions of men to be used as they will. One Islamic tradition even quotes Muhammad saying, "If a husband calls his wife to his bed (i.e., to have sexual relation) and she refuses and causes him to sleep in anger, the angels will curse her till morning."[9] This is not merely an ancient tradition now ignored, but is actually one element of a complex of laws and customs most Muslims don't see as seventh-century relics at all, but as part of Allah's eternal and immutable law, forever applicable in all times and places as the best possible ordering for human society.

AS MANY WIVES AS YOU CAN HANDLE

Islamic law grants a man as many as four wives: "If ye fear that ye shall not be able to deal justly with the orphans, marry women of your choice, two or three or four" (Qur'an 4:3). If a polygamous Muslim man is unhappy with any of his wives, meanwhile, he is under no obligation to put up with a situation that causes him any annoyance: he is free to divorce her by saying "I divorce you."[10] If he says this three times, the divorce is irrevocable, at least to the extent that the couple cannot reunite unless the wife has married and divorced another man. The Qur'an stipulates only that a man wait for a suitable interval in order to make sure that his wife is not pregnant: "Prophet (and you believers), if you divorce your wives, divorce them at the end of their waiting period. Compute their waiting period and have fear of God, your Lord. You shall not expel them from their houses, nor shall they go away, unless they have committed a proven vile deed" (65:1). If the divorcing couple has any children, they ordinarily go with the father, and he owes his wife no financial or any other kind of support.[11]

Divorce, of course, is epidemic in the West, and among the Christian churches only the Catholic church still holds out against it, in accord with Jesus's words—"What therefore God has joined together, let not man put asunder" (Matthew 19:6)—and his direct statement that Moses allowed divorce only "for your hardness of heart" (Matthew 19:8). But the particular Islamic perspective on divorce is by no means identical even to the post-Christian understanding of divorce in the West. Instead, it only reinforces the perception of women as commodities, and subjects them in some cases to degradation: as men can obtain divorces so easily, they often divorce capriciously. But the Qur'an provides for that also: "If a man divorces his wife, he cannot remarry her until she has wedded another man and been divorced by him" (2:230).

This verse is generally understood to refer to a third and final divorce. In such a case, this second marriage must be consummated, as per Muhammad's words when a woman came to him who had been divorced by her husband, had married another man, and now wanted to remarry her first husband. (Her second husband was impotent.) Muhammad was unyielding, telling her that she could not remarry her first husband "unless you had a complete sexual relation with your present husband and he enjoys a complete sexual relation with you."[12] This statement, enshrined in Islamic law, has given rise to the phenomenon of "temporary husbands." After a husband has divorced his wife in a fit of pique, temporary husbands will "marry" the hapless divorcée for one night in order to allow her to return to her husband and family.

The apparent harshness of all this seems to be mitigated by another verse from the Qur'an: "If a woman fear ill-treatment or desertion on the part of her husband, it shall be no offense for them to seek a mutual agreement, for agreement is best" (4:128). But this call for an agreement is not a call for a meeting of equals—at least as it has been interpreted in the hadith. Muhammad's wife Aisha has given an influential analysis of this verse: "It concerns the woman whose husband does not want to keep her with him any longer, but wants to divorce her and marry some other lady, so she says to him: 'Keep me and do not divorce me, and then marry another woman, and you may neither spend on me, nor sleep with me.'"[13]

Yet modern Europe is so thoroughly in thrall to multiculturalism, and so anxious to placate its rapidly growing and increasingly assertive Muslim minorities, that in April 2007 the European Union floated a proposal to allow the divorce laws of non-EU nations to be applied in Europe—effectively opening the door to sharia divorce.[14]

The permission given to men to have as many as four wives is not a relic of the dead past. Muslim immigrants are bringing this practice with them to their new homes in the West. A tragic house fire in March 2007 that killed a woman and nine children in a Bronx row house brought to light a little-noted phenomenon: Islamic polygamy in the United States. Moussa Magassa, the owner of the house and father of five of the children who were killed, had two wives (both of whom survived the fire). The *New York Times* reported that "immigration to New York and other American cities has soared from places where polygamy is lawful and widespread, especially from West African countries like Mali, where demographic surveys show that 43 percent of women are in polygamous marriages."[15]

Mufti Barkatullah, a senior imam in London, stated in 2004 that there were as many as four thousand polygamous families in Great Britain. Dr. Ghayasuddin Siddiqui of the Muslim Parliament in Britain gave a lower estimate that still indicated that the practice was widespread: "I've come across one man who has five wives and I would estimate that there are two thousand men in polygamous marriages in Britain. Of those, one thousand have multiple wives based here and the other one thousand have one here and others in different countries."[16] By late 2004 the British government was considering legalizing polygamy, and in early 2007 it was revealed that Muslim immigrants who arrived in Britain with multiple wives were being allowed to claim extra welfare benefits, even though polygamy remained illegal.[17]

The *Jerusalem Post* reported in July 2005 that polygamy "exists in a vast majority of Islamic countries, where it is permitted by law. And in the twentieth century, it reached European and American shores with the massive wave of immigration from Islamic countries. Interestingly, Europe, while welcoming the reform of the Family Law in Morocco that made polygamy almost impossible, and pressuring Turkey to put an end to the practice (the country's ban on polygamy is commonly overridden), is at the same time turning a blind eye to the existence of the practice within its own borders.... Immigrants from Mali, Egypt, Mauritania, Pakistan, and other countries who come to live in Europe often bring along their extended families, which may contain two, three and even four wives, and all of their offspring."[18]

Polygamy advocates have derided the prevailing Western divorce culture as "serial polygamy." And there is no doubt that there are serious problems for men, women, and children in the prevailing culture of selfishness that derides the notion of a lifelong, total commitment. But the reality of Islamic polygamy makes such a commitment not just difficult, as it is in the West, but completely impossible. Polygamy reduces women to the status of commodities, reinforcing the perspective that men and women are not equal partners, but that women are something that a man may accumulate, like cars or neckties.

"CAPTIVES YOUR RIGHT HANDS POSSESS"

If he has the means to take care of them, a Muslim man may have only four wives at one time, but he is not thus limited in his accumulation of slave girls. The Qur'an directs Muslim men to "marry women of your choice, two or three or four but if ye fear that ye shall not be able to deal justly (with them), then only one, *or (a captive) that your right hands possess*, that will be more suitable, to prevent you from doing injustice" (4:3).

The owning of slave girls is not a thing of the past in Islamic countries. Pakistan, according to Amnesty International, is "both a country of origin and a transit country for the trafficking of women for domestic labor, forced marriage, and prostitution. This form of slavery is organized by crime networks that span South Asia. Some women, both local and trafficked, are killed if they refuse to earn money in prostitution."[19]

The noted feminist activist and author Phyllis Chesler reports that "according to attorney Karima Bennoune, from 1992 on Algerian fundamentalist men have committed a series of 'terrorist atrocities' against Algerian women. Bennoune describes the 'kidnapping and repeated raping of young girls as sex slaves for armed fundamentalists. The girls are also forced to cook and clean for God's warriors . . . one seventeen-year-old girl was repeatedly raped until pregnant. She was kidnapped off the street and held with other young girls, one of whom was shot in the head and killed when she tried to escape.'"[20]

One slave woman in Niger, where, as late as 2005, 8 percent of the population was made up of slaves, was resigned to her fate: "What can I do? I have no money, I need food, I have children, and so if I can work for a man who at least feeds me then that is good."[21]

FOLLOWING IN MUHAMMAD'S FOOTSTEPS: MARRYING CHILDREN

Bennoune's reference to "young girls" could refer even to girls who are prepubescent. Child marriage accords with the example of the prophet

Muhammad: "The Prophet wrote the (marriage contract) with 'Aisha while she was six years old and consummated his marriage with her while she was nine years old and she remained with him for nine years (i.e., till his death)."[22] The Qur'an takes child marriage for granted in its directives about divorce. When speaking about the waiting period required in order to determine if the woman is pregnant, it says: "If you are in doubt concerning those of your wives who have ceased menstruating, know that their waiting period shall be three months. The same shall apply to *those who have not yet menstruated* " (65:4, emphasis added). In other words, Allah is here envisioning a scenario in which a prepubescent girl is not only married, but is also being divorced by her husband.

Imitating the prophet of Islam, many Muslims even in modern times have taken child brides. In some places this even has the blessing of the law: article 1041 of the Civil Code of the Islamic Republic of Iran states that girls can be engaged before the age of nine, and married at nine: "Marriage before puberty (nine full lunar years for girls) is prohibited. Marriage contracted before reaching puberty with the permission of the guardian is valid provided that the interests of the ward are duly observed."[23]

Ayatollah Khomeini of Iran married a ten-year-old girl when he was twenty-eight.[24] Khomeini called marriage to a prepubescent girl "a divine blessing," and advised the faithful, "Do your best to ensure that your daughters do not see their first blood in your house."[25]

Time magazine reported in 2001:

> In Iran the legal age for marriage is nine for girls, fourteen for boys. The law has occasionally been exploited by pedophiles, who marry poor young girls from the provinces, use, and then abandon them. In 2000 the Iranian parliament voted to raise the minimum age for girls to fourteen, but this year, a legislative oversight body dominated by traditional clerics vetoed the move. An attempt by conservatives to abolish Yemen's legal minimum age of fifteen for girls failed, but local experts say it is rarely enforced anyway.[26]

These Islamic practices are even preached in the West. A British television documentary in 2007 taped what goes on in British mosques, and found invocations in favor of killing Jews and homosexuals, advancing jihad, subordinating women, and copying Muhammad's example of marrying nine-year-old girls. Dr. Bilal Phillips, speaking at a mosque in Birmingham, England, was recorded saying: "The prophet Muhammad practically outlined the rules regarding marriage prior to puberty. With his practice, he clarified what is permissible, and that is why we shouldn't have any issues about an older man marrying a younger woman." He continued, "It is looked down upon the society today, but we know that the prophet Muhammad practiced it. It wasn't abuse or exploitation, it was marriage."[27]

That is the attitude of the Islamic world. The United Nations Children's Fund (UNICEF) reports that more than half the girls in Afghanistan and Bangladesh are married before they reach the age of eighteen.[28] In early 2002, researchers in refugee camps in Afghanistan and Pakistan found half the girls married by age thirteen. In an Afghani refugee camp, more than two out of three second-grade girls were either married or engaged, and virtually all the girls who were beyond second grade were already married. One ten-year-old was engaged to a man of sixty.[29] In early 2005 a Saudi man in his sixties drew international attention for marrying *fifty-eight* times; his most recent bride was a fourteen-year-old he married in the spring of 2004.[30]

In early 2007, severe drought in Afghanistan led some Afghanis to sell their daughters into marriages—including girls as young as eight years old—to buy food. One Afghani mother explained: "I need to sell my daughters because of the drought. We don't have enough food and the bride price will enable us to buy food. Three months ago my fifteen-year-old daughter married."[31] Other girls have been sold to make good on opium debts. An Afghani girl named Saliha recounted: "I was thirteen when my father married me off to a twenty-year-old man, whose father had given a loan to my parents and they were unable to return the amount or the quantity of opium."[32]

WIFE BEATING: IT'S IN THE QUR'AN—
AND IN THE ISLAMIC WORLD TODAY

On the heels of child marriage comes more domestic violence: "In Egypt 29 percent of married adolescents have been beaten by their husbands; of those, 41 percent were beaten during pregnancy. A study in Jordan indicated that 26 percent of reported cases of domestic violence were committed against wives under eighteen."[33]

The Qur'an teaches that a husband may beat his wife as the third stage of a disciplinary process that begins with a warning and follows by sending the woman to a separate bed: "Men are in charge of women, because Allah hath made the one of them to excel the other, and because they spend of their property (for the support of women). So good women are the obedient, guarding in secret that which Allah hath guarded. As for those from whom ye fear rebellion, admonish them and banish them to beds apart, and scourge them. Then if they obey you, seek not a way against them. Lo! Allah is ever High, Exalted, Great" (4:34).

Muhammad was once told that "women have become emboldened towards their husbands," whereupon he "gave permission to beat them." When some women complained, Muhammad denigrated those who were complaining: "Many women have gone round Muhammad's family complaining against their husbands. They are not the best among you."[34] He was unhappy with the women who complained, not with their husbands who beat them. At another point he added: "A man will not be asked as to why he beat his wife."[35]

Muhammad even struck his favorite wife, Aisha. One night, thinking she was asleep, he went out; without his noticing, Aisha followed him. When he found out what she had done, he hit her: "He struck me on the chest which caused me pain, and then said: Did you think that Allah and His Apostle would deal unjustly with you?"[36]

These are not just ancient tales to which no one pays attention today. In 1984, Sheikh Yousef al-Qaradawi, who is one of the most respected and influential Islamic clerics in the world, wrote this precise, step-by-step explication of Qur'an 4:34: "If the husband senses that feelings of disobedience and rebelliousness are rising against him in his wife, he should try his best to rectify her attitude by kind words, gentle persuasion, and reasoning with her. If this is not helpful, he should sleep apart from her, trying to awaken her agreeable feminine nature so that serenity may be restored, and she may respond to him in a harmonious fashion. If this approach fails, it is permissible for him to beat her lightly with his hands, avoiding her face and other sensitive parts."[37]

In 2004, an imam in Spain, Mohammed Kamal Mustafa, was found guilty of "inciting violence on the basis of gender" for his book *Women in Islam*, which discussed the methods and limits of administering "physical punishment" of women in accord with Qur'an 4:34.[38]

Even the prominent American Muslim leader Dr. Muzammil H. Siddiqi, former president of the Islamic Society of North America, has said that "in some cases a husband may use some light disciplinary action in order to correct the moral infraction of his wife. . . . The Qur'an is very clear on this issue."[39]

Islamic apologists, including Siddiqi, emphasize that a husband must only beat his wife lightly, so as not to cause her pain or leave any marks. Unfortunately, however, these niceties are all too often overlooked. The Pakistan Institute of Medical Sciences has determined that *over 90 percent* of Pakistani wives have been struck, beaten, or abused sexually—for offenses on the order of cooking an unsatisfactory meal. Others were punished for failing to give birth to a male child.[40] A 2006 study in Syria funded by the United Nations Development Fund for Women found that 25 percent of Syrian women had been victims of domestic violence. One woman commented, "Violence is in every home in the Arab world."[41]

And in the spring of 2005, when the east African nation of Chad tried to institute a new family law that would outlaw wife beating, Muslim clerics led resistance to the measure as un-Islamic.[42] In May 2007, the president of Al-Azhar University and the former mufti of Egypt, Ahmad al-Tayyeb, affirmed the practice's Islamic justification, explaining, "It's not really beating, it's more like punching. . . . It's like shoving or poking her. That's what it is."[43]

COVERING UP

The *burqa* was not invented by the Taliban. The veiling of women is rooted in some of the earliest traditions in Islam. Said Muhammad, "'When a woman reaches the age of menstruation, it does not suit her that she displays her parts of body except this and this,' and he pointed to her face and hands."[44]

While this dictum is not strictly followed in many parts of the Islamic world today, in others women have been brutalized and even killed for not observing it. In February 2007, Zilla Huma Usman, the Pakistani government's minister for social welfare in Punjab province, was shot dead by a Muslim because her head was uncovered. The murderer, Mohammad Sarwar, declared: "I have no regrets. I just obeyed Allah's commandment. I will kill all those women who do not follow the right path, if I am freed again."[45]

When Bangladeshi writer and feminist activist Taslima Nasreen, who has been living in India since she received death threats from Muslims in Bangladesh in 1994, published an article in early 2007 titled "Let's Burn the Burqa," the All India Muslim Personal Law Board reacted swiftly. Nasreen's article, said a board spokesman, was "derogatory and outrageous. . . . She should be thrown out of the country." He announced that the board would approach the government to get Nasreen exiled from Bangladesh.[46]

Phyllis Chesler notes that in Algeria, "as in Iran, 'unveiled,' educated, independent Algerian women have been seen as 'military targets' and increasingly shot on sight." She quotes attorney Karima Bennoune: "The men of Algeria are arming, the women of Algeria are veiling themselves. As one woman said, 'Fear is stronger than our will to be free.'"[47]

In the Muslim holy city of Mecca, fifteen girls perished in a fire at their school in March 2002. The Saudi religious police, the *muttawa*, wouldn't let the girls out of the building: in the female-only school environment, they had shed the concealing outer garments Saudi women must wear in the presence of men. The *muttawa* preferred that the girls die rather than transgress Islamic law, and even battled police and firemen who were trying to open the school's doors.[48]

In line with this kind of thinking, all across the Muslim world women endure restrictions on their movements, their marital options, their professional opportunities, and more. The Qur'an even rules that a son's inheritance should be twice that of a daughter: "Allah (thus) directs you as regards your children's (inheritance): to the male, a portion equal to that of two females" (4:11).

Women have led Muslim countries, but while Tansu Ciller was able to become secular Turkey's prime minister and Benazir Bhutto was even able to rise to leadership in Pakistan, they faced furious opposition from traditionally minded Muslims. Ciller found it necessary to draw ever closer to hard-line Muslim groups.[49] In speaking about opponents to her leadership in Pakistan, Bhutto said that they "saw me as an obstacle in the path of Islamisation of the country."[50] In Kuwait and elsewhere, women cannot vote or hold office. And that's the least of it. According to Amnesty International, in Saudi Arabia "women . . . who walk unaccompanied, or are in the company of a man who is neither their husband nor a close relative, are at risk of arrest on suspicion of prostitution or other 'moral' offences."[51]

PENALIZING WOMEN FOR THEIR OWN RAPES

Accusations of adultery against Muhammad's wife Aisha brought about the requirement that four male Muslim witnesses must be produced in order to establish a crime of adultery or other sexual indiscretions: "Why did they not produce four witnesses? Since they produce not witnesses, they verily are liars in the sight of Allah" (Qur'an 24:13).[52]

Aisha's own word counted for nothing to establish the falsity of the accusations against her—so to this day Islamic law restricts the validity of a woman's testimony, particularly in cases involving sexual immorality. Says the Qur'an: "Call in two male witnesses from among you, but if two men cannot be found, then one man and two women whom you judge fit to act as witnesses; so that if either of them commit an error, the other will remember" (2:282). And Islamic legal theorists have restricted women's testimony even farther, limiting it to, in the words of one Muslim legal manual, "cases involving property, or transactions dealing with property, such as sales."[53] Otherwise only men can testify.

Consequently, even today it is virtually impossible to prove rape in lands that follow these sharia provisions. As long as a man denies the charge and there are no witnesses, he gets off scot-free, because the victim's account is inadmissible. Even worse, if a woman accuses a man of rape, he denies the charge, and she is found to be pregnant, she may end up incriminating herself. If the required male witnesses can't be found, the victim's charge of rape can become an admission of adultery. That accounts for the grim fact that as many as 75 percent of the women in prison in Pakistan are behind bars for the crime of being a victim of rape.[54] Mukhtaran Mai, a rape victim and women's rights activist in Pakistan, said of rape and violence against women: "Such inhuman acts are increasing in Pakistan as the government is not sincere about punishing offenders."[55]

Why not? The former mufti of Australia, Sheik Taj Din al-Hilali, may have given a hint in October 2006. He sparked an international outcry when he explained during a Ramadan sermon that women were usually to blame when they were raped. "If you take out uncovered meat," he said, "and place it outside on the street, or in the garden or in the park, or in the backyard without a cover, and the cats come and eat it . . . whose fault is it, the cats or the uncovered meat? The uncovered meat is the problem. If she was in her room, in her home, in her hijab, no problem would have occurred." Women bore the responsibility in most cases: "It is said in the state of *zina* (adultery), the responsibility falls 90 percent of the time on the woman. Why? Because she possesses the weapon of enticement (*igraa*)."[56]

As outlandish as all this sounds to Western ears, Islamic hard-liners hold such views unapologetically and cling tightly to the Islamic evidence laws set out in the Qur'an. When President Pervez Musharraf's government in Pakistan acted to remove rape from the sphere of Islamic law and have it judged by modern standards of forensic evidence, a group of Islamic clerics were furious. They demanded that the new law be withdrawn: it would turn Pakistan, they said, into a "free-sex zone." Sahibzada Abul Khair Mohammed of the Jamiat Ulema-e-Pakistan (Assembly of Pakistani Clergy) thundered that the new law was "against the teachings of Islam"; other clerics agreed that it "un-Islamic," violating the dictates of the Qur'an and Sunnah, and passed only to appease the West.[57]

Several recent high-profile cases in Nigeria have also revolved around rape accusations reversed by Islamic authorities into charges of fornication, resulting in death sentences that were modified only after international pressure.[58] A seventeen-year-old Nigerian girl named Bariya Ibrahim Magazu was sentenced to one hundred lashes for fornication after she was discovered to be pregnant. She accused several men of possibly being the father; when they all denied having had relations with her, she received an additional eighty lashes for false witness.[59]

Also, in the shame/honor culture of Islam, women who are raped are often seen not as victims but as carriers of shame into the family. In March 2007, a nineteen-year-old Saudi woman received a sentence of ninety lashes. Her crime? She was blackmailed, kidnapped, gang-raped, and beaten: a man threatened to tell her father that they were having an affair unless she met him alone. When she did, she was kidnapped and repeatedly raped, after which her brother beat her because the rapes brought shame to the family. A Saudi court sentenced her to be lashed ninety times because she had met a man alone who was not related to her.[60] According to Phyllis Chesler, "In 2004, a sixteen-year-old girl, Atefeh Rajabi, was hanged in a public square in Iran. Her crime? Rajabi was charged with adultery—which probably means she was raped. Her rapist was not executed. Rajabi told the mullah-judge, Haji Rezaii, that he ought to punish men who rape, not their victims. The judge both sentenced and personally hanged Rajabi because, he said, 'she had a sharp tongue.'"[61]

Time magazine reported in 2004 about "a sixteen-year-old girl named Rana who was raped by her neighbor last April in the city of Nasiriyah [in Iraq]. When her family discovered what had happened, her brothers decided to kill her, since she was no longer a virgin. A cousin who was aware of the plan took Rana to a nearby Italian military base; she was later moved to Baghdad and finally to a secret location farther north. Having fled her family, she is unlikely ever to return home. 'We hope to get a written guarantee from her parents that she will not be killed,' says Zemnakow Aziz, a Workers' Communist Party official. 'Even then we cannot be sure they will stick to it.' Ultimately, Aziz says, he will try to find an Iraqi family abroad to take her in."[62]

FEMALE GENITAL MUTILATION

Yet another source of misery for women in some Islamic countries is female circumcision. This is not a specifically Islamic custom; it's found among a number of cultural and religious groups in Africa and South Asia.

Among Muslims it's prevalent mainly in Egypt and surrounding lands. Yet despite the fact that there is scant (at best) attestation in the Qur'an or hadith for this horrific practice, the Muslims who do practice it invest it with religious significance. One Islamic legal manual states that circumcision is required "for both men and women." An official of Cairo's Al-Azhar, Islam's oldest and most prestigious university, says that this manual "conforms to the practice and faith of the orthodox Sunni community."[63]

To Sheikh Muhammad Sayyed Tantawi, the grand imam of Al-Azhar, female circumcision is "a laudable practice that [does] honor to women."[64] Tantawi is no fringe figure: George W. Bush invoked him in the aftermath of the September 11 terrorist attacks as a Muslim leader who denounced terrorism.[65] Moreover, as the grand imam of Al-Azhar, he is, in the words of a BBC report, "the highest spiritual authority for nearly a billion Sunni Muslims."[66] In endorsing female circumcision he uses this considerable spiritual authority to perpetuate a practice that gives women lifelong pain, which can be quite severe depending on how the procedure is done. But perhaps in the eyes of Sheikh Tantawi the pain is worth the result: most authorities agree that female circumcision is designed to diminish a woman's sexual response, so she will be less likely to commit adultery.

FOR THE SAKE OF HONOR

Honor killing has no sanction in the core Islamic texts, yet it is a byproduct of a culture that focuses far more on shame and honor than on individual responsibility. And this is a development of attitudes inculcated by Islam. Thus it was not surprising when the Jordanian parliament in 2003 voted down a provision designed to stiffen penalties for honor killings. According to al-Jazeera, "Islamists and conservatives said the laws violated religious traditions and would destroy families and values."[67]

In 2006 the Human Rights Commission of Pakistan estimated that about a thousand women are killed for honor every year in that country.[68] Honor killings are also distressingly common in Jordan. The *Chicago Tribune* reported that "On May 31, 1994, Kifaya Husayn, a sixteen-year-old Jordanian girl, was lashed to a chair by her thirty-two-year-old brother. He gave her a drink of water and told her to recite an Islamic prayer. Then he slashed her throat. Immediately afterward, he ran out into the street, waving the bloody knife and crying, 'I have killed my sister to cleanse my honor.' Kifaya's crime? She was raped by another brother, a twenty-one-year-old man. Her judge and jury? Her own uncles, who convinced her eldest brother that Kifaya was too much of a disgrace to the family honor to be allowed to live."[69] Could the rapist have denied his involvement, thus placing all the responsibility on the shoulders of his poor sister? Whatever the case, the court that prosecuted Kifaya Husayn's brother showed how much they valued his sister's life: he was given fifteen years in prison, which was later reduced to seven.

In Jordan in 1999, "a brother put four bullets into his sister's head—in their living room—and was proud of it. His sister's rape had 'dishonored' the family."[70] In 2007, a Jordanian man who murdered his sister because he thought she had a lover was given a three-month sentence, which was suspended for time served, allowing him to walk free.[71] In January of the same year, a father shot his seventeen-year-old daughter dead because he feared she was no longer a virgin; an examination proved her chastity, but he probably need not be concerned that he will serve any significant jail time.[72]

According to *Time* magazine, in September 2003 in Iraq "Ali Jasib Mushiji, seventeen, shot his mother and half-brother because he suspected them of having an affair and killed his four-year-old sister because he thought she was their child. Sitting in a jail cell in the Baghdad slum of Sadr City, he says he wiped out his family to cleanse its shame."

Mushiji was not alone. According to the same report, "last month a Baghdad coroner reported the death of Mouna Adnan Habib, thirty-two, a mother of two, who had been delivered to the city morgue with five bullets in her chest. Habib's left hand had been cut off—a practice common in honor killings, in which men amputate the woman's left hand or index finger to display as proof to tribal leaders and relatives that the deed has been done. In Habib's case, relatives suspected her of having an affair. 'They saw her talking to a man a few times,' said al-Jadr, whose staff investigated the case. Local police have told al-Jadr that they believe Habib was killed by her nephew rather than her husband but that they cannot find the man, who they say has not since returned to the family house."[73]

Such incidents are not at all unusual. Phyllis Chesler reports that in 1997 in Cairo "twenty-five-year-old Nora Marzouk Ahmed's honeymoon ended when her father chopped off her head and carried it down the street. 'Now,' he said, 'the family has regained its honor.' Nora's crime? She had eloped." And "in 2002, in Tehran, an Iranian man cut off his seven-year-old daughter's head after suspecting she had been raped by her uncle. 'The motive behind the killing was to defend my honor, fame, and dignity.' Some people called for this man's death under Islamic law, but ironically, only the father of the victim can demand the death sentence."

Chesler recounts many other such killings. "In 1999, in Lahore, Pakistan, Samia Imran was shot dead in her feminist lawyer's office by a man whom her parents had hired to kill her. Her crime? Seeking a divorce.... In 2001, in Gujar Khan, Pakistan, Zahida Perveen's husband attacked her, gouged out both her eyes, her nose, and her ears. He wrongly suspected her of adultery. He was arrested, but male relatives shook his hand and men decided she 'must have deserved it' and that a 'husband has to do what a man has to do.'... In 2005, in Gaza, five masked members of Hamas... shot Yusra Azzumi, a twenty-year-old Palestinian woman, to death, brutalized her corpse, and savagely beat both her brother, Rami, and her fiancé, Ziad Zaranda, whom she was to marry within days. This self-appointed Morality Squad wrongly suspected Yusra (herself a Hamas member) of 'immoral behavior.'"[74]

A Palestinian Arab girl, Rofayda Qaoud, became pregnant in 2003 after her brothers raped her. Her mother then demanded she kill herself, and killed her when the girl refused. According to a news report: "Armed with a plastic bag, razor, and wooden stick, Qaoud entered her sleeping daughter's room last January 27. 'Tonight you die, Rofayda,' she told the girl, before wrapping the bag tightly around her head. Next, Qaoud sliced Rofayda's wrists, ignoring her muffled pleas of 'No, mother, no!' After her daughter went limp, Qaoud struck her in the head with the stick. Killing her sixth-born child took twenty minutes, Qaoud tells a visitor through a stream of tears and cigarettes that she smokes in rapid succession. 'She killed me before I killed her,' says the forty-three-year-old mother of nine. 'I had to protect my children. This is the only way I could protect my family's honor.'"[75]

Honor killings have come to Western Europe with Muslim immigration. A Turkish Muslim woman, Hatin Sürücü, was murdered in February 2005. The killers were her three brothers, who she had enraged by leaving an arranged marriage. One young Muslim in Germany thought she had earned her death: "Well, she lived like a German, didn't she?"[76]

In early 2007, Soraida Abdel-Hussein of the Women's Center for Legal Aid and Counseling in the Palestinian Arab city of Ramallah blamed Israel for honor killings: "Being under oppressive occupation gives you a feeling of low self-esteem, of being less intelligent, less powerful, less of everything. That hits the masculine identity—and women pay the price. Men internalize the values of violence. They replicate the roles of occupier and victim."[77] But even if this is a factor among Palestinians, it cannot explain honor killings elsewhere in the Islamic world. Islam's culture of shame and honor does.

STONING ADULTERESSES: NOW YOU SEE IT, NOW YOU DON'T

Islamic law mandates stoning for adultery. Some Muslim apologists point out that such a penalty is not specified in the Qur'an, which is true, and that therefore Islamic law has strayed from the purity of the faith, which is not true.

It would be highly unusual to have a stipulation of Islamic law that directly contradicts the Qur'an. The Qur'anic punishment for adultery is one hundred lashes. The penalty is the same for men and women.[78] So where does the stoning for adultery come from? The mystery is solved by Muhammad's companion Umar, who became the second caliph of Islam: "Stoning is a duty laid down in Allah's Book for married men and women who commit adultery when proof is established, or if there is pregnancy, or a confession."[79] Yet there is no such command in the Qur'an. Umar explains that it was originally there, but somehow dropped out:

Allah sent Muhammad with the Truth and revealed the Book (the Qur'an) to him, and among what Allah revealed, was the Verse of the

Rajm (the stoning of married persons—male and female) who commits illegal sexual intercourse, and we did recite this Verse and understood and memorized it. Allah's Messenger did carry out the punishment of stoning and so did we after him.

I am afraid that after a long time has passed, somebody will say, "By Allah, we do not find the Verse of the *Rajm* in Allah's Book," and thus they will go astray by leaving an obligation which Allah has revealed. And the punishment of the *Rajm* is to be inflicted to any married person (male and female) who commits illegal sexual intercourse if the required evidence is available or there is conception or confession.[80]

So while the verse of stoning is not in the Qur'an, it is still enforced in the states that still implement the fullness of Islamic law: Saudi Arabia and Iran. Paradoxically, while the verse of stoning *is* in the Torah, it is not enforced today by Jews. But neither Jews nor Christians regard such works with the strict literalism that is theologically mainstream in Islam. In the Muslim world, sharia provisions may be set aside in favor of Western norms, but they cannot be set aside on Islamic grounds, especially when the provision is a hadith—a tradition of Muhammad—taught by a well-attested source and affirmed by Islamic scholars as authentic.

Accordingly, there have been several high-profile death penalty adultery cases in recent years, notably in Nigeria. Sufiyatu Huseini, a Muslim woman, was given the death sentence for adultery. Her child was evidence enough to establish her guilt, but the man she said had raped her denied the charge. For Sufiyatu Huseini to make her case, she would have had to produce four male witnesses to the actual crime. Aliyu Abubakar Sanyinna, the attorney general of Nigeria's Sokoto state, said that the sentence was "the law of Allah."[81] Huseini's conviction was ultimately overturned after international protests. Other women in the Islamic world, however, haven't been so lucky.

The achievements of a few women in the Islamic world who have risen to political power or other prominence do not outweigh the great burdens the many must carry. Religiously sanctioned wife beating, polygamy, and the prosecution and murder of rape victims—all this and more is what

Islamic law justifies and what jihadists are fighting to implement around the world. To see Christianity as somehow inherently misogynistic, and to see Islam as somehow a bulwark against "sexism," manifests a massive ignorance of the teachings of the respective religions as well as the reality of Christian and Islamic societies today.

CHAPTER TWELVE

YES, VIRGINIA, WESTERN CIVILIZATION IS WORTH DEFENDING

When Dinesh D'Souza stated his startling thesis that "the cultural left in this country is responsible for causing 9/11"[1] in his book *The Enemy at Home*, his point was that the aggressive exporting of degenerate American pop culture all over the world had made Muslims feel they had to fight to defend their traditional values. There is a certain truth to this. With their view of the West as the locus of irreligion and license, most Muslims treat with contempt the idea that America is trying to bring "freedom" to Afghanistan and Iraq. In the words of one young Saudi imam: "Your leaders want to bring your freedom to Islamic society. We don't want freedom. The difference between Muslims and the West is we are controlled by God's laws, which don't change for 1,400 years. Your laws change with your leaders."[2] Jihadists routinely deride Western freedom as libertinism: "In essence," one explained, "the kufr [unbelief] of Western society can be summed up in one word which is used over and over to justify its presence, growth, and its glorification . . . Freedom. Yet what such a society fails to comprehend, is that such 'freedom' simply represents the worship and enslavement to desires, opinions, and whims, a disregard for what is (truly) right, and a disregard for the Creator of the Heavens and the Earth."[3]

MADONNA DOES MECCA

While many of us might deplore the depravity of today's pop culture, we should not let Islamic moral critique put us on the defensive. In reality, the freedom at which the jihadists sneer is an essential component of any genuine morality. "Australian law guarantees freedoms up to a crazy level," remarked the controversial former Australian mufti Sheikh Taj al-Din al-Hilali—but without freedom, even "up to a crazy level," morality is hollow.[4] The secular West, with all its irreligion and debauchery, provides the only authentic framework for genuine virtue. Without the freedom to choose evil, choosing good is not a virtue. It's nothing more than submitting to coercion. And as anyone who has studied Islam knows, the coerced conformity of Islamic society masks a rampant hypocrisy, as was manifested by the September 11 terrorists who—when they weren't plotting to kill innocents—were sitting in strip bars (although they may have been counting on their supreme act of jihad to outweigh all their indiscretions on the divine scales), and by the long tradition of tolerance for pederasty in Islamic society. Islam's moral critique likewise founders on the divine sanction given to violence in the Qur'an and Islamic tradition.

Violent coercion is a fundamental element of sharia law, with its stonings and amputations. Ayatollah Khomeini admitted this without apology: "Whatever good there is exists thanks to the sword and in the shadow of the sword! People cannot be made obedient except with the sword! The sword is the key to Paradise, which can be opened only for the Holy Warriors!"[5] Dinesh D'Souza himself wrote eloquently on this point in 2004: "Consider the woman in Afghanistan or Iran who is required to wear the veil. There is no real modesty in this, because the woman is being compelled. Compulsion cannot produce virtue; it can only produce the outward semblance of virtue." He mocked those who imagined that a cleanup of American pop culture would lessen the force of the jihad: "Some Americans may be tempted to say, 'The Muslims have a point about Jerry Springer and Howard Stern. If they will agree to stop bombing our buildings, in exchange for us sending them Springer and Stern to do with as they wish, why not make the deal? We could even throw in some of Springer's guests.'"[6]

Yet by 2007 D'Souza had joined those he had earlier derided, claiming that the failure to throw Springer and Stern to the wolves was creating more jihadists: "When you make America synonymous with permissiveness, when you dismiss serious moral offenses with a no-big-deal attitude . . . you are driving the traditional Muslims into the arms of the radicals."[7]

It is true that the jihadists' presentation of themselves as holy warriors fighting Western blasphemers and libertines is a potent recruiting tool. But the proper response to their critique of the West is to challenge them on their own ground: to point out that the Judeo-Christian tradition, with its principle of individual freedom as a prerequisite for virtue, offers a superior vision of God and the world than that offered by Ayatollah Khomeini and his sword as the key to paradise.

Western freedom would be more respected in the Islamic world if it were presented in this moral context. In subjugated Eastern Europe during the Cold War, this was understood, because the opposition to Communism was rooted in Christianity. In Islam, it is not understood. In Islam, the recurrent view of the West is of a culture of immorality, which is one reason, but by no means the only reason, why the jihadist critique carries such weight.

The crucial battlefront in defeating the global jihad is ideological, but on this front, so far, only one side is fighting. Defending the Judeo-Christian civilization of the West is indispensable for defeating the jihadists. And for all the faults of Western society, most people in the world still believe it is superior to the Islamic alternative. Roger Scruton points out that "70 percent of the world's refugees are Muslims fleeing from places where their religion is the official doctrine. Moreover, these refugees are all fleeing to the West, recognizing no other place as able to grant the opportunities, freedoms, and personal safety that they despair of finding at home."

Yet Scruton goes on to note that "equally odd, however, is the fact that, having arrived in the West, many of the Muslim refugees begin to conceive a hatred of the society by which they find themselves surrounded, and aspire to take revenge against it for some fault so heinous that they can conceive of nothing less than final destruction as the fitting punishment."[8]

Many Westerners, driven by a similar hatred of the society and culture in which they have always lived, are willing to abet them. The most formidable and determined enemies of Western civilization may not be the jihadists at all, but the leftists who have located all evil in the Christian West of "theocrat" conspirators, the late Jerry Falwell, the white man's burden, the legacy of Western slavery, xenophobia, and the rest. These are people who even at a time of peril from global jihad think the chief danger comes not from militant Islam, but from their churchgoing neighbors, and who deride the very faith that set the course of Western civilization and established our basic values.

Those of us who do not wish to live under sharia need to reclaim our cultural heritage and defend the Judeo-Christian civilization that has given us the freedoms we enjoy. From Western ideas, rooted in the Judeo-Christian tradition, we can build a moral alliance against Islamic supremacism.

THE INVALUABLE ALLIANCE

All the actual and potential victims of jihad violence—Jews, Christians, Hindus, Buddhists, secular Muslims, atheists, and others—need to unite to defend universal human rights in order to defeat the jihadist onslaught. Disagreements among these groups can be sorted out later.

The common enemy is Islamic supremacism. The popular Saudi sheikh Muhammad Saleh al-Munajjid, whose sermons circulate widely in the Islamic world, recently made abundantly clear how sharply Islamic values differ from those that originated in the Judeo-Christian tradition. He warned that "the Muslim should not be deceived by the so-called Western and European 'human rights' organizations, because although they outwardly appear to support the oppressed and to take a stance against torture and undermining of human dignity in prisons and detention centres—which in general terms are good ideas—they also play other roles, and support other principles which are aimed at destroying the family, and opening the door to slander against Islam and the Prophet (peace and blessings of Allaah be upon him), and all his fellow-Prophets."

And what are those "principles aimed at destroying the family"? Do human rights organizations support prostitution or pornography? Polygamy or pedophilia?

None of that was on the sheikh's mind. Rather, he was upset because these organizations oppose sharia at its most draconian: "They are opposed to the rule of sharee'ah which enjoins hard punishments such as stoning for the adulterer, execution for the apostate, and cutting off the hand for the thief, becoming part of legislation and being implemented, which is in fact very rare." He also criticized their opposition to "the shar'i rulings that have to do with women, such as the necessity of her wali's [guardian's] consent for marriage, the command to observe hijab, and the prohibition on her mixing" with men aside from family members.

He then equated Western freedom with libertinism, again demonstrating no grasp of the necessity of freedom for virtue: "To sum up what these organizations promote: it is that man should be able to do whatever he wants, no matter how perverse. They support lesbians, homosexuals and bisexuals, and religious deviance. They regard it as a human right to disbelieve in whatever religions one wants and to express one's opinion—even about the Prophets—without any fear or shame, and they also support the liberation of woman from the control of her father, husband, or religion."[9]

Sheikh al-Munajjid also criticized several sections of the United Nations' 1948 Universal Declaration of Human Rights, including Article 16, which declares that men and women have equal rights in marriage; Article 18, on freedom of conscience; and Article 19, on freedom of expression. He declared that Muslims and non-Muslims should not enjoy equality of rights before the law: "These so-called rights and freedoms which they call for all people to enjoy regardless of religion make the monotheist and the polytheist equally entitled to these rights and freedoms, so the slave of Allaah and the slave of the Shaytaan are placed on the same level, and every worshipper of rocks, idols, or people is given the complete right and freedom to enjoy his kufr and heresy. This is contrary to the laws of Allaah in this world and the Hereafter."[10]

He derides the guarantee of freedom of conscience as "a call to abolish the ruling on apostasy, and to openly flaunt the principles of kufr [unbelief] and heresy. It is a call to open the door to everyone who wants to criticize Islam or the Prophet of Islam Muhammad (peace and blessings of Allaah be upon him) and to have the freedom to criticize and express oneself with no restrictions." And women's rights? "If marriage was left up to the woman without her guardian's consent, you would see most girls marrying those who enchant them of the wolves of men, who are eager to rob them of their chastity then throw them aside. They also give the wife the same rights of divorce as the husband has. This is something that causes women to turn against their husbands and leads to the break up of their families. The one who knows the nature of men and women will not be able to agree to such nonsense. Western families are not so intact that we can say: Look at how they were destroyed. The call for homosexual rights and the rights of women to form any relationship she wants and women's rights in marriage and divorce—what families can be built on such shaky foundations?"[11]

There can be no accord between this view and one based on Jesus's dictum to let the wheat and tares "grow together until the harvest" (Matthew 13:30), which is predicated on the assumption that there is a higher good than the purity of the community. And that higher good is the development of genuine virtue in the individual, by means of choices made difficult by the ease and allure of choosing evil. But it is up to the individual to make the right choices—and it is the exercise of making the right choice that ennobles man.

Thus ultimately the clash between the Islamic world and the Judeo-Christian West is between two fundamentally opposed visions for society: one based on sharia—a true theocracy—and the other based on freedom. In the Christian view freedom is God's gift to and test of man, and church and state are separate ("Render unto Caesar the things which are Caesar's, and unto God the things that are God's"). This is the very opposite of the Islamic view, which insists on submission rather than freedom, and where there is no distinction between religious law and secular law. The Muslim bears with honor the title "slave of Allah," while Jesus says, "I no longer call you slaves, because the slave doesn't know what the master is doing. But you I have called friends, because everything that I heard from my father, I made known to you" (John 15:15). In Jewish tradition also is a strong emphasis on the freedom and responsibility of the individual, cutting against the conformism and fatalism that the jihadists so vividly illustrate.

Man is noble, and worthy, not because he is a slave, but because he is free. That is what distinguishes the Judeo-Christian view from the

Islamic view of mankind. Sheikh Muhammad Saleh al-Munajjid would say that mankind has value because human beings are the slaves of Allah. Jews and Christians, and even the secularists rooted in the Judeo-Christian culture, would say that mankind has value because human beings are free.

That is the difference. And that makes all the difference.

What about Hindus, Buddhists, secular Muslims, and atheists? The answer is the same: if they value individual freedom, they are natural allies against the global jihad.

THE MEDIA JIHAD AGAINST CHRISTIANS

The need for such an alliance, its feasibility, its obstacles—none of this is being discussed in the mainstream media. They are too busy sounding the alarm about Christian theocracy and equating conservative Christians with Islamic jihadists. Reviewing the documentary film *Jesus Camp*, which was dedicated to sneering at evangelical Christians, Stephen Holden wrote in the *New York Times*: "It wasn't so long ago that another puritanical youth army, Mao Zedong's Red Guards, turned the world's most populous country inside out. Nowadays the possibility of a right-wing Christian American version of what happened in China no longer seems entirely far-fetched."[12] Social critic Michael Medved wrote that the film "explicitly compares an enthusiastic Christian summer program for kids to a terrorist training ground."[13]

After seeing the same movie, musician David Byrne, the front man for the 1980s avant-garde pop group Talking Heads, reacted with full-throttle theocracy paranoia, garnished with a healthy dash of moral equivalence. Byrne even compared the jihadists favorably to the Christian villains of his imaginings: "They want to turn the U.S. into the 'Christian' version of Iran or Saudi Arabia. A theocracy. The separation between church and state, already shaky with Bush in charge, is under full frontal assault by this bunch—and they are well organized, too."[14]

Yet neither Holden nor the *Times* seem particularly concerned about the real terrorists. Neither does Byrne. In 2004 the *Times*'s Nicholas Kristof equated the apocalyptic scenes of the popular evangelical Christian *Left*

Behind novel series to jihadist literature. He fumed: "If a Muslim were to write an Islamic version of 'Glorious Appearing' and publish it in Saudi Arabia, jubilantly describing a massacre of millions of non-Muslims by God, we would have a fit."[15] Kristof was apparently unaware that such books have been published in large numbers in the Islamic world, replete with fervid descriptions of the annihilation of the United States and Israel, sometimes by means of a nuclear explosion set off by the mujahedin. Egyptian writer Bashir Muhammad 'Abdallah sketches out a vision of the end times in which "there will be so many killed that there will be no place to bury them and plagues will be many as a result. . . . This will be God's vengeance because of the claims of Zion and its corruption of all of humanity and the great Jewish arrogance." Another apocalypse fantasist, Muhammad 'Isa Da'ud, says that when the end comes, Israel "will seek its own destruction and dig its own grave."[16]

The media and governing elite seem to have an inverted view of reality. A New Jersey public school recently staged a hostage drill. It was not couched as a repeat of the jihadist attack such as occurred in Beslan, Russia, in September 2004, or more recent FBI warnings about terrorists targeting school buses. No, in the New Jersey school the fictive terrorists were Christians: a "right-wing fundamentalist group" called the New Crusaders, who rejected the separation of church and state.[17]

The New Jersey school administrators might have gotten this idea from the BBC. In November 2006, the British network aired a drama depicting Christian terrorists carrying out a series of attacks against Muslims in England, including the assassination of a Muslim imam. The fictional Christian group announces: "Britain is a nation under Christ. We will no longer tolerate the Muslims in our ranks. This is a declaration of war against Islam." One of the leaders of this Christian terrorist group has trained for the priesthood and believes that his acts of terror are restoring "God's kingdom" and doing "God's will."[18]

The liberal West is much more comfortable attacking itself and condemning the Christians and conservatives in its midst than breaking the multiculturalist taboo and admitting that Western civilization might be better than Islamic civilization. In real life, there is no Christian equivalent to the jihadist group in Iraq that terrorized Baghdad Christians in the spring of 2007, demanding that they convert to Islam or pay the non-Muslim tax (jizya) mandated by Qur'an 9:29 and threatening to burn down churches unless their crosses were removed.[19]

Moral equivalence between Christianity and Islam is either fiction or misappropriated and misrepresented ancient history. Michael Medved points out that "when secularists try to insist that all religions, not just Islam, display a dangerous violent streak, it's deeply revealing that they indict Christianity by reaching back five hundred years (to the Spanish Inquisition) or a thousand years (to the Crusades). It's no exaggeration to say that Muslim extremists around the world committed many, many more violent attacks in the last week than have Christian conservatives in the last ten years." Why, then, the animus against Christians? Because of the chimerical fear of theocracy that animates critics of the "Religious Right," whose adherents, in Medved's words, "merely wish to return to the more hospitable attitude to public expressions of faith that flourished in this nation until the 1960s."[20]

THE GREATEST CIVILIZATION

I have not written this book to proselytize, but to state a fact—a fact that many Muslims cheerfully and proudly avow. Christianity is a religion of peace, and it is a religion without a jihadist movement. Islam is a religion of the sword and there are, by even the most conservative estimates, more than one hundred million active jihadists seeking to impose sharia not only in the Islamic world, but in Europe and ultimately in the United States.

And they will succeed, in time, if Westerners continue to delude themselves that Western civilization is uniquely responsible for the evil in the world, that Christianity is just as inherently violent as Islam, that all cultures are equal in their capacity to inspire magnanimity, nobility, generosity, and greatness of soul.

This is a suicidal myth. Daniel Pipes is correct in saying that Western "pacifism, self-hatred, and complacency are lengthening the war against radical Islam and causing undue casualties. Only after absorbing catastrophic human and property losses will left-leaning Westerners likely overcome this triple affliction and confront the true scope of the threat.

The civilized world will likely then prevail, but belatedly and at higher cost than need have been."[21]

Whether one believes in Christianity or not, it is necessary now for all lovers of authentic freedom to acknowledge their debt to the Judeo-Christian West, to the Judeo-Christian assumptions that built Europe and the United States, and to acknowledge that this great civilization is imperiled and worth defending.

On that first step, everything else depends.

ACKNOWLEDGMENTS

This book would never have been written were it not for Regnery's extraordinary Harry Crocker, whose initial idea and ever-keen stylistic and editorial guidance are responsible for whatever virtues it may possess. I am also indebted to Miriam Moore, Paula Currall, Patricia Jackson, and—as always—Jeff Rubin for their always perceptive observations, suggestions, and encouragement.

Meanwhile, I am grateful for the indefatigable labors of my Jihad Watch colleagues Hugh Fitzgerald, Marisol Seibold, and Gregory M. Davis, who helped ensure that that ongoing effort did not founder while I put this book together. Thanks also to Hugh and Andrew G. Bostom for their gracious and generous help with tracking down some hard-to-find and most relevant historical material.

There are many others whom I cannot name for various reasons, but whose contributions to this work are significant and sizable. I mention their existence here as just one small token of my gratitude, which is immense.

NOTES

Chapter One: No, Virginia, All Religions Aren't Equal

1 David A. Yeagley, "What's Up with White Women?" FrontPageMagazine.com, May 18, 2001.

2 David Machlis and Tovah Lazaroff, "Muslims 'about to take over Europe,'" *Jerusalem Post*, January 29, 2007.

3 Alicia Colon, "Raising American Taliban," *New York Sun*, April 10, 2007.

4 Adeel Pathan, "Ulema demand WPA withdrawal, CII reformation," *The News*, December 17, 2006.

5 "Muslims fear Christians waging 'war against Islam,'" Associated Press, August 4, 2004.

6 Bruce Lawrence, ed. *Messages to the World: The Statements of Osama bin Laden* (London: Verso, 2005), 39.

7 Ibid., 208.

8 "Islamist Holiday Video Calls for Jihad and Slaughter of 'Crusaders,'" Middle East Media Research Institute (MEMRI), Special Dispatch Series No. 1333, Islamist Websites Monitor No. 12, October 24, 2006.

9 "Islamist group urges Algerians to target French," Agence France-Presse, January 10, 2007.

10 "Al Qaeda Operative Adam Gadahn, aka 'Azzam the American,' Calls upon Americans to Convert to Islam," Middle East Media Research Institute, TV Monitor Project Clip No. 1257, September 2, 2006.

11 Abdul Hamid Siddiqi and Kitab Bhavan, trans. *Sahih Muslim* (New
    Delhi: Kitab Bhavan, revised edition, 2000), book 19, no. 4294.
12 "The Duty to Integrate: Shared British Values," Speech given by Prime
    Minister Tony Blair, London, December 8, 2006.
13 Fjordman, "Why Europeans Should Support Israel," *Brussels Journal*,
    March 12, 2007.

Chapter Two: Wars of Religion

1   Ann Coulter, "This Is War: We should invade their countries," *National
    Review*, September 13, 2001.
2   Peter Wehner, "The War Against Global Jihadism,"
    RealClearPolitics.com, January 8, 2007.
3   Remarks by President George W. Bush on U.S. humanitarian aid to
    Afghanistan, Presidential Hall, Dwight David Eisenhower Executive
    Office Building, Washington, D.C., October 11, 2002.
4   "U.S. State Department funding mosque building in Bulgaria," Focus
    News Agency, October 4, 2004; "Faithful spurn U.S.-built mosque,"
    News24.com, February 25, 2004.
5   "Christian Zionists Gear Up for the Apocalypse," Muslim Public Affairs
    Committee of the United Kingdom, January 20, 2007.
6   "Bush aims to boost US tsunami aid," BBC News, February 10, 2005.
7   "British tsunami casualties rise," BBC News, January 10, 2005;
    "Tsunami appeal finishes at £300m," BBC News, February 26, 2005.
8   "Tsunami-Katastrophe: Kabinett beschließt 500 Millionen Euro
    Hilfe für Flutopfer," *Der Spiegel*, January 5, 2005.
9   "Tsunami: Response to the Catastrophe," Canadian International
    Development Agency, http://www.acdi-cida.gc.ca/tsunami-e.
10 Ingvild Jensen, "Stortinget gir én mrd. Ekstra," Nettavisen, January
    3, 2005.
11 Nicholas Blanford, "After slow start, Arab countries crank up tsunami
    relief," *Christian Science Monitor*, January 12, 2005.
12 Mel White, *Religion Gone Bad: The Hidden Dangers of the Christian
    Right* (New York: Penguin, 2006, jacket).
13 Damon Linker, *The Theocons: Secular America Under Siege* (New York:
    Doubleday, 2006), 13.

14 Chris Hedges, *American Fascists: The Christian Right and the War on America* (New York: Free Press, 2006), 24.

15 Richard Dawkins, *The God Delusion* (New York: Houghton Mifflin, 2006), 27.

16 Kevin Phillips, *American Theocracy* (New York: Viking, 2006), 41.

17 Sam Harris, *Letter to a Christian Nation* (New York: Alfred A. Knopf, 2006), 91.

18 "Is Religion 'Built Upon Lies'?" debate between Sam Harris and Andrew Sullivan, Beliefnet.com, January 16, 2007. http://www.beliefnet.com/story/209/story_20904_1.html.

19 John Derbyshire, "God & Me," *National Review*, October 30, 2006.

20 Sam Schulman, "Without God, Gall Is Permitted," *Wall Street Journal*, January 5, 2007.

21 Jim Emerson, "Jonestown: The Life and Death of Peoples Temple," RogerEbert.com, November 22, 2006.

22 Scott Whitlock, "Rosie O'Donnell: 'Radical Christianity Is Just as Threatening as Radical Islam,'" NewsBusters.org, September 12, 2006. http://newsbusters.org/node/7577.

23 David Thompson, "Blunting the Senses in the Name of Fairness," *3:AM Magazine*, August 20, 2006.

24 Yaakov Lappin, "Jihadis aspire to 'conquer France,'" *Ynet News*, April 23, 2007.

25 Arnaud de Borchgrave, "Papal cannon misfires," *Washington Times*, September 20, 2006.

26 Ralph Peters, "Islam-Haters: An Enemy Within," *New York Post*, September 8, 2006.

27 Dinesh D'Souza, *The Enemy at Home* (New York: Doubleday, 2007), 187.

28 Jamie Glazov, "Did the Cultural Left Cause 9/11?" Interview with Dinesh D'Souza, FrontPageMagazine.com, January 25, 2007.

29 Interview with Dinesh D'Souza, *To the Source*, January 17, 2007. http://www.tothesource.org/1_17_2007/1_17_2007.htm.

30 Dinesh D'Souza. "The Closing of the Conservative Mind, Part I: Blindsided from the Right," *National Review*, March 12, 2007.

31 "What is Jihad? Is it carrying weapons to attract more adherents to your religion?" *al-Jazeera*, December 29, 2006.

32 For a clear presentation of this point of view, see B. J. Sabri, "The
    Splendid Failure of Occupation," Part 28: Imperialist Expansions
    and 9/11, Online Journal, March 2, 2005. http://www.onlinejournal.
    com/artman/publish/article_119.shtml.

33 Rich Lowry, "Naming the enemy—just not that important," National
    Review.com, September 5, 2006.

34 James Carroll, "The war against Islam," *Boston Globe*, June 7, 2005.

35 Press conference by President Bush and President Havel of Czech
    Republic, Prague Castle, Prague, Czech Republic, November 20,
    2002.

36 "Fighting terrorism is not a fight against Islam: Downer," Agence
    France-Presse, February 27, 2006.

37 Speech by Tony Blair, September 26, 2006. http://www.labour.org.uk/
    index.php?id=news2005&ux_news%5Bid%5D=primeminister&cHash=
    7e84d2fbb8.

38 "President Bush and Secretary of State Rice Discuss the Middle East
    Crisis," White House press release, August 7, 2006.

39 "Blair condemns bombers who 'act in name of Islam,'" Reuters, July 7,
    2005.

40 Cait Murphy, "The poverty/terror myth," *Fortune*, March 13, 2007;
    Henry Schuster, "Terrorists' backgrounds defy conventional wisdom,"
    CNN, May 24, 2005.

41 Meetu Jain, "PM's priority: Muslim development," CNN-IBN,
    December 9, 2006.

42 "Statement by John Wallach, President and Founder of Seeds of Peace,
    in response to the tragedies that took place on September 11, 2001,"
    http://www.seedsofpeace.org/site/News2?page=NewsArticle&id=5355.

43 Phillips, 259.

44 Ibid., 259–60.

45 Ibid., 260.

46 Barbara Stock, "Michael Moore: Master of Propaganda," *American
    Daily*, July 8, 2004.

47 Book description at Amazon.com. http://www.amazon.com/gp/
    product/product-description/1585425516/ref=dp_proddesc_0/102-
    5792489-3944923?ie=UTF8&n=283155&s=books.

48 Dinesh D'Souza, "Bernard Lewis vs. the Islamophobes," Newsbloggers,
    AOL News, March 6, 2007.

Chapter Three: We Have Met the Enemy and He Is...

1   Kevin Phillips, *American Theocracy: The Peril and Politics of Radical
    Religion, Oil, and Borrowed Money in the 21st Century* (New York:
    Viking, 2006), 217.
2   Damon Linker, *The Theocons: Secular America Under Siege* (New York:
    Doubleday, 2006), 5.
3   Phillips, xv.
4   Michelle Goldberg, *Kingdom Coming: The Rise of Christian
    Nationalism* (New York: W. W. Norton & Company, 2006), 7.
5   Mel White, *Religion Gone Bad: The Hidden Dangers of the Christian
    Right* (New York: Penguin, 2006), 110.
6   Ibid., 111.
7   Ibid., 159, 161.
8   Goldberg, 207, 210.
9   Chris Hedges, *American Fascists: The Christian Right and the War on
    America* (New York: Free Press, 2007), 12.
10 Ibid., 12, 10, 19.
11 Barry Lynn, *Piety & Politics: The Right-Wing Assault on Religious
    Freedom* (New York: Harmony Books, 2006), 2–3.
12 Hedges, 35.
13 Ibid., 201–02.
14 Ibid., 152.
15 Lynn, 2–3.
16 Hedges, 207.
17 Goldberg, 207, 210.
18 Hedges, 201–02.
19 White, 159.
20 Ibid., 109–10.
21 John 7:53–8:11. Anti-sodomy laws, however, have been almost
    universal throughout history, and around the world, as violations of
    natural law. For the most part, only in the latter half of the twentieth
    century did some countries start removing these laws.

22 Walter Olson, "Invitation to a Stoning: Getting cozy with theocrats," *Reason*, November 1998.

23 George Grant, *The Changing of the Guard* (Fort Worth, TX: Dominion Press, 1987), 50–51. Quoted in "The Words of Christinian Reconstuctionists," compiled by Paul Thibodeau, http://www.sullivan-county.com/nf0/fundienazis/fundiewords.htm.

24 George Grant, e-mail to the author, February 24, 2007.

25 "Chalcedon Vision Statement," The Chalcedon Foundation, http://www.chalcedon.edu/vision.php.

26 Chris Ortiz, "Talk2Action vs. Christian Dominion," Chalcedon Blog, The Chalcedon Foundation, February 19, 2007. http://www.chalcedon.edu/blog/2007_02_01_archive.php#117189940092542465.

27 "What Chalcedon Believes," The Chalcedon Foundation, http://www.chalcedon.edu/credo.php.

28 Francis A. Schaeffer, *A Christian Manifesto* (Wheaton, IL: Crossway Books, 1981), 120–21.

29 Bernard Goldberg, *Crazies to the Left of Me, Wimps to the Right: How One Side Lost Its Mind and the Other Lost Its Nerve* (New York: HarperCollins, 2007).

30 Paul Weyrich, "The 'Values Summit' series—legislative opportunities," *Renew America*, July 6, 2006.

31 Hedges, 10.

Chapter Four: The Real Threat

1   Umm Saeed, "Dialogue with Sheikh Abu Musab Al-Zaraqawi: Part Two," *Jihad Unspun*, January 11, 2007.

2   "Islamist Leaders in London Interviewed," Middle East Media Research Institute (MEMRI) Special Dispatch No. 410, August 9, 2002.

3   Jon Dougherty, "Muslim Leaders Pledge to 'Transform West,'" WorldNetDaily.com, August 13, 2002.

4   Abu Hamza al-Masri, *Allah's Governance on Earth*, quoted at http://www.islamistwatch.org/.

5   "I have a question about offensive Jihad," Islam Q & A Online with Mufti Ebrahim Desai, Question 12128 from Canada, July 17, 2004, http://www.islam.tc/ask-imam/view.php?q=12128.

6   "A Video Speech from Dr. Ayman al-Zawahiri Regarding the Events in Lebanon and Gaza: 7/27/2006," SITE Institute, July 27, 2006.

7   Steven Stalinsky, "The 'Islamic Affairs Department' of the Saudi Embassy in Washington, D.C.," Middle East Media Research Institute (MEMRI) Special Report No. 23, November 26, 2003.

8   Sayyid Qutb, *Milestones*, The Mother Mosque Foundation, n.d., 130–31.

9   Sayyid Qutb, "A Muslim's Nationality and His Belief." Reprinted at http://www.witness-pioneer.org/vil/Articles/politics/nationalism.htm.

10 Not to be confused with former Afghani president Burhanuddin Rabbani's Muslim Party, which is usually rendered in English as Jamiat-e-Islami.

11 Syed Ubaidur Rahman, "Jamaat-e-Islami: Where it stands today," *Milli Gazette*, January 15, 2002.

12 Syed Abul A'la Maududi, "Jihad in Islam," Address at the Town Hall, Lahore, April 13, 1939. Reprinted at http://www.muhammadanism.org/Terrorism/jihah_in_islam/jihad_in_islam.pdf.

13 Sayyid Abul A'la Maududi [here, Mawdudi], *Towards Understanding the Qur'an*, Zafar Ishaq Ansari, trans. (Leicestershire, England: The Islamic Foundation, revised edition, 1999), Vol. 3, 202.

14 Qazi Hussain Ahmed, "Ijtihad," Jamaat-e-Islami Pakistan, http://www.jamaat.org/qa/ijtihad.html.

15 "Syed Abu-A'la Maududi's Chapter Introductions to the Qur'an," USC-MSA Compendium of Muslim Texts, http://www.usc.edu/dept/MSA/quran/maududi/.

16 Muhammad 'Abdus Salam Faraj, *Jihad: The Absent Obligation*, 43. Quoted at http://www.islamistwatch.org/texts/faraj/obligation/oblig.html.

17 Duncan Gardham, "Tube bomb accused 'left suicide note,'" *Telegraph*, February 25, 2007.

18 "What is the Khilafah?" Risala.org. http://www.risala.org/content/view/89/32/.

19 "The *Al Qaeda* Manual," U.S. Department of Justice translation, usdoj.gov/ag/manualpart1.1.pdf.

20 Kevin Phillips, *American Theocracy: The Peril and Politics of Radical Religion, Oil, and Borrowed Money in the 21st Century* (New York: Viking, 2006), 206.

21 "President Holds Prime-Time News Conference," White House Press Office, October 11, 2001.

22 Phillips, 259.

23 "President's Radio Address," White House Press Office, March 4, 2006.

24 Afghanistan Constitution, adopted January 4, 2004.

25 Bukhari, vol. 9, book 87, no. 6878.

26 Ibid., book 88, no. 6922; cf. vol. 4, book 56, no. 3017.

27 Thomas Patrick Huges, "Apostasy from Islam," *A Dictionary of Islam* (London: W. H. Allen & Co., 1885), 16.

28 Tim Albone, "Anger over Christian convert in Kabul who faces death," *The Times*, March 21, 2006.

29 "U.S. Backs Afghan Man Who Converted to Christianity," Associated Press, March 22, 2006.

30 "Iraq: Kidnappers Behead Priest In Mosul," *Compass Direct*, October 12, 2006.

31 William Dalrymple, "The final place of refuge for Christians in the Middle East is under threat," *The Guardian*, September 2, 2006.

32 "What Will the Wise Men Bring to Bethlehem?" National Review Online, December 20, 2006.

33 "Iraq: Militant Group Threatens Female Students in Kirkuk," AKI, June 6, 2006.

34 Nimrod Raphaeli, "The Plight of Iraqi Christians," Middle East Media Research Institute Inquiry and Analysis Series No. 213, March 22, 2005.

35 Dalrymple, "The final place of refuge for Christians in the Middle East is under threat."

36 Phillips, 250.

37 "Man beheaded, two shot dead in restive Thai south," Agence France-Presse, March 7, 2007.

38 Florida Catholic Conference, "Spare Paul Hill," press release, August 25, 2003. http://www.flacathconf.org/pressreleases/Prsrel03/SparePaulHill.htm.

39 Albert Mohler, "The Execution of Justice: The Real Meaning of Paul Hill," Crosswalk.com, September 4, 2003.

40 Gary North, "Letter to Paul Hill," September 29, 1994. Reprinted by the Center for Reformed Study and Apologetics, http://www.reformed. org/social/index.html?mainframe=http://www.reformed.org/social/let_ 2_paul_hill.html.

41 Cal Thomas, "Pro-Life, Not Play God," Crosswalk.com, September 4, 2003.

42 Council on American Islamic Relations, "U.S. Muslim Religious Council Issues Fatwa Against Terrorism." http://www.cair-net.org/ downloads/fatwa.htm.

43 Daniel Pipes, "Can Infidels Be Innocents?" www.danielpipes.org, August 7, 2005.

44 "Muslim leaders condemn terrorism," BBC News, June 23, 2006.

45 Also "Choudri," "Choudhury," etc.

46 "The Killings of Non-Muslims Is Legitimate," http://www.youtube.com/ watch?v=maHSOB2RFm4. November 24, 2006.

47 Suzanne Goldenberg, "'It's gone beyond hostility,'" *The Guardian*, August 12, 2002.

48 "Arab Liberals: Prosecute Clerics Who Promote Murder," *Middle East Quarterly*, Winter 2005.

49 John L. Esposito, "Practice and Theory: A response to 'Islam and the Challenge of Democracy,'" *Boston Review*, April/May 2003; "Al-Qaradawi full transcript," BBC News, July 8, 2004.

50 "Al-Qaradawi full transcript."

51 The Council on American-Islamic Relations, "About CAIR," CAIR.com.

52 Christopher Goffard, "Controversy follows Dennis Prager to Yorba Linda," *Los Angeles Times*, January 24, 2007.

53 Deborah Solomon, "Questions for Yusuf Islam; Singing a New Song," *New York Times Magazine*, January 7, 2007.

54 Ian Schwartz, "Video: Imam prays to stop 'oppression and occupation' at DNC meeting," HotAir.com, February 2, 2007.

55 Ian Schwartz, "Video: DNC imam Husham al-Husainy on *Hannity & Colmes*," HotAir.com, February 8, 2007.

56 "DNC's Imam al-Husainy Melts Down on the Air," LittleGreenFootballs.com, February 10, 2007.

57 Andrew Sullivan, *The Conservative Soul* (New York: HarperCollins, 2006), 120–21.

58 Michael Freund, "The straightforward arithmetic of jihad," *Jerusalem Post*, January 30, 2007.

Chapter Five: Cherry-Picking in the Fields of the Lord

1   Martin E. Marty, "Them and us," *Christian Century*, October 3, 2006.

2   Ralph Peters, "Islam-Haters: An Enemy Within," *New York Post*, September 7, 2006.

3   Dinesh D'Souza. "The Closing of the Conservative Mind, Part I: Blindsided from the Right," *National Review*, March 12, 2007.

4   "Eyeing the Enemy: Dinesh D'Souza looks left," *National Review*, January 16, 2007.

5   Jamie Glazov, "Did the Cultural Left Cause 9/11?" Interview with Dinesh D'Souza, FrontPageMagazine.com, January 25, 2007.

6   Chris Hedges, *American Fascists: The Christian Right and the War on America* (New York: Free Press, 2006), 6.

7   These and other approaches are discussed in Eryl W. Davies, "The Morally Dubious Passages of the Hebrew Bible: An Examination of Some Proposed Solutions," *Currents in Biblical Research* no. 3, 2005, 197.

8   The Holy Bible, Revised Standard Version, Catholic Edition (Nashville, TN: Thomas Nelson, 1966), 998.

9   *The Navarre Bible Joshua–Kings* (New York: Scepter Publishers, 2002), 48–49.

10 Andy and Berit Kjos, "JOSHUA: Lesson 9; Conquering Jericho," Kjos Ministries Bible Studies, http://www.crossroad.to/.

11 The Holy Bible, Douay 1609 edition, reprinted by Loreto Publications (Fitzwilliam, NH: 2005), 200.

12 Rev. David Holwick, "Holy Violence," sermon outline, October 11, 1998. http://tonga.globat.com/~holwick.com/joshua/joshua6b.html.

13 Christopher Hitchens, *God Is Not Great* (New York: Warner Twelve, 2007), passim.

14 Bernard of Clairvaux, *De Laude Novae Militiae*, trans. David Carbon from J. Leclercq and H. M. Rochais, eds., "Liber ad milites Templi de

laude novae militiae," in *S. Bernardi Opera*, vol. 3. (Rome, 1963), 206–39. http://faculty.smu.edu/bwheeler/chivalry/bernard.html.

15 Ibid.

16 Osama bin Laden, "Declaration of War against the Americans Occupying the Land of the Two Holy Places," 1996. http://www.mideastweb.org/osamabinladen1.htm.

17 Middle East Media Research Institute, "Bin Laden's Sermon for the Feast of the Sacrifice," MEMRI Special Dispatch No. 476, March 5, 2003.

18 "Jihad in the Qur'an and Ahadeeth," http://www.abdulmateen.com/Mail%20Archive/2002/December/Religious/JihadintheQuranandAhadeeth.htm, 2002.

19 Detroit Free Press, "100 Questions and Answers About Arab Americans," http://www.freep.com/jobspage/arabs.htm, 2001.

20 George W. Bush, "Address to a Joint Session of Congress and the American People," White House press release, September 20, 2001.

21 "Robertson: Jihad at heart of Islam," CNN Access, www.cnn.com, November 26, 2002.

22 "India—Eight dead, 90 Hurt in Ongoing Anti-Falwell Riots," Agence France-Press, October 12, 2002; "Cleric demands death for three U.S. Protestant pastors," Agence France-Presse, October 12, 2002.

23 Ibn Warraq, "Introduction," *What the Koran Really Says: Language, Text, and Commentary*, Ibn Warraq, ed. (Amherst, NY: Prometheus Books, 2002), 26.

24 Ibn Ishaq, *The Life of Muhammad: A Translation of Ibn Ishaq's Sirat Rasul Allah*, A. Guillaume, trans. (Oxford: Oxford University Press, 1955), 212–13.

25 Ibid.

26 Qur'an 2:193; Ibn Ishaq, 212–13.

27 'Abdullah bin Muhammad bin Humaid, "The Call to Jihad (Holy Fighting for Allah's Cause) in the Qur'an," Appendix III of *Sahih Bukhari*, vol. 9, p. 462.

28 Sayyid Qutb, *Milestones* (New Delhi: Islamic Book Service, 2006), 64.

29 Ibid., 53–54.

30 Ibid., 57.

31   Ibn Arabi, in Suyuti, *Itqan* iii, 69. Cf. John Wansbrough, *Quranic Studies* (New York: Prometheus, 2003), 184.

32   "Surat at-Tawba: Repentance," *Tafsir al-Jalalayn*, anonymous translation, reprinted at http://ourworld.compuserve.com/homepages/ABewley/tawba1.html.

33   Ibn Kathir, vol. 4, p. 377.

34   "Surat at-Tawba: Repentance."

35   Ibn Kathir, vol. 8, p. 668.

36   Ibn Abi Zayd al-Qayrawani, *La Risala* (*Epitre sur les elements du dogme et de la loi de l'Islam selon le rite malikite*) Translated from Arabic by Leon Bercher. (Algiers, fifth edition, 1960), 165. Cited in Andrew G. Bostom, "Khaled Abou El Fadl: Reformer or Revisionist?" http://www.secularislam.org/articles/bostom.htm.

37   Ibn Taymiyya, "Jihad," in Rudolph Peters, *Jihad in Classical and Modern Islam* (Princeton, NJ: Markus Wiener Publishers, 1996), 49. Cited in Andrew G. Bostom, "Khaled Abou El Fadl: Reformer or Revisionist?"

38   From the *Hidayah*, vol. Ii., 140, quoted in Thomas P. Hughes, *A Dictionary of Islam* (London: W. H. Allen, 1895), "Jihad," 243–48. Cited in Andrew G. Bostom, "Khaled Abou El Fadl: Reformer or Revisionist?"

39   Abu'l Hasan al-Mawardi, *al-Ahkam as-Sultaniyyah* (*The Laws of Islamic Governance*) (London: Ta-Ha Publishers, 1996), 60.

40   Cyril Glasse, "Ijtihad," *The Encyclopedia of Islam* (Lanham, MD: Altamira Press, 2001), 209.

41   Karen Armstrong, *Muhammad: A Biography of the Prophet* (San Francisco: Harper, 1992), 260.

42   "Question #34770: There is no compulsion to accept Islam," *Learn Hajj Jurisprudence*, Islam Q & A, http://63.175.194.25/index.php?ln=eng&ds=qa&lv=browse&QR=34770&dgn=4.

43   Ahmed ibn Naqib al-Misri, *Reliance of the Traveller ('Umdat al-Salik): A Classic Manual of Islamic Sacred Law*, trans. Nuh Ha Mim Keller (Beltsville, MD: Amana Publications, 1999), xx.

44   Ibid., o9.0.

45   Ibid., o9.8.

46   Ibid., o9.6.

47　Craig Pyes, Josh Meyer, and William C. Rempel, "Officials Reveal Bin Laden Plan," *Los Angeles Times,* May 18, 2002.

48　"Algerian terror group seeks Zarqawi's help," United Press International, May 2, 2006.

49　S. K. Malik, *The Qur'anic Concept of War* (New Delhi: Adam Publishers, 1992), 11.

50　Muhammad Sa'id R. Al-Buti, *Jihad in Islam: How to Understand & Practice It,* trans. Munzer Adel Absi (Pittsburgh: Dar Al-Fikr Publishing House, 1995), 91.

51　Ibid., 94.

52　Imran Ahsan Khan Nyazee, *Theories of Islamic Law: The Methodology of Ijtihad* (New York: Other Press, 1994), 251–52.

53　Ibid., 253.

54　Bertrand Russell, *Why I Am Not a Christian* (Carmichael, CA: Touchstone, 1957), 17.

55　Ibid., 19.

56　Bukhari, vol. 4, book 61, no. 3635.

57　Ibn Ishaq, 367.

58　Bukhari, vol. 4, book 61, no. 3635.

59　See, for example, "Fears as young Muslims 'opt out,'" BBC News, March 7, 2004.

60　Tahir Shah, *The Caliph's House: A Year in Casablanca* (New York: Bantam Books, 2006), 126.

Chapter Six: The Cross and the Sword

1　Maggie Michael, "War of Stickers: Christian Fish, Muslim Shark," Associated Press, December 2, 2003.

2　Aqeel Hussein and Colin Freeman, "Pack up or die, street vendors told," *Telegraph,* June 3, 2006.

3　Second Vatican Council, *Lumen Gentium* 16, November 21, 1964; *Catechism of the Catholic Church* 841.

4　Pope Urban II, "Speech at Council of Clermont, 1095, according to Fulcher of Chartres," quoted in Bongars, *Gesta Dei per Francos,* 1, 382 f., trans. in Oliver J. Thatcher and Edgar Holmes McNeal, eds., *A Source Book for Medieval History* (New York: Scribners, 1905), 513–17.

Reprinted at *Medieval Sourcebook*, http://www.fordham.edu/halsall/
source/urban2-fulcher.html.

5   "Khomeini's speech on the day of celebration of the birth of
Muhammad: 1981," FaithFreedom.org. http://www.faithfreedom.org/
Iran/KhomeiniSpeech.htm.

6   Pope Urban II, "Speech at Council of Clermont, 1095, according to
Fulcher of Chartres," quoted in Bongars.

7   John B. O'Connor, "St. Isidore of Seville," *Catholic Encyclopedia*, Vol.
VIII (New York: Robert Appleton Company, 1910). Reprinted at
http://www.newadvent.org.

8   Rodney Stark, *The Victory of Reason* (New York: Random House, 2005),
29.

9   Ibid., 28.

10 William Lloyd Garrison, speech at Charleston, South Carolina, April
14, 1865. http://www.spartacus.schoolnet.co.uk/USASgarrison.htm.

11 Abraham Lincoln, "Reply to Delegation of Baptists on May 30, 1864,"
in Roy P. Basler, ed., *Collected Works of Abraham Lincoln*, Vol. VII
(Rutgers, NJ: Rutgers University Press, 1953), 368.

12 Abraham Lincoln, "Story Written for Noah Brooks," December 6,
1864, in *Collected Works of Abraham Lincoln*, 154–55.

13 Bukhari, vol. 1, book 2, no. 13.

14 Bat Ye'or, *The Decline of Eastern Christianity Under Islam: From Jihad to
Dhimmitude* (Madison, NJ: Fairleigh Dickinson University Press,
1996), 108.

15 Speros Vryonis, *The Decline of Medieval Hellenism in Asia Minor and the
Process of Islamization from the Eleventh through the Fifteenth Century*
(Berkeley: Berkeley Press, 1971), 174–75. Quoted in Andrew G. Bostom,
The Legacy of Jihad (Amherst, NY: Prometheus Books, 2005), 87.

16 K. S. Lal, *Muslim Slave System in Medieval India* (New Delhi: Aditya
Prakashan, 1994), 9.

17 Patricia Crone, *God's Rule: Government and Islam* (New York:
Columbia University Press, 2004), 371–72. Quoted in Bostom, 86.

18 Giles Milton, *White Gold: The Extraordinary Story of Thomas Pellow
and Islam's One Million White Slaves* (New York: Farrar, Straus and
Giroux, 2004), 84.

19 Bostom, 89–90.

20 Hilary Andersson, "Born to be a slave in Niger," BBC News, February 11, 2005.

21 Barbara Ferguson, "Saudi Gets 27 Years to Life for Enslaving Maid," *Arab News*, September 1, 2006.

22 "Egyptians who enslaved girl, 10, get U.S. prison," Reuters, October 24, 2006.

23 "Kuwaiti Diplomat Accused of Domestic Slavery," ABC7 News, January 17, 2007.

24 Coalition Against Slavery in Mauritania and Sudan, "Sudan Q & A," compiled by the American Friends Service Committee, http://members.aol.com/casmasalc/newpage8.htm, 1998.

25 Aid to the Church in Need, "Religious Freedom in the Majority Islamic Countries 1998 Report: Sudan," op. cit. http://www.alleanzacattolica. org/acs/acs_english/acs_index.htm.

26 Joseph Winter, "No return for Sudan's forgotten slaves," BBC News, March 16, 2007.

27 Pascal Fletcher, "Slavery still exists in Mauritania," Reuters, March 21, 2007.

28 *The History of al-Tabari*, Volume XII: The Battle of al-Qadisiyyah and the Conquest of Syria and Palestine, trans. Yohanan Friedmann (Albany, NY: State University of New York Press, 1992), 167. Cited in Andrew Bostom, "The Legacy of Jihad in Palestine," FrontPageMagazine.com, December 7, 2004, http://www.frontpagemag.com/Articles/ReadArticle.asp?ID=16235.

29 Steven Runciman, *A History of the Crusades* Vol. I (Cambridge: Cambridge University Press, 1951), 3.

30 Philip K. Hitti, *The Arabs: A Short History* (Washington, DC: Regnery, 1996), 205.

31 Moshe Gil, *A History of Palestine 634–1099* (Cambridge: Cambridge University Press, 1992), 376.

32 Runciman, *A History of the Crusades*, 36.

33 Ibid., 49.

34 Quoted in Thomas F. Madden, *The New Concise History of the Crusades* (Lanham, MD: Rowman & Littlefield, 2005), 181–82.

35 Steven Runciman, *The Fall of Constantinople 1453* (Cambridge: Cambridge University Press, 1965), 145.

36 Amin Maalouf, *The Crusades Through Arab Eyes* (New York: Schocken Books, 1984), 263.

37 Bernard Lewis, 2007 Irving Kristol Lecture, American Enterprise Institute, Washington, D.C., March 7, 2007.

38 J. H. Robinson, *Readings in European History* (Toronto: Ginn, 1905), 72–73.

39 Tertullian, "To Scapula," S. Thelwall, trans., in "Latin Christianity: Its Founder, Tertullian," in *The Ante-Nicene Fathers*, Alexander Roberts and James Donaldson, eds., Vol. III (Grand Rapids, MI: Eerdmans, 1986), 105.

40 Origen, "Against Celsus," in "Fathers of the Third Century," in *The Ante-Nicene Fathers*, 621.

41 Lactantius, "The Divine Institutes," in "Fathers of the Third and Fourth Centuries," in *The Ante-Nicene Fathers*, 156–57.

42 Optatus of Milevus, "Against the Donatists," book 3, no. 6–7, in O. R. Vassall-Phillips, trans., *The Work of St. Optatus Bishop of Milevus Against the Donatists* (London: Longmans, Green, and Co., 1917). http://www.tertullian.org/fathers/index.htm#Against_the_Donatists.

43 John Chrysostom, Homily XLVI, in George Prevost, trans., "The Homilies of St. John Chrysostom" in Philip Schaff, ed., *A Select Library of the Nicene and Post-Nicene Fathers of the Christian Church* Vol. X (Grand Rapids, MI: Eerdmans, 1986), 288.

44 Augustine, Letter C, in "Letters of St. Augustin," J. G. Cunningham, trans., in *A Select Library of the Nicene and Post-Nicene Fathers of the Christian Church*, Vol. I, 412.

45 Thomas Aquinas, *Summa Theologica*, II.ii.11, translated by the Fathers of the English Dominican Province. Vol. III (Grand Rapids, MI: Christian Classics, 1981), 1220.

46 Joseph Blötzer, "Inquisition," *Catholic Encyclopedia*, Vol. VIII. http://www.newadvent.org/cathen/index.html.

47 Michael T. Ott, "Tomás de Torquemada," *Catholic Encyclopedia*, Vol. XIV. http://www.newadvent.org/cathen/index.html.

48 Juan Antonio Llorente, *Historia Crítica de la Inquisición en España*, Vol. IV (Madrid: Hiperión, 1980), 183.

49 See Henry Charles Lea, *A History of the Inquisition of Spain* (London: Macmillan, 1907).

50 Bukhari, vol. 9, book 88, no. 6922; cf. vol. 4, book 56, no. 3017.

51 *'Umdat al-Salik*, o8.1.

52 Barbara Palmer, "Warfare against religious extremists strengthens their cause, scholar asserts," *Stanford Report*, October 20, 2004.

53 John Lofton, "Timothy McVeigh was not a 'Christian' terrorist, HUMAN EVENTS, May 6, 2002.

54 Ibid.

55 Christopher Hitchens, *God Is Not Great* (New York: Warner Twelve, 2007), 189.

Chapter Seven: Christian Anti-Semitism vs. Islamic "Apes and Pigs"

1 Malcolm Hay, *Europe and the Jews* (Chicago: Academy Chicago Publishers, 1992), 12–13.

2 Ibid., 13.

3 Ibid.

4 Justin Martyr, "Dialogue with Trypho," in "The Apostolic Fathers with Justin Martyr and Irenaeus," in Alexander Roberts and James Donaldson, eds., *The Ante-Nicene Fathers*, Vol. I (Grand Rapids, MI: Eerdmans, 1986), 200.

5 John Chrysostom, *Adversus Judaeos*, Homily I. http://www.fordham.edu/halsall/source/chrysostom-jews6.html.

6 Ibid., Homily I, Homily VI.

7 Hay, 11–12.

8 Quoted in David G. Dalin, *The Myth of Hitler's Pope* (Washington, DC: Regnery, 2005), 17.

9 Dalin, 18.

10 Hay, 70.

11 Ibid., 56; Walter Lacqueur, *The Changing Face of Anti-Semitism* (Oxford: Oxford University Press, 2006), 48.

12 Commission for Religious Relations with the Jews, "We Remember: A Reflection on the Shoah," March 16, 1998.

13 Edward A. Synan, *The Popes and the Jews in the Middle Ages* (London: Macmillan, 1965), 61.

14 Ibid., 60.

15 Ibid., 65.

16 Ibid., 106.

17 Ibid., 108.

18 Ibid., 120; Hay, 73.

19 Synan, 121.

20 Ibid., 131.

21 David I. Kertzer, *The Kidnapping of Edgardo Mortara* (New York: Vintage, 1998).

22 Dalin, 18.

23 Ibid., 19.

24 Synan, 46.

25 Ibid., 49, 58.

26 Ibid., 68–69.

27 Ibid., 70–74.

28 Dalin, 20.

29 Synan, 75.

30 Hay, 43.

31 Ibid., 55.

32 Ibid., 56.

33 Ibid., 91.

34 Innocent III, "Constitution for the Jews (1199 AD)," Medieval Sourcebook, http://www.fordham.edu/halsall/source/in3-constjews.html; Hay, 78.

35 Dalin, 20.

36 Ibid., 23, 29, 32; Synan, 119.

37 Hay, 75.

38 Dalin, 20–25, 31.

39 Ibid., 27–28.

40 The Catechism of Trent, Article IV: "Suffered Under Pontius Pilate, Was Crucified, Dead, and Buried." http://www.cin.org/users/james/ebooks/master/trent/tcreed04.htm.

41 Dalin, 32.

42 Ibid., 33.

43 Ibid., 34.

44 Ibid., 38.

45 Pius XI, *Mit Brennender Sorge*, March 14, 1937; Dalin, 39.

46 Ibid.; Ibid., 67.

47 Dalin, 39.

48 Ibid., 40.

49 Second Vatican Council, "Declaration on the Relation of the Church to Non-Christian Religions (Nostra Aetate)," October 28, 1965.

50 Pope John Paul II, "Visit to the Chief Rabbis of Israel, March 23, 2000," *L'Osservatore Romano*, March 29, 2000.

51 Dalin, 15.

52 Etgar Lefkovits, "Priests: Remove anti-Semitic liturgy," *Jerusalem Post*, April 20, 2007.

53 Norman Cameron and R. H. Stevens, trans., *Hitler's Table Talk 1941–1944* (New York: Enigma Books, 2000), 342.

54 Ibid., 144.

55 Ibid., 322, 288.

56 Ibid., 7, 146.

57 Ibid., 142.

58 Albert Speer, *Inside the Third Reich: Memoirs*, Richard and Clara Winston, trans. (New York: Simon & Schuster, 1970), 96.

59 Cameron and Stevens, 667.

60 Ibid., 51.

61 Ibid., 6.

62 Ibid., 343.

63 Ronald Rychlak, *Hitler, the War and the Pope* (Huntington, IL: Our Sunday Visitor, 2000), 76.

64 "German War Christmas (1944)," Calvin College German Propaganda Archive, http://www.calvin.edu/academic/cas/gpa/weihnacht44.htm.

65 Christopher Hitchens, *God Is Not Great* (New York: Warner Twelve, 2006), 240.

66 Dalin, 8.

67 Ibid., 15.

68 Pierre Blet, S.J., "Response to Accusations Against Pius XII: Myth vs. Historical Fact," *L'Osservatore Romano*, April 29, 1998.

69 Dimitri Cavalli, "Was Pius XII really 'Hitler's pope'?" *Jerusalem Post*, June 5, 2006.

70 Stephen M. DiGiovanni, "Pius XII and the Jews: The War Years, as reported by the *New York Times*," *Catholic Social Scientist Review*, Vol. VI, 2001.

71 Cameron and Stevens, 521.

72 DiGiovanni, "Pius XII and the Jews."

73 Cavalli, "Was Pius XII really 'Hitler's pope'?"

74 DiGiovanni, "Pius XII and the Jews."

75 Rychlak, 205.

76 Donald DeMarco, "800,000 Saved by Pius XII's 'Silence,'" *Catholic Register*, May 18, 1998.

77 Dalin, 14.

78 DeMarco, "800,000 Saved by Pius XII's 'Silence.'"

79 Moshe Perlman, *Mufti of Jerusalem* (Philadelphia: Pavilion Press, 2006).

80 Quoted in Andrew Bostom, *The Legacy of Islamic Antisemitism* (Amherst, NY: Prometheus, 2007).

81 John Esposito, "Practice and Theory: A response to 'Islam and the Challenge of Democracy,'" *Boston Review*, April/May 2003; "Al-Qaradawi full transcript," BBC News, July 8, 2004.

82 1. These include, among others, 3:75; 5:64; 3:181; 5:41; 5:13; 2:109; 3:120; 2:61; 2:74; 2:100; 59:13-14; 2:96; and 2:79.

83 Ibn Kathir, *Tafsir Ibn Kathir* (Abridged), vol. 1 (London: Darussalam, 2000), 254.

84 Aluma Solnick, "Based on Koranic Verses, Interpretations, and Traditions, Muslim Clerics State: The Jews Are the Descendants of Apes, Pigs, and Other Animals," Middle East Media Research Institute Special Report No. 11, November 1, 2002.

85 Aaron Klein, "Abbas urges: 'Raise rifles against Israel,'" WorldNetDaily.com, January 11, 2007.

86 "Jews as Depicted in the Qur'an," Islam Online, March 23, 2004.

87 Yaakov Lappin, "Iran: Israel, US will soon die," *Ynet News*, January 23, 2007.

88 Quoted in Bostom.

89 Ibn Kathir, 245.

90 Quoted in Bostom.

91 Ibn Kathir, 193.

92 Bukhari, vol. 4, book 56, no. 2925.

93 Itamar Marcus and Barbara Crook, "Hamas Spokesman: Genocide of Jews remains Hamas goal," *Palestinian Media Watch*, April 12, 2007.

94 Philip K. Hitti, *The Arabs: A Short History* (Washington, DC: Regnery, 1996), 137.

95 Quoted in Bat Ye'or, *The Dhimmi: Jews and Christians Under Islam* (Madison, NJ: Fairleigh Dickinson University Press, 1985), 376.

96 Quoted in ibid., 352, 354.

97 Karen Armstrong, "The curse of the infidel: A century ago Muslim intellectuals admired the West. Why did we lose their goodwill?" *The Guardian*, June 20, 2002.

98 Scott Bohlinger, "First U.S. Museum Devoted to Islam Based in Jackson, Mississippi: Museum Fosters Tolerance, Multicultural Understanding," U.S. Department of State, March 27, 2003. http://usinfo.state.gov/usa/islam/a032703.htm.

99 Quoted in Bostom.

100 María Rosa Menocal, *The Ornament of the World: How Muslims, Jews, and Christians Created a Culture of Tolerance in Medieval Spain* (New York: Little, Brown, 2002), 72–73.

101 Richard Fletcher, *Moorish Spain* (Berkeley: University of California Press, 1992), 172–73.

102 Andrew G. Bostom, "An Apology for Koranic Antisemitism?" *American Thinker*, April 20, 2007.

103 Fletcher, 108.

104 Ibid., 96–97.

105 Quoted in Bostom.

106 Ibn Ishaq, *The Life of Muhammad: A Translation of Ibn Ishaq's Sirat Rasul Allah*, A. Guillaume, trans. (Oxford: Oxford University Press, 1955), 461.

107 Bostom.

108 Bernard Lewis, *What Went Wrong?* (Oxford: Oxford University Press, 2002), 114.

109 Jamie Glazov, interview with Dinesh D'Souza, "Did the Cultural Left Cause 9/11?" FrontPageMagazine.com, January 25, 2007.

110 Ibn Warraq, *Why I Am Not a Muslim* (Amherst, NY: Prometheus, 1995), 21.

111 "'Wave of hatred' warning as attacks on Jews hits record high," *Daily Mail*, February 1, 2007.

112 Tom Harper and Ben Leapman, "Jews far more likely to be victims of faith hatred than Muslims," *Sunday Telegraph*, December 17, 2006.

113 "'A good way to show they have regrets,'" *Flanders News*, January 5, 2007.

114 "Jews warned against harassment," *Aftenposten*, July 20, 2007.

115 Bruce Bawer, *While Europe Slept* (New York: Doubleday, 2006), 143–44.

Chapter Eight: The West Calls for Dialogue; Islam Calls for Jihad

1   "Slaughter and 'Submission,'" CBS News, August 20, 2006.

2   Toby Sterling, "Dutch Filmmaker Theo Van Gogh Murdered," Associated Press, November 2, 2004.

3   "Van Gogh murder suspect confesses to killing," MSNBC, July 12, 2005.

4   Philippe Naughton, "Van Gogh killer jailed for life," Times Online, July 26, 2005.

5   Condoleezza Rice, "Statement on Palestinian Elections, Remarks at the World Economic Forum in Davos, Switzerland," U.S. Department of State, January 26, 2006.

6   "Hamas rules out talks with Israel," *Jerusalem Post*, January 25, 2006.

7   "Faith, reason, and the university: memories and reflections," Papal address at University of Regensburg, September 12, 2006.

8   "Pakistan: Pope's Jihadi Comments Shows His Ignorance of Islam, Official Says," AKI, September 14, 2006.

9   "Turkish cleric attacks pope's Islam remarks," Associated Press, September 14, 2006.

10 Malcolm Moore, "Turkish hosts scold conciliatory Pope," *Telegraph*, November 29, 2006.

11 "Muslim leaders condemn Pope's speech, want apology," Reuters, September 15, 2006.

12 "Fears of violent Mideast backlash to pope," Agence France-Presse, September 15, 2006.

13 "Shiite Cleric Hails Hezbollah Militants," Associated Press, August 3, 2006.

14 Ibn Ishaq, *The Life of Muhammad: A Translation of Ibn Ishaq's Sirat Rasul Allah*, A. Guillaume, trans. (Oxford: Oxford University Press, 1955), 511–15; Ibn Sa'd, *Kitab Al-Tabaqat Al-Kabir*, Vol. II, S. Moinul Haq and H K. Ghazanfar, trans. (New Delhi: Kitab Bhavan, n.d.), 132–37.

15 "Muslim anger over papal comments grows," Associated Press, September 15, 2006.

16 Roee Nahmias, "Arab op-ed: Pope's remarks may lead to war," *Ynet News*, September 16, 2006.

17 "Pope's comments on Islam unite Iraqis," Associated Press, September 15, 2006.

18 "Somali cleric calls for pope's death," *The Age*, September 17, 2006.

19 "Islam row raises pope safety fears," Reuters, September 15, 2006.

20 Ryan Jones, "Gaza's Christian Arabs Living in Fear," CNSNews.com, September 20, 2006.

21 "Report: Rome tightens pope's security after fury over Islam remarks," *Haaretz*, September 17, 2006.

22 "'Jihad' vowed over Pope's speech," Reuters, September 18, 2006.

23 "Christian Killed in Iraq in Response to Pope's Speech: Islamic Website," Assyrian International News Agency, September 16, 2006.

24 Michael Luo, "Iraq's Christians Flee as Extremist Threat Worsens," *New York Times*, October 17, 2006.

25 "Witnesses: Italian nun killed in Somalia," Associated Press, September 17, 2006.

26 "Just outside Westminster Cathedral today," Joee Blogs: A Catholic Londoner, September 17, 2006. http://catholiclondoner.blogspot.com/2006/09/very-rushed-post.html.

27 "The Pope must die, says Muslim," *Evening Standard*, September 18, 2006.

28 "Church elder murdered in Mosul, priest kidnapped in Baghdad," *Compass Direct*, December 4, 2006.

29 Khaled Abu Toameh, "Gazans warn pope to accept Islam," *Jerusalem Post*, September 18, 2006.

30 Muhammed Ibn Ismaiel al-Bukhari, *Sahih al-Bukhari: The Translation of the Meanings*, Vol. 4, book 56, no. 2941, trans. Muhammad M. Khan (London: Darussalam, 1997).

31 "Top Muslim avoids meeting with pope," ANSA, March 22, 2007.

32 Daniel Pipes, "A Look at Islamic Violence," *New York Sun*, September 26, 2006.

33 Hassan M. Fattah, "At Mecca Meeting, Cartoon Outrage Crystallized," *New York Times*, February 9, 2006.

34 "Cartoon Body Count," http://www.cartoonbodycount.com/.

35 "Gaza EU offices raided by gunmen," BBC News, January 30, 2006.

36 "Gazans burn Danish flags, demand cartoon apology," Reuters, January 31, 2006.

37 "EU Press Reprints Explosive Cartoons," IslamOnline, February 1, 2006.

38 "Open Letter to Pope Benedict XVI," *Islamica* magazine, September 12, 2006, http://www.islamicamagazine.com/issue18/openletter18_lowres.pdf.

39 Ibid.

40 Muslim, book 19, no. 4294.

41 Bukhari, vol. 1, book 2, no. 25. The transliterated Arabic of the Muslim confession of faith has been omitted from this translation for ease of reading. The same statement is repeated in Bukhari, vol. 1, book 8, no. 392; vol. 4, book 56, no. 2946; vol. 9, book 88, no. 6924; and vol. 9, book 96, nos. 7284–85, as well as in other hadith collections.

42 Abu Hamid al-Ghazali, *The Incoherence of the Philosophers*, trans. Michael E. Marmura (Provo, UT: Brigham Young University Press, 2000), 2.

43 Ibid., 8.

44 Tilman Nagel, *The History of Islamic Theology from Muhammad to the Present*, translated by Thomas Thornton, Markus Wiener Publishers, 2000, 211.

45 Al-Ghazali, *Kitab al-Wagiz fi fiqh madhab al-imam al-Safi'i*, quoted in Andrew Bostom, *The Legacy of Jihad* (Amherst, NY: Prometheus, 2005), 226. Emphasis added.

46 Ibid., 199.

47 Ibid., o9.8.

48 Imran Ahsan Khan Nyazee, *Theories of Islamic Law: The Methodology of Ijtihad* (New York: Other Press, 1994), 251–52.

Chapter Nine: Faith and Unreason

1 Quoted in Thomas Woods, *How the Catholic Church Built Western Civilization* (Washington, DC: Regnery, 2005), 81.

2 "Faith, reason, and the university: memories and reflections," Papal address at University of Regensburg, September 12, 2006.

3   Quoted in James V. Schall, S. J., *War-Time Clarifications: Who Is Our Enemy?* TCR News, 2001, from Stanley Jaki, *Chance or Reality* (Lanham, MD: Rowman & Littlefield, 1986), 242.

4   Stanley Jaki, *The Savior of Science* (Washington, DC: Regnery Gateway, 1988), 43.

5   Rodney Stark, *The Victory of Reason* (New York: Random House, 2005), 20–21.

6   Moses Maimonides, *The Guide for the Perplexed*, M. Friedländer, trans. (New York: Barnes & Noble, 2004).

7   Jaki, *The Savior of Science*, 43.

8   Ibid., 44.

9   Stark, 46–47.

10 St. Thomas Aquinas, *Summa Contra Gentiles*, "Book Two: Creation," trans. James F. Anderson. (Notre Dame, IN: University of Notre Dame Press, 1975), chapter 25, section 14.

11 Stark, 22–23.

12 Philip K. Hitti, *The Arabs: A Short History* (Washington, DC: Regnery, 1996), 120, 5.

13 Caesar E. Farah, *Islam*, sixth edition (Hauppauge, NY: Barrons, 2000), 198.

14 Elias B. Skaff, *The Place of the Patriarchs of Antioch in Church History* (Manchester, NH: Sophia Press, 1993), 169.

15 Bat Ye'or, *The Decline of Eastern Christianity Under Islam* (Madison, NJ: Fairleigh Dickinson University Press, 1996), 78.

16 Hitti, 145.

17 Ibid., 141–42.

18 Ibid., 142–44.

19 Bernard Lewis, *The Arabs in History* (Oxford: Oxford University Press, 1993), 147; A. Zahoor, "Abu 'Uthman 'Amr ibn Bahr al-Basri al-Jahiz," http://users.erols.com/gmqm/jahiz.html.

20 Dennis Overbye, "How Islam Won, and Lost, the Lead in Science," *New York Times*, October 30, 2001.

21 Stark, 21.

22 http://www.1001inventions.com/.

23 Woods, 68.

24 Ibid.

25 Stark, 48.

26 Bernard Lewis, *What Went Wrong?* (Oxford: Oxford University Press, 2002), 118.

27 Ibid., 125.

28 Ibid., 127.

29 Woods, 67.

30 Quoted in Woods, 71.

31 Quoted in Woods, 72.

32 Quoted in Woods, 74.

33 Pope John Paul II, "Lessons of the Galileo Case," Address to the Pontifical Academy of Sciences, October 31, 1992.

34 Pope John Paul II, "Truth cannot be subject to negotiation," Address to the Pontifical Academy of Sciences, November 13, 2000.

Chapter Ten: Democracy, Whiskey, Sexy

1 Jim Dwyer, "Exuberant Crowd's Most Urgent Request: Water," *New York Times*, April 3, 2003.

2 Nimrod Raphaeli, "The Plight of Iraqi Christians," Middle East Media Research Institute Inquiry and Analysis Series No. 213, March 22, 2005.

3 "Iraq: Militant Group Threatens Female Students in Kirkuk," AKI, June 6, 2006.

4 Thom Shanker, "Perhaps Thinking of Legacy, Bush Has Rice on the Move," *New York Times*, January 19, 2007.

5 Dinesh D'Souza, *The Enemy at Home* (New York: Doubleday, 2007), 279.

6 Abdulwahab Alkebsi, "Human dignity, the rule of law and limits on the power of the state are clearly mandated by Islam's holy book," *Insight*, April 1, 2003.

7 Amir Taheri, "Amir Taheri's Remarks at Debate 'Islam Is Incompatible with Democracy,'" *Benador Online*, May 19, 2004.

8 Ibid.

9 Quoted in Amir Taheri, *The Spirit of Allah: Khomeini and the Islamic Revolution* (Bethesda, MD: Adler & Adler, 1986), 90–91.

10 Sultanhussein Tabandeh, *A Muslim Commentary on the Universal Declaration of Human Rights*, trans. F. J. Goulding (London: F. T. Goulding and Co., 1970), 18.

11 "Bangladeshi Muslim editor faces death penalty for moderate views," *Jerusalem Post*, September 22, 2006.

12 Jürgen Kremb, "Sliding Towards Conservative Islam: Indonesia's Secular State under Siege," Spiegel Online, April 6, 2007.

13 "Indonesia: Justice in Religious Conflicts Appears Uneven: More Christians may face death penalty; Islamists get light sentences for beheadings," *Compass Direct*, April 4, 2007.

14 "Indonesia executes Christians," *Daily Telegraph*, September 22, 2006.

15 Paul Stenhouse, "Forced Islamisation," *Jihad Watch*, December 10, 2006.

16 "Indonesia: Angry Mob Attacks Church in Aceh," *Compass Direct*, September 8, 2006.

17 D'Souza, 280.

18 Baradan Kuppusamy, "Malaysia: Temple Demolitions Spell Creeping Islamisation," Inter Press Service News Agency, June 1, 2006.

19 "Incentives for marrying and converting orang asli," *The Star*, June 27, 2006.

20 "Malaysian police arrest two Americans suspected of promoting Christianity," Agence France-Presse, April 27, 2005.

21 "Malaysia rejects Christian appeal," BBC News, May 30, 2007.

22 "Malaysia's Islamic officials seize baby from mother who sought a Hindu life," Associated Press, April 6, 2007.

23 "Woman fails in bid to renounce Islam," *New Straits Times*, March 29, 2007.

24 "Malaysian switched at birth wants to switch religion," Reuters, February 3, 2007.

25 "Statement saddens Evangelicals," *Star Online*, April 16, 2005.

26 "Christmas without Jesus in Malaysia," *AsiaNews*, December 14, 2004.

27 Leapman and Wynne-Jones, "Prescott heaps praise on 'tolerant' Malaysia, despite its crumbling human rights."

28 Andrew Mango, *Atatürk: The Biography of the Founder of Modern Turkey* (New York: Overlook Press, 2000), 438.

29 Ibid., 471.

30 "Albright says U.S. not happy about Turkey's Islamic drift," CNN, February 12, 1997.

31 Suna Erdem, "Turks protest amid fears of 'secret plan' to overturn secular state," *The Times*, April 16, 2007.

32 "Vatican: Pope Asks Turkey to Give Church Legal Status," AKI, January 19, 2007.

33 "Christian converts on trial in Turkey," Associated Press, November 24, 2006.

34 "Turkey: Attackers Firebomb Protestant Church," *Compass Direct*, November 9, 2006.

35 "Turkey: Authorities 'Harass' Orthodox Patriarchate Staff," *Compass Direct*, December 8, 2006.

36 Roger Scruton, *The West and the Rest: Globalization and the Terrorist Threat* (Wilmington, DE: Intercollegiate Studies Institute, 2002), 4.

37 Seyyed Hossein Nasr, *Ideals and Realities of Islam*, new revised edition (Chicago: ABC International Group, Inc., 2000), 87.

38 Sayyid Qutb, *Social Justice in Islam*, John B. Hardie, trans., translation revised by Hamid Algar (North Haledon, NJ: Islamic Publications International, 1953), 317.

39 Scruton, 4.

40 Ibid., 5.

41 Ibid., 6.

42 Mohamed Elhachmi Hamdi, "Islam and Liberal Democracy: The Limits of the Western Model," *Journal of Democracy* 7.2, 1996, 81–85.

43 Ibid.

44 Syed Abul Ala Maududi, "Jihad in Islam," Address at the Town Hall, Lahore, April 13, 1939. Reprinted at http://host06.ipowerweb.com/~ymofmdc/books/jihadinislam/.

45 "The Charter of Allah: The Platform of the Islamic Resistance movement (Hamas)," translated and annotated by Raphael Israeli, The International Policy Institute for Counter-Terrorism, April 5, 1998. http://www.ict.org.il/documents/documentdet.cfm?docid=14.

46 "Al Qaeda group claims Iraq parliament attack," Agence France-Presse, April 13, 2007.

47 Fawaz Turki, "Of Democracy and Coercion," *Arab News*, November 13, 2003.

48 Mark O'Keefe, "Has the United States Become Judeo-Christian-Islamic?" Newhouse News Service, May 16, 2003.

49 Michael Novak, *On Two Wings: Humble Faith and Common Sense at the American Founding* (New York: Encounter Books, 2002), 28–29.

50 Sayyid Qutb, *Milestones* (New Delhi: Islamic Book Service, 2006), 61.

51 Ibid., 57.

52 Art Moore, "Did CAIR founder say Islam to rule America?" WorldNetDaily.com, December 11, 2006.

53 John Perazzo, "Hamas and Hizzoner," FrontPageMagazine.com, March 5, 2003.

54 *Minneapolis Star Tribune*, April 4, 1993, quoted in Daniel Pipes and Sharon Chadha, "CAIR: Islamists Fooling the Establishment," *Middle East Quarterly*, spring 2006.

55 Joel Mowbray, "Democrats' dilemma," *Washington Times*, September 25, 2006.

Chapter Eleven: Women in the West vs. Burqas and Beatings

1 "Lawyer Convicted of Helping Terrorists," Associated Press, February 10, 2005.

2 "Full text: bin Laden's 'letter to America,'" *Observer*, November 24, 2002.

3 Muslim Women's League, "Gender Equality in Islam," September 1995, http://www.mwlusa.org/pub_gender.html.

4 Sayyid Qutb, *Social Justice in Islam*, John B. Hardie, trans., translation revised by Hamid Algar (North Haledon, NJ: Islamic Publications International, 1953), 77–78.

5 Quoted in Muhammad Ali al-Hashimi, *The Ideal Muslimah: The True Islamic Personality of the Muslim Woman as Defined in the Qur'an and Sunnah* (Raleigh, NC: International Islamic Publishing House, 1998), http://www.usc.edu/dept/MSA/humanrelations/womeninislam/idealmuslimah/.

6 James Palmer, "Extremists force women to hide under head scarves," *Washington Times*, April 10, 2007.

7 Muhammed Ibn Ismaiel al-Bukhari, *Sahih al-Bukhari: The Translation of the Meanings*, trans. Muhammad M. Khan (London: Darussalam, 1997), Vol. 7, book 77, no. 5825. Bukhari (810–870) is generally considered by Muslims to be the most reliable source for traditions about Muhammad.

8 Quoted in al-Hashimi.

9 Bukhari, vol. 4, book 59, no. 3237.

10 *'Umdat al-Salik*, n3.2.

11 Ibid., m11.10 (1).

12 Bukhari, vol. 3, book 52, no. 2639.

13 Ibid., vol. 7, book 67, no. 5206.

14 "Opposition to EU divorce rules plan," Deutsche Presse Agentur, April 19, 2007.

15 Nina Bernstein, "In Secret, Polygamy Follows Africans to N.Y.," *New York Times*, March 23, 2007.

16 Lewis Smith, "Muslim men use law loophole to get a harem of 'wives,'" *The Times*, October 21, 2004.

17 Nicholas Hellen, "Muslim second wives may get a tax break," *The Times*, December 26, 2004; "Polygamous husbands can claim cash for their harems," *Evening Standard*, April 17, 2007.

18 "Two wives," *Jerusalem Post*, July 12, 2005.

19 Amnesty International, "Pakistan: Violence against women on the increase and still no protection," April 17, 2002, http://web.amnesty.org/ai.nsf/Index/ASA330082002?OpenDocument&of=THEMES\WOMEN.

20 Phyllis Chesler, "What Is Justice for a Rape Victim?" *On the Issues*, winter 1995.

21 Hilary Andersson, "Born to be a slave in Niger," BBC News, February 11, 2005.

22 Bukhari, vol. 7, book 67, no. 5134.

23 Sarvnaz Chitsaz and Soona Samsami, "Iranian Women and Girls: Victims of Exploitation and Violence," in *Making the Harm Visible: Global Sexual Exploitation of Women and Girls*, Donna M. Hughes and Claire M. Roche, eds. The Coalition Against Trafficking in Women, 1999. http://www.uri.edu/artsci/wms/hughes/mhviran.htm.

24 Amir Taheri, *The Spirit of Allah: Khomeini and the Islamic Revolution* (Bethesda, MD: Adler & Adler, 1986), 90–91.

25 Ibid., 35.

26 Lisa Beyer, "The Women of Islam," *Time*, November 25, 2001.

27 http://www.ynetnews.com/articles/0,7340,L-3353122,00.html.

28 "Child marriage 'violates rights,'" BBC News, March 7, 2001.

29 Andrew Bushell, "Child Marriage in Afghanistan and Pakistan," *America*, March 11, 2002.

30 "Saudi man with 58 wives stirs polygamy debate," Associated Press, January 1, 2005.

31 Peter Beaumont, "Starving Afghans sell girls of eight as brides," *The Observer*, January 7, 2007.

32 "Afghanistan: Girls and women traded for opium debts," Reuters, January 25, 2007.

33 Bushell, "Child Marriage in Afghanistan and Pakistan."

34 Abu Dawud, book 11, no. 2141.

35 Ibid., no. 2142.

36 Muslim, book 4, no. 2127.

37 Steven Stalinsky and Y. Yehoshua, "Muslim Clerics on the Religious Rulings Regarding Wife-Beating," Middle East Media Research Institute Special Report No. 27, March 22, 2004.

38 "Muslim author of book advocating wife-beating jailed," Agence France-Presse, January 15, 2004.

39 Steven Stalinsky and Y. Yehoshua, "Muslim Clerics on the Religious Rulings Regarding Wife-Beating," Middle East Media Research Institute Special Report No. 27, March 22, 2004.

40 See Amnesty International, "Media briefing: Violence against women in Pakistan," April 17, 2002, http://web.amnesty.org/ai.nsf/Index/ASA330102002?OpenDocument&of=THEMES\WOMEN.

41 Rhonda Roumani, "Study reveals domestic abuse is widespread in Syria," *Christian Science Monitor*, April 25, 2006.

42 "Chad Struggles to Pass New Family Law," *VOA News*, April 15, 2005.

43 "President of Al-Azhar University and Fomer Mufti of Egypt Ahmad Al-Tayyeb Explains Wife Beating in Islam," Middle East Media Research Institute TV Monitor Project, Clip No. 1478, May 25, 2007.

44 Abu-Dawud Sulaiman bin al-Aash'ath al-Azdi as-Sijistani, *Sunan abu-Dawud*, Ahmad Hasan, trans. (New Delhi: Kitab Bhavan, 1990), book 32, no. 4092.

45 Devika Bhat and Zahid Hussain, "Female Pakistani minister shot dead for 'breaking Islamic dress code,'" Times Online, February 20, 2007.

46 "Throw Taslima out of India: Muslim law board," Rediff.com, January 20, 2007.

47 Chesler, "What Is Justice for a Rape Victim?"

48 See Christopher Dickey and Rod Nordland, "The Fire That Won't Die Out," *Newsweek*, July 22, 2002.

49 See Ustun Reinart, "Ambition for All Seasons: Tansu Ciller," *MERIA (Middle East Review of International Affairs) Journal*, March 1999, http://meria.idc.ac.il/journal/1999/issue1/jv3n1a6.html.

50 Quoted in Harvey Morris, "The West and Islam: An interview with Benazir Bhutto," *ForeignWire*, October 21, 1998, http://www.foreignwire.com/benazir.html.

51 Amnesty International, "Saudi Arabia: End Secrecy End Suffering: Women," http://www.amnesty.org/ailib/intcam/saudi/briefing/4.html.

52 See also Bukhari, vol. 3, book 52, no. 2661.

53 Ahmed ibn Naqib al-Misri, *Reliance of the Traveller ['Umdat al-Salik]: A Classic Manual of Islamic Sacred Law*, translated by Nuh Ha Mim Keller (Beltsville, MD: Amana Publications, 1999), o24.8.

54 See Sisters in Islam, "Rape, Zina, and Incest," April 6, 2000, http://www.muslimtents.com/sistersinislam/resources/sdefini.htm.

55 "Pakistani rape victim says attacks increasing," Reuters, February 1, 2007.

56 Richard Kerbaj, "Muslim leader blames women for sex attacks," *Australian*, October 26, 2006.

57 Adeel Pathan, "Ulema demand WPA withdrawal, CII reformation," *The News*, December 17, 2006.

58 Stephen Faris, "In Nigeria, a Mother Faces Execution," www.africana.com, January 7, 2002.

59 Ibid.

60 "Gang-rape victim faces lashes," Agence France-Presse, March 6, 2007.

61 Phyllis Chesler, *The Death of Feminism: What's Next in the Struggle for Women's Freedom* (New York: Palgrave Macmillan, 2005), 12.

62 Vivienne Walt, "Marked Women," *Time*, July 19, 2004.

63 *'Umdat al-Salik*, e4.3. The certification of the book's Islamic orthodoxy is on page xx of its introductory material.

64 Quoted in Geneive Abdo, *No God But God: Egypt and the Triumph of Islam* (Oxford: Oxford University Press, 2000), 59.

65 Later this turned out to be not quite accurate: Tantawi endorsed suicide bombing. See "Leading Egyptian Government Cleric Calls For: 'Martyrdom Attacks That Strike Horror into the Hearts of the Enemies

of Allah,'" Middle East Media Research Institute Special Dispatch Series No. 363, April 7, 2002.

66 Frank Gardner, "Grand sheikh condemns suicide bombings," BBC News, December 4, 2001.

67 "Jordan quashes 'honour crimes' law," *al-Jazeera*, September 7, 2003.

68 "U.N. women's rights group criticized Pakistan for honor killings, trafficking," Associated Press, June 8, 2007.

69 *Chicago Tribune*, May 3, 1998, quoted in Yotam Feldner, "'Honor' Murders: Why the Perps Get Off Easy," Middle East Media Research Institute, April 16, 2001.

70 Chesler, *The Death of Feminism*, 11.

71 "Jordanian given reduced sentence in 'honor killing,'" Agence France-Presse, February 1, 2007.

72 Shafika Mattar, "Father kills daughter; doubted virginity," Associated Press, January 25, 2007.

73 Vivienne Walt, "Marked Women," *Time*, July 19, 2004.

74 Chesler, *The Death of Feminism*, 11–12.

75 Soraya Sarhaddi Nelson, "Mother kills raped daughter to restore 'honor,'" Knight Ridder Newspapers, November 17, 2003.

76 Tony Paterson, "'How many more women have to die before this society wakes up?'" *Telegraph*, February 27, 2005.

77 "Palestinian honor killings linked to travails of occupation," IRIN News.org, March 9, 2007.

78 Qur'an 24:2.

79 Muslim, book 17, no. 4194.

80 Bukhari, vol. 8, book 86, no. 6830.

81 Quoted in Mark Goldblatt, "Why the West Is Better," *New York Post*, January 30, 2002.

Chapter Twelve: Yes, Virginia, Western Civilization Is Worth Defending

1 Dinesh D'Souza, *The Enemy at Home* (New York: Doubleday, 2007), 1.

2 Karen Elliott House, "Host of Conflicting Forces Has Saudis on a Tightrope," *Wall Street Journal*, April 10, 2007.

3 Ali Bekhan, "Western Society: A Culture of Paganism and Disbelief," KavkazCenter.com, December 1, 2006.

4   "Hilali in hot water again," *The Age*, January 11, 2007.

5   Quoted in Amir Taheri, *Holy Terror: Inside the World of Islamic Terrorism* (Bethesda, MD: Adler & Adler, 1987), 241–43.

6   Dinesh D'Souza, "Land of the Free: The Islamic critique cuts deep, but there is an answer," *National Review*, July 2, 2004.

7   Jamie Glazov, Interview with Dinesh D'Souza, "Did the Cultural Left Cause 9/11?" FrontPageMagazine.com, January 25, 2007.

8   Roger Scruton, *The West and the Rest: Globalization and the Terrorist Threat* (Wilmington, DE: Intercollegiate Studies Institute, 2002), ix.

9   Muhammad S. al-Munajjid, "Western human rights organizations and the ruling on referring to them for judgement," Islam QA, Question No. 97827, http://islam-qa.com/index.php?ref=97827&ln=eng#.

10   Ibid.

11   Ibid.

12   Stephen Holden, "Children's Boot Camp for the Culture Wars," *New York Times*, September 22, 2006.

13   Michael Medved, "Religion, madness, and secular paranoia," Townhall.com, October 4, 2006.

14   David Byrne, "American Madrassas," *David Byrne Journal*, August 2, 2006. http://journal.davidbyrne.com/.

15   Nicholas D. Kristof, "Jesus and Jihad," *New York Times*, July 17, 2004.

16   David Cook, *Contemporary Muslim Apocalyptic Literature* (Syracuse, NY: Syracuse University Press, 2005), 73, 76.

17   Jim Brown, "Hostage drill at NJ school features mock 'Christian terrorists,'" OneNewsNow.com, April 2, 2007.

18   Paul Revoir, "Christian groups accuse BBC drama of inciting anti-Christian bias," *Daily Mail*, November 1, 2006.

19   "Muslims Forcing Christian Assyrians in Baghdad Neighborhood to Pay 'Protection Tax,'" Assyrian International News Agency, March 18, 2007; "Islamic group in Baghdad: 'Get rid of the cross or we will burn your churches,'" *AsiaNews*, April 18, 2007.

20   Medved, "Religion, madness, and secular paranoia."

21   Daniel Pipes, "How the West Could Lose," *New York Sun*, December 26, 2006.

INDEX